Southwest

Volume 3 – A guide to the
natural landmarks of
Colorado & New Mexico

Second Edition

Laurent Martrès

This guidebook will take you on a remarkable journey of discovery from the vast plains of Northwestern Colorado to the deserts of Southern New Mexico, exploring geological marvels, sand dunes, the alpine scenery of the San Juan and Rocky Mountains with their incredible wildflowers and fall colors, ancient cliff dwellings, old mining towns, Spanish New Mexico, and Indian Pueblos. We also make a short foray into Texas to visit Big Bend National Park.

PHOTOGRAPHING THE SOUTHWEST (SECOND EDITION)
VOLUME 3 – COLORADO & NEW MEXICO

Published by PhotoTripUSA™
An imprint of

GRAPHIE
INTERNATIONAL, INC.
8780 19th Street, Suite 199
Alta Loma, CA 91701, USA

All photography by Laurent Martrès, Copyright © 2002-2007, except where noted.
Cover photo: Square Tower House Sunset (Mesa Verde Nat'l Park)
Title page: Bisti Badlands
Overleaf: Sprague Lake Sunrise (Rocky Mountain Nat'l Park)
End of book: Bisti Badlands

Visit Laurent's web sites: **http://www.martres.com** and **http://www.phototripusa.com**

Also available in this series:
Photographing the Southwest – Volume 1 Southern Utah ISBN 978-0-916189-12-9
Photographing the Southwest – Volume 2 Arizona ISBN 978-0-916189-13-6

Printed in China

Disclaimer
Some of the locations described in this book require travel through remote areas, where footpaths and 4-wheel drive trails can be difficult, even dangerous. Travel at your own risk and always check conditions locally before venturing out. The author and publisher decline all responsibility if you get lost, stranded, injured or otherwise suffer any kind of mishap as a result of following the advice and descriptions in this book. Furthermore, the information contained herein may have become outdated by the time you read it; the author and publisher assume no responsibility for outdated information, errors and omissions.

Publisher's Cataloging-in-Publication

    Martrès, Laurent.
        Photographing the Southwest / by Laurent Martrès. --
    2nd ed.
        v. cm.
        Includes bibliographical references and index.
        CONTENTS: v. 1. Southern Utah -- v. 2. Arizona -- v.
    3. Colorado & New Mexico.
        ISBN-13: 978-0-916189-12-9 (v. 1)
        ISBN-10: 0-916189-12-0 (v. 1)
        ISBN-13: 978-0-916189-13-6 (v. 2)
        ISBN-10: 0-916189-13-9 (v. 2)
        [etc.]

        1. Southwest, New--Guidebooks. 2. Landscape
    photography--Southwest, New--Guidebooks. I. Title.

    F787.M37 2005   917.904'34
                         QBI05-200068

PREFACE
by Tom Till

I've often said that the Colorado Plateau is a place where two divergent forces, the world's best light and the world's most interesting landscapes, seamlessly combine to create a photographer's paradise. Having been lucky enough to travel worldwide in pursuit of landscape and nature imagery, and also lucky enough to have lived my entire adult life in canyon country, I believe I have the standing to make such a claim, although anyone who has spent much time here knows my words to be utterly true.

As I looked at the places mentioned in the text, I was flooded with a lifetime of memories of the great times I have had exploring, hiking, jeeping, river running and making photographs in the Four Corners area. I was fortunate, beginning in the 1970's, to be one of the first photographers to visit the Subway in Zion National Park, to cruise around the White Rim in Canyonlands without a permit, and to be the only photographer in Antelope Canyon for weeks at a time.

Photographers coming to the area now have a challenge I never faced in those early years: other photographers. Over the decades serious photography has become one of the major activities pursued by visitors to the region. As such, we have an increased responsibility to leave the land as we find it, behave ourselves around other photographers and visitors, and place the integrity of the land above our desire to create images. After you leave this magnificent place, you can also provide a valuable service and help insure its survival as a viable ecosystem by supporting national and local environmental groups who lavish a great deal of needed attention on the preservation of our spectacular deserts. These groups include The Sierra Club, The Grand Canyon Trust, The Southern Utah Wilderness Alliance, The Nature Conservancy, and The Wilderness Society.

I congratulate Laurent on the fine work he has done with these books, on his own wonderful photography, and on his mission to give many other photographers a forum for disseminating their great work. In this regard, he is unique among established western landscape photographers.

Photographing the Southwest will be a helpful tool for me when I return to many of my favorite haunts in the future, but I'm also glad that an infinity of canyons, arches, ruins, springs and secret places have been left out of this book. These places are the true heart of the wilderness desert southwest. They are available to all who push a little beyond the established scenic hot spots, and all who are willing to risk equipment, creature comforts, and at times, life and limb. It's all worthwhile in pursuit of the magical light that calls us onward around the next bend of the canyon.

Tom Till

ACKNOWLEDGEMENTS

As with any book of this scope, many individuals have contributed one way or another to a better experience for the reader.

My deepest gratitude goes to Philippe Schuler, whose careful editing of the manuscript and innumerable enhancements to its contents have resulted in a much better book. Philippe—who shares with me an intense passion for the Southwest—brought to these guidebooks a level of precision and excellence that I would not have been able to achieve on my own. He co-wrote several sections and contributed informative textual and pictorial content throughout the various volumes and chapters. He also spent countless hours verifying the relevance and accuracy of the practical information and helped immensely in restructuring the presentation of this Second Edition to make the three books a better read. Human error is always possible, but Philippe did everything he could to ensure that I provided the most accurate information about the locations.

Tom Till's wonderful photography has consistently inspired me. Tom kindly wrote the Preface to *Photographing the Southwest* and some of his photography is also featured in this series.

Sioux Bally, of Heartstone Arts (siouxbally.com), lent her considerable artistry to designing the cover, as well as the anchor pages of each chapter.

Danelle Bell created the base maps of the territory covered in this book.

Thanks to Tony Kuyper (goodlight.us) who substantially edited and improved the Introduction and Photo Advice chapters; I'm very grateful for his help.

The following individuals contributed information and/or suggested corrections to the manuscript: Isabel Czermak, Ron Flickinger, Jan Forseth, Leona Hemmerich, Bill Mitchem, Kathi Muhlich, Benjamin Parker, Mark Ruehmann, Jerry Sadler, Steffen Synnatschke, Steve Traudt, Greg Vaughn, Victoria White, and David Whitman.

The following photography & hiking partners: Gene Mezereny, Sid Moore, Denis Savouray, as well as my wife Patricia accompanied me on some of my trips to Colorado, New Mexico and Texas and I'm grateful for their company.

Finally, I thank the photographers who have contributed their talent to enrich the pictorial content of this book and I encourage you to visit their web sites: Ron Flickinger (ronflickinger.com), Jan Forseth (imagesofcolorado.com), Barry Haynes (maxart.com), Steve Larese (stevelarese.com), QT Luong (terragalleria.com), Bill Mitchem, Mike Norton (mikenortonphotography.com), Benjamin Parker (southwesthorizons.net), Alan Plisskin (aspimages.com), Jerry Sadler, Philippe Schuler (phschuler.com), Denis Savouray (americainmyheart.com), Adam Schallau (recapturephoto.com), Jesse Speer (jessespeer.com), and Tom Till (tomtill.com).

ABOUT THIS BOOK

Welcome to the Second Edition of *Photographing the Southwest.*

I like to think of this book as a resource for visitors and photographers to the natural landmarks of the Southwest. The present Volume 3 covers Colorado, New Mexico, as well as the southwestern portion of Texas. Volume 1 covers Southern Utah and Volume 2 covers Arizona and a small portion of Nevada.

The purpose of these books is to document natural landmarks of the American Southwest from a photographic perspective. Some of these landmarks are well known; but, many are off the beaten track and seldom featured in more traditional guidebooks. Many are easily accessible and will provide you with unforgettable images and memories.

Some human activity is also covered in the books, but it is essentially limited to pre-Columbian dwellings and rock art of ancestral native Americans. This is due to the fact that cliff dwellings and rock art are tightly integrated into the landscape and can be interpreted as an extension of the natural world. I believe that most landscape photographers would agree with that.

On rare occasions, mention is made of more recent sites due to their proximity to natural landmarks. In Volume 3, I also stray from the strict landscape-centric focus of the previous volumes by including two seminal New Mexico events that are of interest to a great number of photographers: the sandhill cranes and arctic snowgeese wintering at Bosque del Apache, and the Balloon Fiesta in Albuquerque.

If you're not a photographer, you'll find in these books lots of information that more traditional guides leave out. The location of a hidden site, the most beautiful angle, and the best time of the day to view it are equally as valuable for seeing with your own eyes as for photography. These books are for everyone with a passion for the Southwest.

Each volume of *Photographing the Southwest* should be seen as a resource, rather than strictly a guidebook. It supplements other—more traditional—travel guides with specialized photographic information. The information is arranged by geographic areas. Locations whose photographic interest is particularly impressive are listed under these main headings. It also describes how to get there, as well as how and when to get the best shots. It purposely leaves out logistical concerns such as restaurant and hotel accommodations as there are already more than enough excellent travel books on that subject.

In addition to all the new areas covered in this Second Edition of *Photographing the Southwest*, all three volumes include a lot of new commentary and advice concerning previously visited sites.

The chapter on photography has been expanded, despite my initial reluctance to dispense this kind of advice. While I hope you'll benefit from my suggestions if you are a beginning photographer, my primary goal remains to provide you with a comprehensive location resource with which you can unleash your very own photographic talent.

In this series of guidebooks, coverage of pre-Columbian sites has been increased, reflecting the growing interest on the part of the public for exploring the heritage of native Americans and interpreting their rock art. As Val Brinkerhoff, photographer of *Architecture of the Ancient Ones* puts it: "Visit one ancient dwelling site and you're likely to be drawn to experience another, and another, and another."

With these three greatly expanded volumes, my goal is to give readers from all over the world the best practical information to discover and photograph the Southwest. I believe you'll enjoy experiencing the infinite photographic possibilities of the Southwest and make some truly amazing discoveries of your own in the course of your travels.

May this book bring you a slew of new ideas for your creative photography of the Southwest. ✿

—*Laurent Martrès*

KEEPING CURRENT

We live in a world where things change rapidly, this is particularly true of the Southwest, which has recently experienced an influx of tourism, as well as of special interests: trails become paved or deteriorate, road numbers change, some sites become off-limit to visitors while new ones open up, quota systems become mandatory, and new rules supersede all ones. The rapid pace of these changes is well beyond the capacity of a publisher to update their guides at regular interval, but the internet is our savior:

You'll find errors, omissions and updates to this book and others in the series on our web site at *http://www.phototripusa.com/updates/index.htm*.

Conversely, should you notice an error or change in one of the descriptions of this book, kindly let us know about it by e-mailing us at *updates@phototripusa.com*. The entire community will benefit from it.

TABLE OF CONTENTS

Koan

Chapter 1

INTRODUCTION

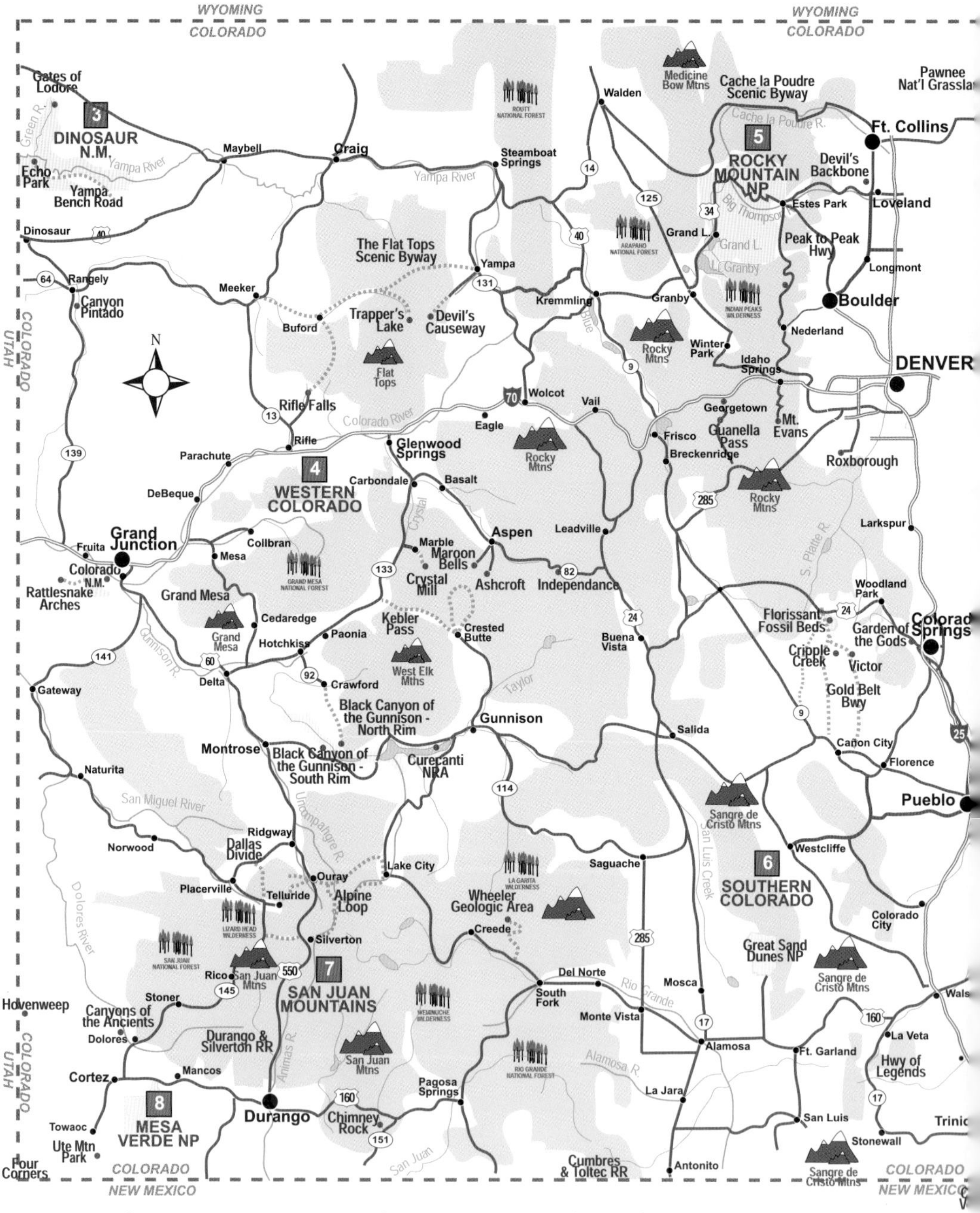

These two maps represent the territory covered in Volume 3. Chapters describing sites located in Colorado are on the above map. Chapters dealing with New Mexico and Texas are on the next page. The purpose of the maps is to indicate in a very general way the location of the chapters and some of the sites. The maps do not attempt to be accurate and are no substitue for real maps. More information on maps can be found in *Appendix*.

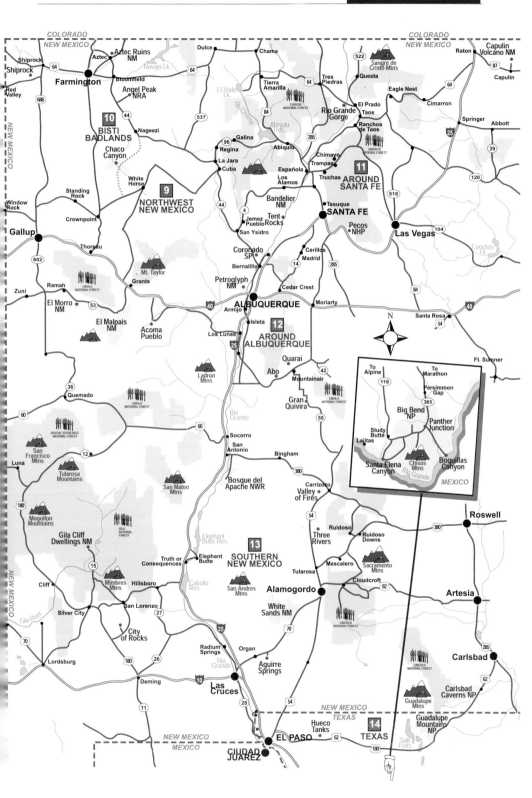

This chapter deals with the logistics of a trip to the Southwest. Information concerning the geology, fauna & flora, and history of the Southwest can be found in Chapter 1 of *Photographing the Southwest Volume 1 – Southern Utah*.

Maps

You may find it surprising that this book doesn't contain any detailed maps other than the simple ones on the previous pages, which describe the general location of the chapters and some of the more prominent sections. The reason for this is that *Photographing the Southwest* has a different purpose than other guidebooks: I like to think of it as an illustrated location resource, providing ideas for discovering or expanding on your previous knowledge of the Southwest. Also, had I chosen to illustrate with numerous maps the locations covered in the three volumes of *Photographing the Southwest*, it would have dramatically increased the size, weight and price of the books, making them impractical to carry on a trip. Any number of small maps I could have included would still be no substitute for the real thing. The reality is that even with these books, you will need several different kinds of maps to effectively use the information.

Maps play a huge role in several respects. Large scale maps are necessary to get a global perspective of your trip and make initial decisions. Detailed road maps are necessary in order to follow the instructions in the "*Getting there*" sections of the book. You'll find a list of recommended maps in *Appendix*, along with a short description of each. One particular map—the *AAA Indian Country* map—stands out as an excellent asset in the preparation and enjoyment of your trips. This remarkable map covers about 90% of the territory of *Volume 1* and about half the terrain of *Volumes 2* and *3*.

Additionally, since many of the locations I describe are off the beaten path, 7.5 minute US Geological Survey maps are necessary. Although the information on these maps is sometimes outdated, they are an indispensable tool for locating remote sites and navigating the backcountry. As it can become expensive and impractical to buy so many different topographic maps, I suggest that you purchase the remarkable *National Geographic Topo! State series* maps for your computer. These Digital Rasterized Graphics files allow you to print your own maps for specific locations. You can print only the portion of map corresponding to your needs, including markers and annotations. While the initial investment in the four *Topo! State series* maps covering the three volumes of *Photographing the Southwest* is sizeable, it will prove economical in the long run if you're going to make extensive use of the books.

The *National Geographic Topo!* maps become a powerful tool when installed on a laptop computer. Used in tandem with a GPS unit, you can track your precise location in real time on your monitor while driving on remote dirt roads. Consider this simple scenario: Driving back from your sunset shoot, you find yourself at a fork and do not remember which branch you came in on earlier. The digitized map and GPS combination makes it extremely easy to find your location and hence the correct turn in order to return home. It's true that you can do this with a mapping GPS alone, but tracking your progress on a computer screen with all the fine detail of a *Topo! State series* map provides a degree of accuracy and comfort that is not possible with the GPS' tiny screen. Entering waypoints from a computer keyboard is also easier and navigating the maps on the computer screen provides a better understanding of the topology—hills to climb, gullies to bypass, etc.—especially if you use relief shading or, better yet, 3-dimensional viewing. If you haven't purchased these maps on CD-ROM, I suggest at least preparing your trips using the excellent *www.topozone.com* web site. Here you can access and print at no charge small-sized excerpts of topographic maps. There are also commercial web-based topographic services allowing you to print maps with various degrees of information for a fee.

So now that we've entered the realm of digital mapping, let's talk about this other useful tool: the GPS.

GPS considerations

In the previous edition, I considered it inappropriate to give away GPS points. My philosophy at the time was that readers needed to make their own adventure, performing a minor amount of effort in researching locations. I also considered, and still consider, GPS usage fraught with dangers in the hands of inexperienced users. Knowing GPS coordinates is one thing, but it is no substitute for a topographic map, particularly when it comes to understanding relief.

I have noticed that novice users tend to rely on the "GOTO" function of their GPS, without consideration for the topology. Rarely can one follow the straight line indicated on the GPS. Gullies too deep for crossing and vertical cliffs too high for scaling are common occurrences.

In the early 2000s, a majority of friends and government agency officials shared my concern. The consensus at the time was that giving away GPS coordinates could make things too easy and perhaps dangerous for novice users.

Circumstances have changed substantially since then. Today, GPS coordinates can be found on the Internet for just about any location of interest and the information is freely exchanged between peers with similar pursuits. In this rapidly evolving context, it would be counterproductive to force readers to seek GPS information outside of this book.

Therefore, in this edition, I have chosen to provide GPS coordinates very selectively. I do not want to entice readers to rely totally on their GPS unit. Instead, you'll find coordinates whenever they are truly useful or even indispensable.

I'll reiterate my warning, however. The GPS is no substitute for a topographic map and a compass, and in some cases for plain old instinct and navigational skills. Batteries eventually die, but the compass will continue to indicate your direction. You should always carry spare batteries, a compass and a map... and of course know how to use them.

If you are a novice user, I suggest that you attend a clinic. GPS clinics are available for free at many outdoor equipment stores in cities across the country.

One last bit of advice: do not walk with your eyes riveted to your GPS. Instead, try finding your way around by observing landmarks and following natural paths. Not only will you become a better routefinder, but you'll enjoy your surroundings a lot more. Your GPS is not a toy; use it only when necessary, to make sure that you are on course. Once you've mastered its use and are aware of its potential pitfalls, you may wonder how you got along without it.

The coordinate system used in this book is Degrees, Minutes, Seconds in WGS84 datum. It is the simplest to understand for novice users. It is also the best choice in terms of readability and ease of input: The popular UTM system may have some pluses, but it is not as immediately descriptive when comparing two waypoints. Coordinates expressed in UTM are also easier to mistype. Once typed into your GPS unit, *Topo!* program, or on-line web site, you can simply convert the coordinates to your preferred reference system.

Driving around

The question of the best vehicle to use may naturally arise when you visit an area as vast as the American Southwest. In this *Volume 3* of *Photographing the Southwest*, about 82% of the sites are accessible via paved roads or tracks adequate for passenger cars. An additional 8% of the sites can be accessed via rougher tracks that are still potentially passable by passenger cars if driven with caution in dry weather. The rest necessitate an SUV or some kind of high clearance vehicle. In a number of cases—not the majority—use of a four-wheel drive (4WD) vehicle and some experience with this kind of driving is required. High-clearance is generally associated with larger tires than on the typical passenger car and is often necessary to negotiate the irregularities of a track, prevent damage to the undercarriage, and avoid becoming high-centered. Complementing high clearance, 4WD, especially in low-range, is useful on sandy or muddy tracks or tracks presenting rock steps and/or particularly steep angles—a small minority of locations in this book.

Road difficulty is examined in detail for each location in the text. Also, in the Ratings section at this end of the book, I rate the difficulty of vehicular access under "normal" conditions, i.e. always in dry weather and long after a rain. In wet conditions or after violent thunderstorms, a track rated accessible by passenger car can become impassable even to a high-clearance 4WD vehicle. The ratings provided should always be confirmed with visitor centers or local authorities, as track condition change frequently based on recent weather and the elapsed time since the last road maintenance. Don't take any unnecessary risks. Towing may cost hundreds or even thousands of dollars should you become stranded in some remote location.

Undoubtedly, using an SUV to explore the locations in this guidebook—even if it isn't 4WD—provides a degree of flexibility and comfort not offered by passenger cars and limits the risk of damage to your vehicle. If you are considering car camping on your trip, you may even be able to sleep in your vehicle. Assuming you have a flat surface after folding down the rear seats, a person of average height can usually fit quite well. If you own a pick-up, a shell will provide inexpensive and effective protection against the elements.

If you're traveling in your own SUV or pick-up truck, you should always carry a tow strap, a shovel and a small air compressor. The latter will allow you to reinflate your tires after airing down in particularly sandy terrain. If you fly in from another part of the country (or the world) and rent an SUV from a major rental company, be aware that it will rarely offer 4WD. Furthermore, your rental agreement usually prohibits taking the rental vehicle off paved roads, so think twice about where you want to go, as you'll be assuming a major financial risk. One last piece of advice concerning rental vehicles: Always verify the presence of an adequate spare tire and tools to change it. You don't want to be stuck on a remote road just because the crank to operate the jack is missing.

Hiking

I'm often asked about the level of difficulty of the hikes involved in visiting various locations. The answer depends on a plurality of factors. Many readers are not necessarily avid hikers. While a majority are probably content to carry a lightweight camera, some may be hauling heavy photographic equipment. At the other end of the spectrum, some folks prefer long hikes so they can "get away from the crowds". In *Volume 3*, about 2/3rd of the locations can be visited and photographed with almost no hiking at all or else an easy stroll lasting less than an hour round-trip. An additional 17% of the sites should be accessible to most readers, requiring between one to three hours round-trip with moderate difficulty. About 11% are more demanding, as they require up to six hours round-trip and/or involve some kind of difficulty such as elevation change, orienteering, tougher terrain, obstacles or other risks. A minority require longer, more strenuous hiking or backpacking (mentioned only marginally in this guidebook).

In addition to the descriptions in the text, hiking difficulty is summed up in detail at the end of the book, with ratings on difficulty of access on foot for each location. These ratings are done with the average hiker in mind, i.e. neither a person with mobility problems, nor a marathon runner, in average physical shape (exercising regularly, preferably walking) and having a reasonably good sense of orientation, under normal hiking conditions (in dry weather and average temperatures).

Reading this guidebook, you'll see that visiting the Southwest—even off the beaten track—is not the exclusive domain of hard-core hikers. You'll come to realize that ordinary city folks can find plenty of trips to satisfy their photographic pursuits with only a modest amount of effort. Obviously, you need to set reasonable goals for yourself. Begin your trip with easy hikes, increasing your mileage progressively and alternating hard and easy days. Pay particular attention to the duration of your hikes; some people tend to be overly optimistic, especially if taking lots of pictures.

Always heed the advice of park rangers and professional guides, even if it feels a little too conservative. This is particularly important when hiking in canyon country. Flash floods are a not so rare occurrence in all seasons, although they tend to happen much more frequently during summer. You don't want to find yourself trapped in a slot canyon when that happens.

Hiking equipment should also be considered carefully. It can make a significant difference in terms of security and comfort. Security should not be taken lightly as there is a very real risk of getting lost on backcountry hikes without trails. Although a minority, there are a few such hikes in this guidebook. Start with the Ten Essentials:

- ❐ A first aid kit
- ❐ Waterproof matches or a small lighter
- ❐ A pocket knife
- ❐ A headlamp (there are very small, lightweight LED models)
- ❐ Sunglasses (polarized types are nice for photography)
- ❐ A loud whistle (so you can be located by your party or a rescue team in case of mishap)
- ❐ High-energy food (trail mix or energy bars)
- ❐ A topographic map of the area
- ❐ A compass and if possible a GPS unit (always take a waypoint of your vehicle's location)
- ❐ Extra clothing in case of a sudden change in weather.

Your digital camera can also be a useful tool when hiking in the backcountry, where there is no trail or no obvious landmark and you'll be returning the same way you came. At each strategic location (such as a spot where you need to go down or ascend a cliff, an intersection of side canyons, or when leaving the course of a wash) turn around and take a snapshot, taking care to place the direction to be followed on returning in the center of the frame. If you have any doubt as to the correct course when you return, just examine the shots you took on your camera's LCD.

A good pair of hiking shoes with good ankle support is essential for hiking in the Southwest. You want good ankle support and soles with good traction on small pebbles and slickrock. Sneakers are definitely inadequate for the trail and should stay in your car. If you're going to wade inside streambeds, a second pair of shoes, specialized for water activities, will come in handy. This type of shoe usually has excellent anti-slip soles. Although not indispensable, they offer an additional level of comfort when hiking in water. Use them with a pair of wool socks or synthetic liners to avoid blisters. For pants, shorts, and shirts, the newer synthetic fibers work very well in the Southwest environment. They breathe well, transferring body moisture away from the skin, and they dry extremely fast (on you or after being washed). Don't forget the indispensable fleece jacket and/or windbreaker, which you should always have handy as temperatures can change radically throughout the day. Don't be fooled by the fact that the land looks like a desert; it can get cold very fast, especially at elevation, during the spring and fall months. When hiking in full sun—a common occurrence in the Southwest—consider a solar cap with a "legionnaire" attachment to protect your ears and neck. Also, frequent application of sunscreen to sun-exposed areas is recommended. Sunburn can hurt like hell and has potentially life-threatening health consequences.

There are many good daypacks and photo packs available. Consider one with sufficient capacity to carry not only your photo equipment but also your additional clothing, safety gear and, above all, plenty of water. In summer, dehydration may come easily and without warning. Some of the day-hikes in this book may require a full gallon of water. When hiking in the backcountry, I sometimes encounter photographers carrying "specialized" photo packs for their equipment and only a small hip-bag with just enough space for a couple of energy bars and two pints of water. Not having enough water places you at serious risk in case of unplanned occurrences. Taking the wrong turn or simply extending your visit because every bend of the canyon brings more captivating beauty requires additional resources, especially water. On long day hikes, I usually stash a water bladder behind a tree for the return trip. On extended trips, I carry and use a water filter.

Trekking poles can be very helpful on hikes that involve lots of ascents and descents. They propel you forward going up and relieve pressure on your knees going down. Your poles can also aid in keeping your balance when wading rocky streams. Note that a trekking pole with a hole on top to screw in your camera is no substitute for a steady tripod!

A word about lodging

I provide no information or advice concerning accommodations, although I occasionally mention campgrounds. I have found that my readers have very different traveling styles depending on their individual goals, time constraints, and the level of comfort they require. There are excellent travel guides available that can assist the reader in finding the specific type of accommodations they desire.

Keep in mind, however, that you'll take many of your best photos during the so-called "golden hour", soon after sunrise and just before sunset. As many of the locations discussed in this book are on dirt roads far away from motels, you may have to camp close to the site to be present during the best light. Doing so, you avoid driving at night on backcountry tracks. What would pass as minor impediments during the day can become very dangerous when you discover them at the last second with your headlights. Depending on the situation, you may be able to opt for organized campgrounds, such as the ones found in many national or state parks (where camping is prohibited outside the official campgrounds).

Alternatively, there may be primitive camping where you'll just pick your site in the middle of the backcountry if this is authorized, which is the case most on BLM-administered land.

Even if you're following a classic regimen of motels every night, you may want to carry in your car a small tent, a sleeping pad, a sleeping bag, as well as a stash of food and several gallons of water. Should some unforeseen circumstances prevent you from going back to town, you'll be able to improvise a night in the backcountry. You may even become addicted once you get a taste of it!

When to visit

Colorado and New Mexico can both be visited year-round. Each season possesses its unique charm and presents various advantages and disadvantages.

Summer monsoon storms make for sublime skies, occasional rainbows, soft lighting due to the haze and spectacular sunsets, but there is a high price to pay for that. It's the busiest time of the year on the roads and in the parks. In the last two decades, foreign visitors en masse have also discovered the American West, in organized tour groups or as individuals, crowding the roads and parks, not to mention the motels. In the most popular places, reservations become indispensable and need to be made in advance to guarantee a place for the night. This can create a serious obstacle to the flexibility of your itinerary by imposing a measure of control on your evening's destination.

The intense heat is not generally a problem in the car or on short walks, but it is a factor on long hikes, especially in the Rocky Mountains. Summer sees frequent afternoon thunderstorms with all the risks they entail, especially when hiking the numerous mountain trails described in this guidebook. Additionally, unpaved roads are sometimes closed by water runoff.

Insects can pose a problem in certain areas, particularly at the beginning of summer when mosquitoes, deerflies and biting gnats or "no-see-ums" will attack your skin relentlessly. Unfortunately, it is impossible to predict when and where they will hang out in a particular year.

Finally, the days are at their longest; this allows you to cover a lot of ground and visit many sites. On the other hand, this can considerably limit your photographic opportunities during the day when the sun is high in the sky and your shots will be way too contrasty and without nuance. Bear in mind that the angle of the sun is at its highest in summer. There is no such thing as a "golden hour" at the height of summer, merely fifteen minutes of very good light after sunrise and before sunset. As a photographer, I find summer rather exhausting in the Desert Southwest. I recommend concentrating on the mountainous parts of Colorado and New Mexico, where morning and midday clouds can be stunning. Summer is also wildflower season in Colorado, usually between mid-July and mid-August.

Autumn is the best time to discover Colorado and New Mexico. It's still warm at lower elevations, but the heat is less ferocious. Autumn also brings cool nights in the mountain areas. In the first part of autumn, days are still long but less grueling. Kids and the majority of grown-ups have returned to work and school after Labor Day. The motels empty out. Prices lower to a reasonable level, the parks are less congested and parking near the panoramic vistas no longer requires you to drive around for ½ hour to find a spot. Hazy days become rare and insects no longer make your life miserable.

Fall colors begin in mid-September in the high country and usually last until mid-October. Late September is absolutely marvelous in the San Juan Mountains and the Rockies as the aspens turn and a new, multi-colored palette of yellow, ocher and red appears with a much softer illumination than in summer. Strong rains are relatively rare at lower elevations, but snow storms are possible in the mountains. Finally, the sun rises and sets at a lower angle and the "golden hour" lasts quite a bit longer than in summer. This is my favorite season for general travel in the Southwest at large, as well as for photography.

Winter is the off-season in Northwest Colorado and Southern New Mexico. Elsewhere, huge crowds flock to the mountain resorts. Winter's short daylight hours, as well as the low trajectory of the sun on the horizon, are a real asset to the photographer.

Winter storms often bring rain in the lowlands and heavy snow to the higher elevations and can last several days. However, a fresh snowfall on the passes and summits is a magical experience when, with these alternate periods of beautiful weather, the air attains an unequaled purity and the sky is an intense blue. By the same token, there are few clouds in the sky and it can be tough to come up with spectacular photography including much sky. Nonetheless, unobstructed views reveal extraordinary distances when there is no pollution, as is rarely the case in summer. Large animals descend from the higher elevations and are frequently and easily observed in the valleys.

The main drawback is that some sites become inaccessible without proper equipment, especially in the high mountains. Another negative factor is the lack of color in the vegetation. You'll have to be careful not to include bare vegetation in your images; bare branches and bushes don't make very nice foregrounds.

Spring is a magnificent season, although the weather can be very unpredictable. You are as likely to encounter stormy, wet days as warm and sunny weather. Rain and snow are frequent and the rivers and waterfalls are at their highest. The high country is still snowbound and snow melt can be a problem. In the lowlands, greenery is sprouting, the trees are leafing out and wildflowers abound in wet years. Temperatures are still tolerable. It's a good time to visit New Mexico.

The days are getting longer and prices are still not as expensive as during the height of the season. In late spring, insects can be a great nuisance. No-see-ums, fond of blood and terribly annoying, as well as aggressive deerflies are to be found along watercourses and in washes.

Archeological Sites Etiquette

Rock art and ancient dwellings are a most precious heritage of Native American Indians and humanity at large. They are obviously extremely fragile and when not protected, are often the unfortunate object of vandalism. When photographing rock art and ruins, the first and foremost rule is: Don't touch. Natural oils from human skin can and will affect glyphs and paintings. Even though a slight touch may only remove a minute amount of pigment or sandstone, when you multiply that by many years and many visitors it will eventually lead to irreparable degradations. Even worse than that is the use of chalk or crayon to enhance or highlight the art for photographs. It compromises the integrity of the art by becoming a permanent part of the design and paves the way for others to add their own mark, thus destroying the precious heritage forever. This is a sad and irresponsible act, which I have observed too many times on otherwise beautiful rock art throughout the Southwest. Another reprehensible practice is the wetting of rock art with water to accentuate contrast and texture. Needless to say, you should not cut, chip, or try to remove rock art.

A word now about the looting of antique objects and rock art for profit. This criminal activity has markedly increased in recent years—almost exclusively on BLM lands—according to a study by the National Trust for Historic Preservation. Both the BLM and the Trust concur on the root causes of this phenomenon: decreased funding resulting in understaffed BLM field offices and new roads into once-inaccessible areas, for the purpose of oil and gas exploration.

The Antiquities Act protects antique structure, objects, and rock art; infractions are subject to very high fines, but this is not enough to deter vandals and looters. The best way to prevent this from happening is through education, in school and at the sites. As observers and photographers of our era, it is our responsibility to treat antique sites properly, so that they may be preserved as a testimony to those who came before us and for the benefit of future generations.

Please don't blame me as an author for disseminating information about public or lesser-known archaeological sites. Vandals don't read books such as this one, looking for information. In 99% of cases, rock art is defaced by teenagers, mostly males, often drunk, and happening to pass by in groups. As for the recent surge in looting, according to the BLM it is mostly a crime of opportunity taking place near new oil fields.

Some of the best places to admire and photograph ancient dwellings and rock art in Colorado and New Mexico are Dinosaur NM, Mesa Verde NP, Canyons of the Ancients NM, Petroglyph NM, Three Rivers Petroglyph Site.

To visit hard-to-find panels and significantly increase your enjoyment and understanding of rock art, consider joining the American Rock Art Research Association, aka ARARA (see *Appendix*). ✿

Aspen Sky

Chapter 2

SOME PHOTOGRAPHIC ADVICE

Photographing the Southwest makes no assumptions about your ability with respect to photography. Whether you are an enthusiastic beginner or a seasoned pro is irrelevant. While this book is essentially a location resource, it also provides specific photographic advice for almost every location to allow you to be better prepared for your visit. The advice is based on my experience in the field, having been at many of these locations several times and under different lighting conditions. In many cases, I have also checked my notes against those of knowledgeable friends or acquaintances.

After examining the indispensable photographic equipment, I'll discuss how to handle a number of generic situations you'll encounter in the field so you can create better images. I ask the more advanced photographers to be understanding if this advice seems trivial; drawing on the feedback from the past edition, many readers seem to appreciate having this quick photographic reference.

ABOUT EQUIPMENT

Terminology

The myriad of existing film and digital camera formats creates confusion when discussing lens focal length expressed in the metric system, i.e. millimeters. Since most people understand focal length based on the 35mm camera, I'll be using this as the reference camera throughout the book. Medium and large format photographers should have no problem recognizing the equivalent lens focal length. Newcomers starting with a digital camera, however, may find it more difficult. The digital camera's sensor size determines the angle of vision for a lens at a given focal length. The focal length inscribed on the lens simply reflects its effective focal distance from the sensor in millimeters. This is the distance the lens must be from the sensor in order to provide sharp focus for an object located at infinity. For each camera system with a different size image capture device, the inscribed focal length will provide a different angle of vision. A focal length that appears to be a very wide angle to a person using a 35mm system may in fact be a normal lens for a person using a digital camera. The difference is due to the size of the sensor in relation to the 24x36mm film size for a 35mm film camera. This size differential is known as the "crop factor". With a 1x crop factor—which exists only for the "full-size sensor" of some high-end digital cameras—the angle of vision is the same as on a 35mm film camera. Cameras with smaller sensors will have crop factors of 1.5x, 2x or even larger. Take a 20mm lens for example. On a 35mm camera or a camera with a "full-size sensor" its angle of vision will be very wide angle. For a sensor with a 1.6x crop factor, the 20mm lens becomes equivalent to a 32mm lens on a 35mm film camera. Therefore, a 28mm lens is considered a "normal" lens on a camera with a 1.6x crop factor. On a digicam equipped with an even smaller sensor, this 28mm focal length could actually provide a small telephoto effect. Since the final angle of vision is what really matters,

I sometimes use additional terminology to describe what the lens does. A 40 to 50mm lens could be described as a normal lens, while 24 to 35mm is standard wide-angle range and anything below 24mm is considered super-wide angle. A 70 to 140mm lens provides a short telephoto effect and from 140 to 300mm is medium telephoto. Larger than 300mm is simply a very long telephoto lens.

Film vs. Digital

The technology of traditional film and camera equipment is very mature. There is little room for improvement, especially in image quality. Any further improvements in terms of lower grain or better color are likely to be trivial. Traditional film-based photography will eventually become obsolete, although, especially for landscape photography, it will coexist with digital for quite some time. For fine-art photographers, film retains definite advantages. It holds the edge in terms of color subtlety and smoothness, feeling of depth and presence, and the capacity to produce huge, incredibly sharp prints. This advantage is mostly limited to medium and large format cameras. In most regards digital has already equaled or surpassed 35mm in terms of quality and is knocking at the door of medium format.

My advice to newcomers is to go straight to digital, the key operative word being instant gratification. Digital camera technology, although already very usable, will see spectacular development in years to come. Having spent twenty years in the computer industry, I am a firm believer in "Moore's Law", which states that technological capacity doubles every 24 months. There is little doubt that we will see a similar rate of expansion in the digital camera industry, albeit perhaps not quite as rapid. Although there are still a few stumbling blocks, the shortcomings of sensor size, limited storage capacity, and short battery life have been overcome for the most part. New sensors are able to produce digital files that are sufficient for most needs, including commercial photography. The last bastion to fall will be big enlargements of digitally-captured landscape scenes. However, it's only a matter of time until they compare to film. Economies of scale will keep driving prices down. After critical mass is achieved, we will have cameras capable of producing astonishing results at a very reasonable cost.

As of this writing, many of the early limitations of digital have been overcome or, at least, greatly improved. Storage, for example, is no longer an issue if you shoot lots of high-quality images during a long trip. Standalone devices are replacing laptops to help you download, archive and review your images on the road. It is becoming increasingly easy to perform a quick review of your images "in-camera" almost in real time. At the end of the day and with the help of a large LCD display a more in-depth review can occur. Anything that isn't a "keeper" can be discarded to make room for more photographs. While improving rapidly, battery life still presents a bit of a challenge in the field. Digital photography requires a lot more energy to power the camera, store the image file, and pre- and post-visualize images on the LCD.

One side benefit of digital photography compared to film—at least with small-sensor cameras—is to allow telephoto lenses to act as if they were even longer. As I explained earlier, the source of this phenomenon is the fact that the footprint of a sensor is in most cases smaller than that of a 35mm film window. A 200mm lens may give you the magnification ratio and angle of view of a 320mm when used with a digital camera with a crop factor of 1.6x—although it won't provide the same nice blur in out-of-focus areas. While this is a tremendous boon for photographing wildlife, it is not necessarily so for landscape photography where a wide angle and its associated depth-of-field are more useful. In the case of a digital camera with a crop factor of 1.6x, you'll need to use a 17mm lens to get the actual angle of vision provided by a 28mm wide-angle lens on a 35mm film camera. To minimize distortion, a digital lens must be built to very high standards, which means additional costs. This explains why a majority a digicams do not have wide-angle lenses and also why quality wide-angle lenses for digital SLR cameras are so expensive. On the other hand, for an equivalent angle of vision, digicam lenses with a short focal length offer remarkable depth-of-field, which is perfect for landscape photography.

Digital files are also much more practical than film for creative manipulation. Since no scanning is required for digitally-captured images they are more easily made available for computer management. This naturally enhances the photographer's capacity to interpret his work in new ways and to share images with others for fun and to garner feedback.

One final aspect where digital shines is in the area of noise, which is equivalent to grain in film. High-end digital cameras are able to produce clean images with no visible noise, up to 400 ISO or more. This allows you to shoot handheld while preserving quality. Even when noise is present, it can be almost entirely removed without degrading detail using specialized noise reduction algorithms. The images produced by digital cameras can also be more easily enlarged than those that come from film. Because images from digital cameras are inherently clean, they can be more easily interpolated, or "up-rezed," a computer method for increasing the file size, to produce larger prints with excellent results.

What to take on your Trip

You will notice that I do not talk much about equipment throughout the book. That is essentially because gear is not a decisive factor in the quality of your photography. Light, the ability to "see", and an eye for composition are much more likely to affect the results than simply pointing an expensive camera at a well-known landmark and shooting.

❐ The camera body is at the center of your photographic equipment, although it is not the most important component in terms of results. Modern camera bodies offer a tremendous number of functions—too many in my opinion. Some of these functions are nonetheless useful, if not indispensable, if you want to go beyond simple snapshots. Single-lens reflex cameras (SLR or dSLR in the case of the digital SLR) have through-the-lens viewing capability which is helpful for precise framing, although many people are just as happy with a rangefinder, optical or electronic viewfinder. Note that the optical viewfinders in digital point-and-shoot cameras usually show only about 70% of the image forcing you to use the LCD for accuracy. This can sometimes result in fuzzy pictures shot with extended arms.

In traditional photography, aperture-priority mode is essential to maximizing depth-of-field. You'll be able to preview the depth-of-field if your camera has depth-of-field preview. Some sophisticated cameras have special modes allowing you to maximize depth-of-field automatically. While this is fine for non-critical shooting, it is no substitute to setting the depth-of-field manually.

Aperture compensation allows you to manually correct exposure under difficult lighting circumstances. Exposure bracketing is very useful to guarantee correct exposure for those critical shots. An all-metal lens mount is recommended over polycarbonate if you're planning to change lenses often.

One function that has completely vanished on entry-level film cameras is mirror lockup. This is sad because it has been scientifically demonstrated that pictures taken with the mirror up have a higher count of lines per millimeter, producing sharper enlargements. Fortunately, manufacturers have resurrected this functionality on affordable dSLRs. Rangefinder cameras eliminate the mirror shock problem completely, but they come with their own set of limitations.

❐ Lenses are the most important component of your camera system. High optical quality glass is crucial for producing quality results. Single focal length lenses used to be better than multi-focal length zooms, but high-end zooms are now equally as good and are extremely practical, both in terms of speed, weight and protection of the mirror and internal mechanism from dust and wind. Stay away from low-cost consumer zooms; they yield disappointing results. Digital sensors are even more demanding. High quality lenses are absolutely essential if shooting digitally. A bright zoom covering 28mm to 105 or 135mm works well in the Southwest. If you take a digital or analog point-and-shoot camera, be sure not to settle for 35mm or 38mm at the wide end. It will be not be sufficient in the field. You'll find yourself using the wide angle range most of the time. Needless to say, a super wide-angle (24mm or less) and a long telephoto (200mm and above) will significantly enhance your potential for original shots.

Wide-range zooms (28-200mm and 28-300mm) are deservedly popular as versatile lenses for travel photography, but be aware that they are usually soft at the telephoto end. They are adequate for small prints up to 5"x7", but do not expect high-quality enlargements.

One new development that offers a lot of value to the photographer on the go is the emergence of stabilized sensors and gyro-stabilized zooms. This technology allows you to gain at least two stops, which may be enough to forego a tripod in non-critical 35mm or digital landscape photography. While this doesn't completely obviate the use of the tripod, especially to maximize depth-of-field, it offers greatly improved sharpness at speeds in the 1/30th and 1/60th range. It allows you to quickly capture those fleeting moments—a furtive ray of light or a rainbow—with increased chances of getting good results.

As for teleconverters, which generally come with a 1.4x and 2x magnifying factor, only use prime models in conjunction with high-quality lenses in order to get good results. A factor of 1.4 is less radical and less detrimental to overall picture quality.

Whatever lenses you decide to buy, don't be frugal. Too many people buy an expensive body, only to equip it with a mediocre zoom lens. Major manufacturers always have two or even three lines of lenses: a consumer line, a so-called "prosumer" line, and a high-end more expensive line. My advice is to buy the best possible lens you can afford. It will result in sharper, higher contrast pictures, with better color.

❏ I do occasionally recommend the use of filters to enhance and compensate for the shortcomings of film. A UV or Skylight 1B filter will protect your lens without diminishing image quality, but use them with caution on a zoom lens. Zooms, due to their complex optical construction involving the use of many elements and groups, are particularly prone to flare—the phenomenon of light entering the lens and causing unwanted reflections. I do not personally use these filters, relying instead on my lens shade to protect the lens, but this advice is not for everybody.

A graduated neutral-density filter (or ND Grad) is an essential piece of equipment, especially if you shoot transparencies. It will help keep contrast in check and open up shadow areas. Split neutral-density filters work great when the separation line between lit subject and shadow is very obvious, but these instances are rare in Canyon Country. By all means, use a high-quality filter. Cheap ND grad filters are not neutral and will give a nasty color cast to your skies. In my opinion, you'll be better served by a two-stop filter than one with three stops. Also, a model you can slide up and down in a holder is more flexible than a simple screw-in filter.

A mild warming filter such as an 81a, KR 1.5 or Nikon A2 is also an important filter. It is useful under many circumstances, but most particularly in the shade to remove the blue cast from the sky and when photographing under a strong sun. It adds a slight warmth to your images, without introducing a color cast. These filters work very well in the Southwest.

Most books and articles enthusiastically endorse the use of a polarizing filter, or "polarizer", as a vital piece of equipment to carry in your bag. I am not so enthusiastic and recommend that you use your polarizer with moderation with anything other than print film. This advice also applies to digital cameras. If you have high-quality, high-contrast lenses and shoot on a highly saturated film, such as Fuji Velvia, you won't need one most of the time. Used indiscriminately a polarizer may create skies that are too dark. Also, in combination with a wide-angle lens, the polarizing effect can become too strong, resulting in light falloff in one or more corners of the image. I use my polarizer mostly to eliminate glare on foliage, streams or various textures, but generally keep it in the bag during broad daylight unless the sky is full of fluffy clouds. If you use a rangefinder, carry a pair of polarizing sunglasses and look straight into the lens to see the effect of the filter. Then, based on your experience, apply the proper amount of exposure compensation for your particular filter, usually 1½ to 2 stops. It is also not too hard to use an ND grad with a rangefinder with a little practice.

❐ A lens shade is helpful in preventing flare. Be sure it is designed for your lens to avoid the phenomenon of vignetting, which is light falloff in the corners of your image. This is particularly nasty with blue skies.

❐ Now we come to what I consider the second most important piece of equipment after your lenses: the tripod. A tripod is nearly indispensable for landscape photography, particularly if you shoot transparencies. Good slide film is inherently slow and doesn't lend itself to handheld photography. A tripod also allows you to compose your images more carefully and to keep the horizon straight. Unfortunately there is also price to pay when you need to carry a four-pound tripod on long hikes, especially if some scrambling is involved. Carbon fiber tripods are a good alternative albeit quite expensive. They can shave a couple of pounds from an otherwise heavy piece of equipment. I recommend buying a headless tripod and purchasing your own ballhead. I personally use a combination carbon-fiber tripod and magnesium ballhead. There are now smaller, lighter-weight, and less expensive tripods that do a great job with small digicams and lightweight dSLRs. If you have never used a tripod before when shooting landscapes, you'll be surprised at how much it can improve your photography.

❐ The natural companion of the tripod is fortunately very lightweight: a cable release. It is useful in avoiding camera movement when releasing the shutter, even when the camera is mounted on a tripod. A good quality one costs only a few dollars more than a small flimsy model and is much nicer to use. If you don't want to bother with one, you can also use your camera's built-in timer release. There is one potential pitfall with the timer technique on entry-level cameras: someone may walk right in front of your camera just when it's taking the picture. I can almost guarantee that this will happen in highly visited places, such as Mesa Verde. Most digital camera manufacturers offer remote control devices, which take care of this problem.

❐ You shouldn't carry your camera and lenses without some form of protection. It is risky to switch lenses in an environment where dust and sand are present, especially with a dSLR. Be sure to protect your camera from the wind when changing lenses and to blow away dust every time you load a new roll or sheet if you shoot film. Fine dust suspended in the air can lodge in your camera when you change lenses, eventually settling on your sensor. Some dSLRs now incorporate vibrating sensors to shake the dust off, apparently with very good results. A digital point-and-shoot camera, with its permanently attached lens, is almost impervious to this type of misadventure. Dust can also cause malfunctioning of the storage media. If you use film, you run the risk of having lines etched across your entire roll. A single speck of dust can ruin all the frames when you rewind. You should carry a soft airbrush with which to blow away dust from the lens and from the inside of the camera between rolls.

If you carry several lenses, consider a photo backpack. It will also take your tripod and, hopefully, your water bottles. For reasons I explained in Chapter 1, I think it is essential to use a backpack capable of carrying your water. If you are going to venture into wet canyons when the water level is high, you should carry your photo equipment in sealable plastic bags. If your photo adventure involves swimming, a dedicated dry bag is a must to protect your equipment.

❐ If you use expensive, bulky or slow-to-operate equipment, such as medium or large format, I recommend that you take along an auxiliary digicam with a good lens. It will prove invaluable for photographing difficult sections of trails or narrows. A small digicam is also useful for shooting test images before exposing large-format film. Finally, as noted in Chapter 1, a digital point-&-shoot camera can prove very useful in helping you "remember" your way while hiking in the backcountry.

IN THE FIELD

In the following sections, I'll discuss how to handle a number of common situations you'll encounter in the course of photographing the Southwest. This advice is based on what has consistently worked for me in the field. It doesn't replace a good book specializing in lighting and composition, and it certainly is no substitute for a workshop with an experienced instructor. If you are a novice user wanting to explore the locations in this guidebook without bothering too much about learning photography, I hope this advice will come handy and will help you bring home better pictures.

Using Reflected light

I'll start this discussion with what is arguably the quintessential element of photographing the Southwest: reflected light. Let's define reflected light first. Reflection involves two rays of light. One incidental ray strikes a given surface, which in turn sends out a reflected ray. You can immediately guess that the reflective properties of the surface in question impact the quality of the reflected rays. This is where the second ingredient comes into play: sandstone. People often ask me what I consider so special in the Southwest. My answer is it has the greatest body of sandstone on the planet and that sandstone comes in a great variety of flavors.

Doors at Aztec Ruins

The combination of sandstone and reflected light is what sets the Southwest apart. When light strikes sandstone directly, the reflected light has a much warmer color. If the reflected light happens to reach another patch of sandstone that is not illuminated by direct light, it will cause it to glow with warm colors ranging from deep red to soft yellow. Reflected light is the main ingredient of the best photos of the Southwest. It should always be given priority over direct light.

Photographing Scenics including close Subjects

If your scenic composition includes a close subject, it is often necessary to work with the smallest possible aperture, i.e. the highest settings such as f/22, or even f/64 if you shoot large format, to guarantee maximum depth-of-field. It is very disappointing to view a "grand scenic" photograph in which some parts are not razor-sharp. This is even worse if you enlarge the photo.

If you use a sophisticated SLR or dSLR, you may be able to visualize depth-of-field in the viewfinder. For critical landscape work, it is preferable to work with the manual focusing option and to set the distance not as the exact focus when viewed through the lens, but by using the depth-of-field marks of your lens to maximize sharpness within the particular range of distance pertaining to your shot. Unfortunately many modern lenses, particularly zooms, lack depth-of-field marks so it is often necessary to improvise. Another way to guarantee sharpness and to maximize depth-of-field is by using the hyperfocal distance method. As an example, a 35mm lens focused at 10 feet at f/16 yields a sharp image from 5 feet (which is half the hyperfocal distance) to infinity. There are some handy charts you can buy for a few dollars for every camera format. This method is a sure bet to create a sharp-focused image from close range to infinity. In certain cases, you may want to purposely blur the background to isolate your foreground and create an artistic effect using *bokeh* (a Japanese term signifying the out-of-focus area of a photograph).

Photographing on River Trips

Your primary concern on a rafting trip is to keep your camera equipment dry. This includes not only the body but also your lenses, batteries, film and/or storage devices. It's one thing to have a splash-proof camera, but you'll need to protect your lenses too and take all precautions to avoid immersion. Some cameras are designed to survive a short immersion in clean water, but few will resist dirty water full of tiny particles of sediment. Your film would not like it either.

To keep your camera and small personal items dry, you'll receive a supposedly waterproof "ammo can". Ammo cans work well as long as the rubber gasket in the lid is in good condition; they tend to deteriorate over time after being repeatedly drenched and cooked in the sun and few clients bother reporting leaks at trip's end. If possible, I suggest you test it in a bathtub prior to your departure.

Rafting the Green River (photo by Philippe Schuler)

Another concern with ammo cans is that your gear risks being knocked around badly when your craft is tossed about in the rapids.

Serious photographers have to look into more secure alternatives for their gear. Waterproof camera bags work well but it can be difficult to keep the sand out when handling the bag in camp, which is always a sandy beach.

Personally, I use a Model 8 waterproof, transparent Sealline bag while on the boat, in which I carry a small digital camera equipped with an image stabilizer. When crossing rapids, the bag quickly clips to the top strap of my life jacket and the camera can be stored or retrieved in a matter of seconds. The digital camera is the only thing I need to shoot from the boat, when movement and speed preclude anything else than snapshots and require you to work fast. Meanwhile, my main equipment is safely stowed in my camera backpack, which is itself hermetically sealed in a waterproof Pelican hardcase strapped on deck. My tripod is also strapped until we land, but can be retrieved immediately. Upon landing for a hike, the camera bag goes directly from the Pelican case to my back. Admittedly, this setup will only work with a relatively small bag.

If you have a large amount of gear, the specialized waterproof photo backpack is the best solution. I recommend using a solid carabiner to strap the pack somewhere on deck so it's not constantly in your way. If you do go with only one camera and one zoom lens, consider taking only a Sealline bag; it is highly practical and perfectly adapted to the rigors of rafting.

Photographing Running Water

Waterfalls and running water are great subjects for photography. Many people wonder how to create the so-called "angel hair" effect of soft water. It is actually quite simple: use a long exposure. To get the smooth flowing look but also retain a bit of detail or "texture" in the water, try shooting at 1 to 3 seconds. It's not always possible to achieve such slow shutter speeds under normal circumstances and chances are you'll need a bit of help from some extra equipment. Your first option is to use the lowest ISO possible. If you have a polarizing filter, you can use it to further reduce the aperture by 1½ to 2 stops, thus almost quadrupling the exposure. In most cases, this is still not going to be enough. To get a truly beautiful effect you'll need to resort to a neutral density filter (non-graduated). The most common ND filter adds 6 stops to a scene, so what was a 1/30 second exposure at f/8 now becomes a 2 second exposure—enough for a wonderful image of nicely blurred water. Obviously, you'll need a tripod and some kind of mechanical or electronic shutter release. If you are using an SLR or dSLR, I can't emphasize enough the benefit of mirror lockup.

In some cases, a bluish cast can enhance the beauty of running water. To add a bluish cast, photograph the water in indirect light with the high color temperature of the blue sky providing the illumination. A film such as Fujichrome Velvia, which is optimized for warm color temperature will produce some truly exquisite enhanced blue. Using a digital camera, you may have to experiment a bit with the white balance to achieve the results you're looking for.

Photographing Water Reflections

There are several key elements to obtaining great reflections on a body of water. First you need side light or backlight—the latter works great as long as it is not directly in your field of vision and you're using a shade. The light should be soft, so as not to overwhelm the scene, eradicating details and creating nasty shadow areas. Next, you need the ambient air to be perfectly still. The slightest trace of wind will agitate the surface and create ripples that will mar your subject's reflection. If the wind shows no sign of abating, try using it to your advantage and concentrate on playing with colors in the reflection. You'll also need some strong foreground element to anchor the composition and add depth, making the viewer feel immersed in the scene.

In most cases, the reflection is significantly less bright than the actual subject. If it occupies a large portion of the frame, such as in the case of a reflection in a lake, you need a split or graduated neutral density filter to compensate the exposure and keep some detail in what would otherwise be a shadow area in an uncorrected photograph.

Zen Pond

Photographing Dunes and Lava Beds

Crest of the Wave

Sand and lava are two subjects that can easily fool your built-in meter and you may get unpleasant results if you use it. Many new automatic cameras have programs that supposedly compensate for specific lighting conditions; however, you will get better results by compensating the exposure manually based on the lighting conditions. For brown and red sand, you should bracket your exposure in small increments of ½ to 1 f/stop based on the effect you want to achieve. For deeply saturated red sand in the evening sun, try ½ stop under and over exposure, as well as whatever your meter says. For extremely white sand in bright daylight 1½ f/stops overexposure works best; in early to mid-morning, late afternoon or when it's overcast, try ½ f/stop overexposure for scenics and 1 f/stop for sand patterns.

Depending on the light, lava usually doesn't need as much correction, as it is more gray rather than pure black. However, if you want to make it darker, underexpose by ¼ or ½ f/stop.

Photographing Snow & Ice

If you shoot in autumn, winter or spring in Colorado, you're bound to encounter snow and ice and you may want to integrate them into your compositions, either as part of a scenic landscape or by themselves.

Your camera's built-in meter is programmed to render everything a neutral grey, which is of course not what you want with snow and ice. To avoid this, you need to compensate by opening your aperture between 1 and 2 f/stops depending on how bright the scene is. Exposing snow and ice correctly is tricky because you don't want to lose detail in the highlights. In broad daylight, I usually start with a +1½ stop compensation in order to expose the snow so it will be white. If snow is just a background, you'll want to expose your main subject correctly, particularly if it's a person, and let the snow be overexposed.

As with any ordinary scene, shooting snow during the golden hour creates nice shadows, making your photos more interesting. I usually prefer a fair amount of sunlight to make the snow shine.

A bright sunny sky will create a strong blue cast in the shaded areas, especially when your subject is extremely bright. If you don't want the blue cast, use an 81a or 81b filter to provide warmth but making sure that the snow or ice doesn't look reddish or adjust the white balance of your digital camera manually.

A polarizing filter can accentuate the contrast, eliminate glare and restore proper exposure for the sky if the latter is somewhat hazy. If the sky is already very blue, be sure not to overdo the polarizing effect or your sky will be too dark; even more when the sun is at a 90° angle.

An overcast sky during a clearing storm can also work to your advantage by filtering the light, making the snow act as a soft reflector. Digital cameras have an advantage over film as you can fine-tune the white balance by checking for immediate results on your LCD.

Photographing Wildflowers

The two most important factors in photographing wildflowers are the presence of soft, diffused light and the absence of wind. In the case of the light, one thing to avoid is direct illumination by the sun. A cloudy, overcast day always works best. Partly cloudy skies may provide intermittently suitable conditions.

If you are really serious about your wildflower photography, you may need a diffuser and/or reflector for the light and a small tent for the wind (and light) if you do macro photography. An acquaintance of mine has built a wonderful little tent/diffuser using a cheap laundry bag, so it is definitely possible to improvise.

Two filters are essential for wildflowers. A warming filter will always come in handy to remove the blue cast, particularly at higher elevations and if you shoot during the day. An 81a warming filter works best. A polarizing filter is also very useful to remove glare.

I find that high-end digital cameras work well for close-ups of flowers against a blurred background. I still prefer film with

Storm & Wildflowers (photo by Adam Schallau)

medium and large format, however, to shoot scenes involving large fields of flowers. On the other hand, this point may be moot by the time you read this.

When shooting fields of wildflowers, avoid placing your camera too high. You'll get more dynamic results if you shoot at the flower's level. Large format cameras with tilt and shift movements have an enormous advantage. They allow you to concentrate on a close group of flowers while keeping the background in focus to infinity. Digicams with small size sensors can also do the same thing but at a tremendous cost in terms of detail and sense of three-dimensionality.

One common mistake is to be in too big a hurry to take pictures when arriving on the scene. Instead, scan the field for the best flowers, making sure you have an interesting background and paying attention not to include any white or grey sky. Don't be overwhelmed by the color alone; be sure that the flowers you are photographing appear fresh and are wide open. Some older flowers may still look good to you in the viewfinder but may not look their best on a large print.

Colorado is usually great for shooting wildflowers from mid-July to mid-August. There are some excellent online resources for monitoring wildflowers' bloom.

Photographing Fall Colors

Photographing fall colors in Colorado is an exhilarating experience. While it may lack the red foliage of autumn in New England, it adds the incredible yellow and rust colors of cottonwoods and aspens to the grandiose backgrounds of valleys, mountain sides and snowy peaks. Many outstanding fall color locations are discussed in this volume.

One filter you absolutely need for fall colors is a warming filter. Once again a Skylight or 81a filter is usually sufficient to get rid of the bluish cast, which is particularly noticeable at higher elevations. A polarizing filter may also be useful when used in moderation. I use it essentially to remove glare on foliage.

Film, particularly medium and large format transparency film, will continue to give better results than digital for a number of years, not necessarily in terms of sharpness, but for tonality, overall smoothness and three-dimensionality. Fujichrome Velvia 100 is the classic film for shooting fall colors. Fujichrome Velvia 100F does a good job with the reds and is a little tamer when it comes to controlling contrast. I also like Astia 100F for its ability to hold detail in shadows. Kodak film usually does a better job with subtle orange hues.

Photographing Rock Art

Rock art tends to be quite contrasty; therefore it is prone to color casts when photographed with highly saturated films under strong reflected light. Puebloan ruins, often tucked inside deep alcoves, bring the danger of reciprocity failure, particularly for those who shoot large format.

If you shoot under strong reflected light, you are bound to have an exaggerated amount of red on films such as Fujichrome Velvia and Ektachrome VS. If you shoot in dark areas, Velvia will tend to give you an excess of green. In both cases, a slightly lower contrast film such as Fuji Provia will serve you better. The latter offers the finest grain of any slide film as of this writing and it is well suited to accurately reproduce the delicate textures and subdued golden browns of rock art. With large format, an exposure of 30 seconds is common in low light situations. With an additional one stop, you can reduce this to fifteen seconds, thus limiting the color shift.

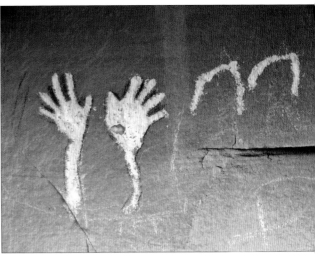

Waving Hands

Large format photographers have the advantage of being able to change plates to match a particular lighting situation. 35mm and medium format photographers must be more careful with the kind of film they load before shooting rock art and small ruins. If you shoot digitally, it might be a good idea to take a custom white balance measurement on the panel, especially if you shoot Jpeg. If you shoot Raw, it doesn't make much difference as you'll be able to adjust the white balance when post-processing your file. In general, I find that shooting rock art digitally gives excellent results.

Photographing Night Scenes

Shooting scenery at night can be a lot of fun and, with a little experience, can yield surprisingly good results. Although it is fraught with technical challenges, it's becoming easier than ever with recent advances in digital technology. The only real drawback remaining is that it requires very long exposures to maintain adequate depth-of-field.

If you are shooting film, you're faced with two disadvantages compared to digital, one purely technical and the other practical: On the technical side, the phenomenon of "reciprocity failure" requires that progressively more light impresses the film as the exposure time increases. While your meter might indicate an exposure time of 4 minutes, you might have to double that to compensate for the reciprocity failure characteristics of your particular film. This example is purely for the purpose of explaining the phenomenon, you will have to check the specs given by the film manufacturer to calculate how much additional exposure time is needed. Reciprocity failure tables are available for the major brands of film. Unfortunately, you can't see the results until your film is processed. As night photography involves a fair amount of guesswork, you may not get the results you expect and you won't find out until your film comes back.

Digital, by contrast, lets you view your results if not immediately, at least just after you've taken the shot, so if you are patient enough, you will get a picture. Reciprocity failure does not affect sensors, so long exposure times are drastically reduced. Digital night photography has its own problem, however, and it's called noise. Small digicams and even some dSLRs produce unacceptable amounts of noise. Some cameras use aggressive noise reduction techniques, which tend to remove a lot of detail. As digital technology matures, however, nighttime photography is bound to become easier and better, thanks to low-noise, high-ISO sensors become more prevalent. Be sure to have a spare battery as long exposures tend to consume power exponentially.

Photographing Lightning

This section should perhaps be called Photographing scenics with lightning, as the idea is to capture lightning as it strikes near an interesting landmark. There are different techniques for photographing lightning. The one I use is rather low tech but it usually works adequately with a digital camera. It can be done whenever you have some interesting scenery and an electrical storm at night dur-

Shiprock Lightning (photo by Tom Till)

ing the monsoon season. Set up your camera on a sturdy tripod, use a low ISO, set the focus to infinity, and choose an aperture of f/5.6. Take repeated exposures of about 30 seconds to a minute each, depending on the frequency of the lightning. After you catch some lightning, evaluate the results and reduce or increase the aperture accordingly. Just discard the frames when you caught nothing.

You can also try to shoot at dusk, using the same technique, with a 6 f/stop ND filter and an exposure time of a few seconds to 30 seconds. You'll actually have to meter it. It's trickier, but it's great fun and you can see instantly if it works. The results can be spectacular if it's dark enough; otherwise the bolts of lightning tend to be absorbed by the daylight.

In all cases, choose a shooting location that is safe and be sure to be far enough from the storm. When you see lightning, count the seconds until you hear thunder. Sound travels 1 mile in about five seconds. If the time is thirty seconds or less, it means the thunderstorm is within 6 miles, and therefore dangerous.

More on Exposure

If you are working with transparency film and wish to obtain the best results without concerning yourself too much about determining the right exposure, take five different shots at ½ stop intervals—i.e. two on either side of the setting you think is correct. In the case of negative film, this is unnecessary since the density of the highlights and shadows can easily be altered during the printing process. Negative film tolerates up to 2 stops of overexposure fairly well, but does poorly with underexposure. If you are a perfectionist, you can always take a second shot with one stop of overexposure—it is useless to try more. If you are using a digital camera, you have the advantage of seeing the results immediately on your LCD. While this is not very precise, it at least gives you a starting point. Also, the more advanced digital cameras have the ability to display a histogram, which allows you to check exposure with a high degree of accuracy.

Attention should also be paid to the reciprocity failure characteristics of film, especially if you are using a tripod and slow transparency film. With exposures of several seconds, certain slide films display a tendency towards incorrect exposure and you risk underexposing the film, as mentioned earlier. There are reciprocity failure tables for the major brands of film on the market. Unless you are taking exposures of four seconds or more, you shouldn't have to worry about this.

Some Advice on Composition

Composition is fortunately not an exact science or else it would be the domain of engineers. Rather, it is a subtle blend of classic established rules, specific properties of your subject and, perhaps most importantly, your own artistic sensibility. While I can't help you with the last two, this short refresher course might help you remember and use "the rules" during your visit to the Southwest.

❒ Before you think about composition, remember that lighting is everything in landscape photography. An image is rarely attractive without interesting light.

❒ Remember the "rule of thirds" to avoid an unaesthetic horizon line in the middle of your picture or a main subject that is too centered. Visualize your image overlaid by an imaginary grid dividing it into thirds horizontally and vertically. Try placing your key elements at the bottom left or right intersections of the grid, or at the upper left or right intersections if there is an interesting foreground, but avoid the middle of the picture.

❒ Be sure to check that the horizon doesn't appear tilted in your viewfinder. Using a tripod and taking your time is the best way to avoid an unpleasant surprise. If you're having trouble, use a small level in your camera's hot shoe.

❒ Resist the urge to squeeze too much of a grand panorama into a small picture. Results are almost always disappointing due to the lack of a center of interest, unless the sky is particularly exciting. Your image will usually be more interesting if you zoom in on a small portion and include some of that nice sky.

❒ Fill most of the frame with your main subject. Too many secondary subjects create clutter and become indistinguishable in a small picture, even though they look good to the naked eye.

❏ Include an interesting foreground and put your main subject slightly off-center when it is distant. This will create depth in your image and reinforce the feeling of presence. Make sure the foreground is not just empty fill-in space, however. If this is the case, it is often better to give the distant subject more prominence rather than having the bottom two-thirds of the frame filled with a boring subject. Always think depth and presence. Some imposing formations may appear smallish in your image if you do not include a reference object, such as trees, a trail or a human silhouette, to provide a sense of scale.

❏ Thoughtfully consider the benefit of telephoto lenses. Long telephotos serve three purposes: extracting details from the landscape, making a subject stand out through creative use of *bokeh* (the unsharp area in a photograph) and compressing the perspective. The compression effect makes your photographs appear rich and dense by allowing several planes to cohabit in one image.

❏ Super wide-angle lenses give excellent results with very tightly-framed close subjects by accentuating—or even esthetically distorting—the graphic, geometric or even abstract properties. Rocks with interesting colors or texture, shapes in sand dunes or badlands, and trees and bushes are examples.

❏ Be mindful of shadows, and make use of a graduated neutral density filter if necessary. So called "golden hour" photography is great, but what appears to you as a simple shaded area may look completely black on your photo.

❏ Above all, be constantly on the lookout for photogenic details around you—rock texture, natural elements with abstract shapes, uncommon colors, reflections, transparent views, interesting vegetation, or tracks and leaves on the ground. Using these elements, you can create some wonderfully original compositions. Not all of them will be keepers, but some will yield beautiful images that are a welcome departure from the common "grand scenic" images. Digital photography can help you in that regard, as it costs nothing to experiment.

Photographing in National Parks

Most people carry some form of camera and are eager to capture memories of their trip using the recognized icons of the West as a background. National Parks have become incredibly recognizable through movies, advertisements, park literature, and coffee table books, not to mention guidebooks such as this one. No wonder people want to show that they've been there. The glorification of the West creates a desire to accumulate photographs as trophies, and cheap film and easy-to-use digital cameras make this almost effortless. In view of the massive onslaught of people in relatively concentrated areas, we must be mindful of our collective impact on the land.

So far the National Park Service has maintained the view that photographers—whether amateur or professional—should be treated like any other visitors. While there are no specific restrictions imposed on us, we are also expected to obey the rules. Some large-format photographers talk of a stigma attached to carrying a tripod and bulky equipment in remote places. I carry a tripod at all times and I have never felt singled out in my interactions with park rangers. So should we worry? I personally don't think so. Federal legislation (Public Law 106-206), which has been around for several years, stipulates that the National Park Service cannot require a permit or assess a fee for still photography if the photography takes place where members of the public are generally allowed and the photography does not involve models or props which are not a part of the site's natural or cultural resources or administrative facilities. The Park Service once floated the possibility of requiring permits for professional photographers, but the idea was abandoned.

My credo is that we, as privileged visitors to pristine areas, should act as good citizens and be mindful of the environment so that our impact on the land not force closures of sensitive areas. We must do everything we can to tread lightly, on foot and on the back roads, to avoid damaging the land and to preserve it for generations to come.

Parting Shots

There is another less palpable, but no less essential ingredient to good landscape photography: an unbridled love for nature and strong emotional connection to the land and your subject. The act of photographing should be an exten-

Hello-o-o-o-o-o

sion of that love, to record the memories and share with others the joy of being there. If your fascination with camera equipment or the physics of photography take precedence over your love of nature in an unbalanced way, it is doubtful that you'll ever achieve great results. Your craft may become technically excellent and you may acquire a nice portfolio to show friends, but you won't be able to communicate emotions if they weren't present when you took the picture. Most people I know who seriously pursue photography of the Southwest have this love of the land within them. Sometimes, however, I meet folks who are more interested in the act of photographing than in enjoying the beauty around them. Over the years I have taken pleasure in asking people whether they would do a particularly strenuous hike to a beautiful spot if they had to leave their camera at home. I have had a few people flatly—and honestly—tell me that they wouldn't. This isn't necessarily a criticism; photography doesn't have to equate to love of nature to be enjoyed as a hobby. I do say, however, that simply being there, quietly enjoying the place and the moment, is in my opinion far more important than bringing back a few pictures.

Another important axiom of good landscape photography is that it rarely happens by accident. In all probability you'll need to visit a location several times, to see it under different light and in different seasons—perhaps even a few times without a camera—to start pre-visualizing your image. As you observe, think and feel during your time there, you will learn to refine your past experience to anticipate a change of light or a break in the clouds. Your best images—those which carry the most emotional content—will be the result of careful planning and pre-visualization.

Finally, with your pre-visualized image in mind, you'll rise early—very early—and drag your sleepy body inside a freezing car. You'll drive on the edge of your seat to the now familiar location, peering at the darkness to spot deer on the road through the partially frozen windshield, nervously glancing at the clock and worrying about the changing light on the horizon. Perhaps you'll be chewing on a hard power bar between nervous sips of coffee to warm you up a bit and get your mind in gear. You will walk to your location briskly, plant your tripod firmly, ready-up filters and lenses. You'll wait, floating in a dual state of serene peace and nervous anticipation. And then, the momentous event you came for will happen: sunrise. The land will be bathed in hues of yellow and red and you will understand the reason you must take this journey.

But there is little time for reflection. There is a job to be done—photos to be taken. The adrenaline kicks in and you are totally focused. You shoot like a maniac, oblivious to everything else but your subject, annoyed if someone else suddenly shows up. You shoot and shoot until the incredible light finally becomes a little too bright, a little too crude. When you're done you smile and bask in the deep feeling of joy that overtakes you as you feel one with this place that you love so much. You linger a while to make the feeling last, letting the sun warm you up, your body still weary from lack of sleep. As you walk back to the trailhead you let your mind wander and play like a puppy. You're proud and ecstatic at having experienced this cosmic moment. You suddenly become part of the great brotherhood of early-rising nature lovers, and, unbeknownst to you, you've just bonded with the fly fisherman in Montana, the ice fisherman in Minnesota and the deer hunter in Idaho!

Months later you sit in your living room looking at the big, majestic enlargement hanging on the wall and you grin happily at the beloved landscape basking in the morning sun. But you also feel something deeper—a special connection. The memories that you bring back from such incredibly poignant and precious moments are treasured as much as the print itself. You may not have the words to express it, but that's okay. The picture will speak for you. ✿

Steamboat Rock

Chapter 3

DINOSAUR NATIONAL MONUMENT

Echo Park (aka Center of the Universe)

DINOSAUR NATIONAL MONUMENT

Straddling the northeast corner of Utah and northwest corner of Colorado, Dinosaur National Monument is a bit out of the way for most people, but the rewards from a visit are many: fantastic mountain and canyon scenery, two wonderful rivers offering great rafting, outstanding Fremont rock art, great camping, spectacular fall colors and few crowds. Oh, and I almost forgot... a remarkable Dinosaur Quarry exhibit!

Most people think of the Monument in terms of the Dinosaur Quarry, but the real star attraction is the 210,000 acres of rugged and beautiful country. Not that the Dinosaur Quarry isn't a wonderfully instructive attraction, but as a photographer the remarkable landscape of the park will be the main focus of your visit. Dinosaur is one huge park and very much an open book of geology with its tortured uplifts and exposed rock layers. It is also a rewarding place if you are looking for solitude and silence; Dinosaur sees less than 300,000 visitors per year—70% of which come in summer. This lack of heavy crowds, even at the height of summer, greatly contributes to a quality experience of the high desert. A scientific study conducted in the nineties has found the ambient noise in Dinosaur to be less than that of a recording studio. Take a hike on the Sound of Silence or Desert Voices trails early in the morning and you'll be able to experience this firsthand.

The solitude and silence are for a large part the result of the Monument's lack of through-access roads. Despite its enormous acreage, only four rather sinuous paved roads provide access close to the Monument's borders—and in one case a deeper foray inside its interior. Although these roads allow you to see some of the park's highlights, you'll need to take dirt roads, do a few dayhikes, or even consider a rafting trip, in order to see the park in-depth. Given the distances involved, count on spending three to five days to discover and photograph the park at an unhurried pace.

The Monument has two Visitor Centers: one is located 1.5 miles east of the small town of Dinosaur, CO on US 40; the other is at the Dinosaur Quarry on UT 149, a few miles from Jensen, UT. All the comforts and trappings of civilization are available in nearby Vernal, UT west of the Monument on US 40.

The Dinosaur Quarry

The remarkably well designed Quarry structure houses fossilized dinosaur skeletons—with about 1500 bones purposely left exposed on the cliff face to be observed at close range by the public. The cliff containing the fossils can be viewed from two levels, but don't expect too much photographically. There are numerous exhibits explaining the evolution, reign and disappearance of dinosaurs, as well as how the bones ended up getting buried, then excavated, in this particular area. It is believed that 150 million years ago, this area was part of a riverbed with a sand bank where dead dinos and other prehistoric creatures became deeply buried after eons of flooding. In later times, uplift and erosion caused the soft sedimentary layers to wash away, exposing the fossilized bones.

Despite the excellent exhibits, your curiosity about dinosaurs and paleontology will be better rewarded by attending one of the excellent short Ranger talks.

Needless to say, the place is a magnet for families with kids and school groups, but during springtime and autumn, you'll find the place very quiet, beautiful and enjoyable. From Memorial Day through Labor Day you must park at the lower Visitor Center and walk the short quarter mile road to the upper Visitor Center and Quarry, or use the shuttle bus if you are rebuked by the slope.

Getting there: The quarry building is located ¼ mile from UT 149—the west entrance road to the Monument—about 7 miles north of Jensen on US 40.

Time required: 1 to 2 hours, depending on your interest in paleontology, preferably around midday when the light is too crude to photograph outdoors.

Around Split Mountain

UT 149 continues for almost 11 miles past the Quarry turnoff, providing spectacular views of Split Mountain along the way. This road is known as Tour of the Tilted Rocks and a sign warns visitors that there are no fossils on display along the road. In fact, there are no fossils to be seen anywhere else inside the Monument.

Darn, no more dino bones, only superlative mountain, river and canyon scenery! About 1 mile past the Quarry turnoff, you'll come to the Swelter Shelter on the north side of the road, a small cave used for thousands of years with a few Fremont petroglyphs and pictographs. About a mile further, you'll encounter the 2.8-mile long Sound of Silence loop route, providing a glimpse at the arid desert environment and aiming to teach people how to find their way in the desert through a series of explanatory markers. The route follows Red Wash for about a mile before leaving it to enter reddish badlands. Bear right at all the junctions until you exit the narrow labyrinth and catch a glimpse of Split Mountain. The route continues on the

Massive Uplift near Split Mountain

bench with nice open views, forcing you to do some easy routefinding through gullies and ridges before rejoining the wash. It's a good idea to take the leaflet at the trailhead before embarking on this hike.

About 2.5 miles from the quarry turnoff, take the paved road to your left leading north to the actual Split Mountain area with its beautiful campground, picnic area and boat ramp. Stop at the scenic overlook to photograph the uplift and the massive bent dome in the background. This is a spectacular place and the closest you'll get to Split Mountain. Close to the campground entrance and boat ramp, you'll find the Desert Voices loop trail. The 1.5-mile loop is one of the most educative and thought-provoking interpretive trails you'll find in any National Park or Monument. Although the signs were primarily designed to challenge young minds by raising their awareness of the desert and mankind's interaction with it, adults will do well to reflect on it too. A 0.5-mile connector trail links the Sound of Silence and Desert Voices trails together, forming a nice loop. Both trails are best hiked in the morning, before the sun gets too high.

After coming back to the Split Mountain turnoff, the tour road follows the Green River to the east, affording highly photogenic views from the low plateau. It then traverses the beautiful private Chew Ranch after crossing the Green River. It follows Cub Creek before turning into a gravel road as it reenters the Monument. Shortly after the mildly interesting Elephant Toes Butte comes into view, you'll find two pullouts in succession with trails leading to the north to petroglyph sites. Both are a must for photographers, but the second one is particularly spectacular. A well-graded trail leads to the bottom of a sandstone cliff harboring petroglyphs of uncommonly large lizards and a Kokopelli.

The road continues for another mile to reach the historic Josie Morris Cabin, set under a canopy of trees at the mouth of a 1000-foot deep box canyon. Time permitting, explore the coolness of nearby Hog Canyon on a 1-mile walk.

Photo advice: The Tour of the Tilted Rocks road is excellent mornings and evenings. Although I tend to prefer late afternoon, there are outstanding morning views of the back of Split Mountain in the early morning from near Josie Morris' cabin. The best vantage point in the area is the Scenic Overlook above the Split Mountain campground. It offers a bird's eye view of the campground and the Green River with the red monocline directly ahead. Gazing at this vista, you'll have to admit that Split Mountain's name is well deserved. From here, it does look like it's been pried open and torqued by colossal tectonic forces, exposing remarkably colorful rock strata.

Time required: 1½ hour up to half a day if you choose to hike.

Island Park Road & McKee Spring

The 18-mile long Island Park gravel road provides access to this remote section of the park that sees little visitation outside summer. Yet it provides access to some exquisite petroglyphs as well as spectacular views of the Green River. Although it is quite a long drive from the Quarry and Split Mountain, this road is actually located just to the north and behind Split Mountain as the crow flies.

Almost 11 miles from the beginning of the Island Park Road is one of the most outstanding Fremont petroglyph panels in the area: the McKee Spring site. Although the site is not marked, you'll have no trouble locating it. About 0.6 mile after passing the interpretive booth marking the Monument's entrance on the right side of the road, you'll notice a couple of pull-outs and a well-worn trail on the left side of the road, leading north toward a low cliff. A short loop takes you through a few panels consisting of anthropomorphs and geometric designs, superbly chiseled and preserved in the beautiful ocher-colored sandstone cliff and providing outstanding photographic opportunities under the right lighting conditions.

About 1.5 miles further, and time permitting, you may want to take the 0.75-mile

McKee Spring Petroglyphs

spur road to Rainbow Park, which is essentially a boat ramp and a couple of primitive campsites with a mildly interesting view of the Green River as it enters Split Mountain. Instead, I recommend that you proceed directly to the Island Park Overlook for its superlative panoramic view of the large open valley formed by the Green River. From the Rainbow Park turnoff, continue for another 1.5 miles and turn right; it's another 0.3 mile to the top. This is an amazing sight in the fall when the cottonwoods have turned. From the last turnoff, another 5 miles brings you to beautiful Island Park, with its banks well shaded by large tracts of cottonwoods.

Photo advice: The McKee Spring petroglyphs can be photographed at close range and a normal lens works well. The cliff is facing south and the glyphs can be photographed all day, with a preference to the early morning. The panoramic view from the Island Park Overlook requires at least a 24mm lens to take it all in. The view is toward the east so it's better to be here in mid to late afternoon.

Getting there: About halfway between Jensen and the Dinosaur Quarry on UT 149, turn northwest on Brush Creek Road for about 5 miles then turn right on a dirt road and drive 4 miles until you reach the marked Island Park Road. If you're coming from downtown Vernal, leave US 191 for 500N Street heading east for about 3 miles. Leaving Brush Creek Road to your right, turn left on Jones Hole Road (aka Diamond Mountain Road) for about 5 miles until you reach an unmarked road veering to the right; after a little less than a mile on this road, turn right at the T and another mile brings you to the marked Island Park Road to your left. From there, it is about 10 miles to the Monument's entrance on a graded gravel road. This road is open year-round and is usually suitable for passenger cars, but becomes impassable when wet.

Time required: at least 3 hours from Jensen or Vernal.

Jones Hole

During the week you will encounter few cars along the narrow but very good paved road to Jones Hole and the Fish Hatchery, even at the height of summer. There are apparently few people willing to tackle the 80-mile round-trip drive from Vernal to this remote location and hike the 8-mile round-trip Jones Creek Trail to the Green River. It's a pity because this is one of the easiest and most beautiful trails in the Southwest, on a par with the Lower Calf Creek Falls (see *Photographing the Southwest - Volume 1*) as one of the top hikes for families with children. There is plenty to see and enjoy even a short distance from the trailhead. Although the elevation loss to the Green River is about 500 feet over 4 miles, the trail feels essentially flat. What makes this hike so beautiful is exquisite Jones Creek, constantly bubbling and scintillating at your side. This is one spectacular creek and a favorite of local fishermen on week-ends. The Fish Hatchery taps directly into the natural spring of Jones Creek and releases some of the purest waters you can find (it must nonetheless be filtered).

The trail begins at the bottom of the fish ponds and immediately enters a lush riparian environment. After about 1.5 miles, just past a wooden footbridge, you'll reach the spur trail for the colorful Deluge Shelter pictograph panel. Shortly after that is the junction with the Ely Creek Trail, leading to a nice waterfall in about 0.3 mile and, further, to a box canyon area known as the Labyrinth. At the junction, there is also a tiny but extremely pleasant backcountry campground (permit required). From this point on the canyon widens, revealing beautiful tall cliffs made of very ancient sandstone and limestone layers. During the remaining 2.2 miles from the Ely Creek Trail to the Green River, you're bound to encounter rafters on a short day hike to the petroglyphs and the waterfall; you may also encounter deer. The trail ends at the Green River in Whirlpool Canyon, which is wide and beautiful at this spot. Upstream, to your left,

Jones Hole Trail (photo by Philippe Schuler)

was the planned location for the dam that would have flooded Echo Park and surrounding canyons without the active opposition of environmental groups.

Getting there: From downtown Vernal, leave US 191 for 500N Street heading east for about 3 miles. There, bear left on Jones Hole Road (aka Diamond Mountain Road) and follow the signs until the end of the road at the National Fish Hatchery

Time required: 4 to 5 hours for the hike, with enough time to photograph and relax by the river, plus almost 2 hours for the round-trip drive from Vernal to the Fish Hatchery trailhead.

Harpers Corner & the Journey Through Time Road

The 31-mile Journey Through Time road leading to Harpers Corner traverses a high plateau providing wide-ranging views of an immense wilderness with pristine habitat and virtually no human presence. The main vista points are located close to 8000 feet in elevation, allowing you to look down on a vast landscape of canyons, mesas, so-called "parks" and colorful geologic features. The journey begins at the Monument's Headquarters and Visitor Center on US 40, 1.5 miles east of Dinosaur, CO.

The first overlook on the Harpers Corner Road is Plug Hat Butte, reached after about 4 miles and a short climb from the valley floor. The 0.5-mile nature trail offers panoramic views toward the south. There is good color from a fault down below, but the panorama is too vast for photography and lacks drama.

The road continues its ascent of the plateau toward Escalante Overlook, about 4 miles further, offering a similarly distant panoramic view to the west.

Having reached the high plateau, the road meanders through several miles of rather arid sagebrush steppe, eventually reaching the short Canyon Overlook road to your right, about 12 miles from the Escalante Overlook. Canyon Overlook provides great views of the Yampa Bench and the rugged canyons carved by the Yampa River. One can easily imagine the abundance of wildlife in such a huge wilderness.

A little over a mile past the sign marking the Colorado-Utah border, you'll see a road to the left with a sign announcing the hang gliding takeoff place. Reset your odometer here and about 1 mile beyond this road, look to the left for a large slab of flat slickrock covered by desert varnish close to the road. Pull off the road and find a suitable location to park your car away from traffic. The best spot is actually on the left side of the road, so you might consider stopping here on the return trip from Harpers Corner. A barbed wire fence needs to be crossed in order to get to the slickrock slab, but don't be alarmed, you won't be trespassing on private property. The reason for the fence is that the park road is an NPS easement in the midst of BLM-administered lands; its purpose is to prevent range animals from wandering on the park road. The fence is low and stones have been strategically arranged to let you scale it easily. Once on the slickrock, you'll immediately spot some photogenic petroglyphs carved on the ground into the desert varnish. This kind of horizontal carving is rare in the Southwest. If you enjoy rock art, you can easily spend an hour here scouting and photographing. Some of the most prominent petroglyphs include figures of cute little humanoids sporting antennas, footprints and bighorn sheep.

At about mile 25, you'll pass the Echo Park Road to your right; we'll leave it for the next section. For now, continue for less than a mile to Island Park Overlook to catch a distant glimpse of the canyon formed by the Green River.

Shortly thereafter comes Iron Springs Bench Overlook with a superb view to the east toward the Yampa Bench canyons. I rate this overlook second only to the Harpers Corner Overlook.

A little over 3 miles further, the Echo Park Overlook has a picnic area and allows you to see Steamboat Rock in Echo Park, but the view is still too distant for interesting photography.

At last, you reach the Harpers Corner trailhead at the end of the road. The 2-mile round-trip trail straddles a narrow ridge; it is relatively easy, with spectacular openings on both sides particularly to the west as you near the end. Nothing prepares you, however, for the breathtaking bird's eye view from Harpers Corner itself.

It is difficult to describe Harpers Corner without resorting to superlatives. I'll say only that it is one of the top panoramic views in the Southwest. The view is extremely open on all sides. Whirlpool Canyon appears below to your left.

The amazing upturned layers of the giant monocline caused by the Uinta uplift rise at an impossible angle 2400 feet below, with Lodore Canyon in the back. To your right, you can see the Mitten Park fault and the long slender silhouette of Steamboat Rock's ridge with the Green River in front, and the Yampa River nearing the confluence in the back. If you're going to spend any time in the Monument, you could return one last time to Harpers Corner so you can contemplate all the places you've been to!

Photo advice: Harpers Corner isn't a great place for sunrise or sunset. It is best photographed in mid-morning or afternoon light under a soft or dramatic stormy sky. Don't come too early in the morning or most of the views will be backlit, with the exception of Whirlpool Canyon to the west. Likewise, don't arrive too late in the afternoon or the jutting promontory at the end of the trail will cast a giant shadow on the Mitten Park fault in front of you. Don't get there in the middle of the day either or everything will appear washed out. If the light isn't right, forget photography and simply enjoy this truly unique view.

Getting there: The road leaves from the main Dinosaur National Monument Visitor Center, which also serves as Park headquarters. It is located 2 miles east of the junction of US 40 and CO 64 in Dinosaur, CO. Coming from the Quarry/Split Mountain area, you can also use County Road 16s as a shortcut; it leaves about 12 miles east of Jensen and joins the Harpers Corner Road 12 miles north of the Visitor Center. This road crosses BLM land and can provide alternate camping in case the Echo Park campground is full or closed. During wintertime, Harpers Corner Road closes at Plug Hat when snow drifts become too deep.

View from Harpers Corner

Nearby location: The little community of Dinosaur! Where else can you live on a street named Tyrannosaurus Rex? Be sure to stop for refreshments at the BedRock Depot and admire the photography of Bill Mitchem, a longtime local resident. His collection of photographs of the Monument is very extensive. The excellent Colorado Welcome Center has up-to-date information on the area and the entire State.

Time required: about 4 hours round-trip from Dinosaur.

Echo Park

Echo Park ranks as one of my favorite places in the Southwest. It is a place of great power, beauty and spirituality; a temple of nature radiating a quiet energy that pervades our consciousness in a positive, soothing way; a place where one feels humbled by nature but also very safe in her hands. Some people call Echo Park the Center of the Universe. Although the two places are very different, I can't resist a comparison with Upper Cathedral Valley in Capitol Reef (see *Photographing the Southwest - Volume 1*). If you've experienced this special connection with nature in Cathedral Valley, I believe you'll be affected in the same way at Echo Park. Go preferably after the rafting season is over (the rafting season lasts from mid-May to mid-September) or you may miss the feeling of remoteness, which is an important part of the experience. The perfect time to visit Echo Park is in the autumn when cottonwoods turn bright yellow against the deep blue sky and most visitors have left.

Let's begin where we left off at the previous section. Returning from Harpers Corner toward the Visitor Center, turn left after about 6 miles onto well-marked Echo Park Road. This is a fairly well-graded dirt/gravel road and although high-clearance vehicles are recommended, passenger cars can use it with caution, unless it has been damaged by recent rains. It is best to inquire on its current condition at the Visitor Center before you go.

The road descends steadily through the Iron Springs Bench before re-entering the Monument (as well as the State of Colorado) after almost 3.5 miles, then follows Sand Canyon and its exquisite cream-colored sandstone cliffs. After about 7.5 miles from the top, you come to the junction with the Yampa Bench Road. Bear left on marked Moffat County Road 156 to meet in less than 1.5 miles lovely Pool Creek Canyon near the historic Chew Ranch. From there, the road follows the creek down to Echo Park for another 3 miles.

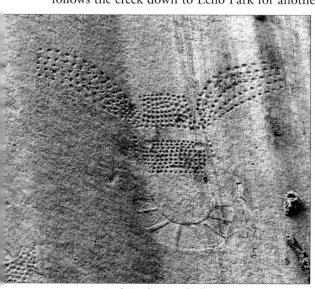

Pool Creek Petroglyph

Almost 2 miles past the first Pool Creek crossing you'll come to the Pool Creek Petroglyphs, located to the left on the cliff above the stream. These Fremont petroglyphs are particularly interesting due to their intricate pointillist technique, consisting of closely spaced holes pecked into the sandstone. Although there are several petroglyphs, you'll be hard-pressed to observe the smaller ones without binoculars. The main one is located 35 feet above ground, requiring a 200mm telephoto.

About 0.5 mile further, you'll come to Whispering Cave—a long, shallow crack in the sandstone approximately 100 feet wide and situated at the base of a huge cliff. You can walk about 50 feet or more inside a narrow passage right behind the sandstone wall. The difference in temperature with the outside is striking. This is a good place to photograph from the inside, because you'll get a wonderful red glow.

Whispering Cave

Another 0.5 mile brings you to Echo Park—a marvelous riparian oasis at the meeting point of the two awesome rivers: the Green and the Yampa. Echo Park is a superlative place for camping and you shouldn't miss the opportunity. You'll enjoy great photography and exceptional silence and solitude, as well as the constant company of deer.

Steamboat Rock is the obvious photographic subject here, with its odd bent shape. John Wesley Powell, who named Echo Park, climbed Steamboat Rock—not a small feat considering the lack of use of his partially severed arm. During his climb of Steamboat Rock, he almost lost his life after having extended himself past his climbing ability. Powell found himself trapped on a tiny ledge and unable to move. It is said that one of his companions rescued Powell from his predicament by stripping off his long johns and using them as a rope to pull Powell up to safety.

There are three interesting walks you can take from Echo Park; information on these three hikes is posted on the campground's bulletin board by the restrooms. The Sand Canyon Trail starts along the east side of Steamboat Rock, passing the confluence of the Green and Yampa rivers and continuing along the Yampa where it meets with Sand Canyon to the right. Most people stop here but it is possible to enter Sand Canyon and hike up southward to the Yampa Bench Road or along the rim and back down into Pool Creek Canyon (more on the last part of this hike below.) The Yampa River is the last major free-flowing tributary of the Colorado River system, although it narrowly escaped being dammed in the early 1950s, which would have put Echo Park and Steamboat Rock under water. A large public outcry helped defeat the Echo Park Dam project—a powerful reminder of how vital it is to let your voice be heard whenever we must fight back to preserve wilderness areas.

Another popular trail is Pat's Draw, located halfway between the campground and Whispering Cave on the west side of Echo Park Road. This canyon is located directly below Harpers Corner Road, discussed in the previous section.

The most popular trail is the Mitten Park Trail which follows the sandstone wall at the back of the campground. It then ascends on a ledge above the Green River, with some petroglyphs, before dropping down into Mitten Park, where you find yourself right below the great Harpers Corner uplift.

There is one more "unlisted" hike that I strongly recommend to photographers; this hike leads to the top of the bench, just above Steamboat Rock and continues above the Green, providing an extraordinary view of the *Center of the Universe*. Although relatively short mileage-wise, this hike is mostly off-trail and requires some routefinding skills and a bit of preparation. A topo map, as well as a compass or GPS, is highly recommended. If you've never hiked off-trail but have "successfully" completed the Sound of Silence trail earlier *(see Around Split Mountain section)*, now is a good time to apply your newly-acquired experience in a real world situation. To find the trail, drive back into Pool Creek Canyon and locate the one-car pullout on the left side of the road, less than 0.2 mile past the petroglyphs. Look straight toward the cliff just ahead of you to the left and you'll see the Picasso Face—a striking disfigured human face sculpted into the sandstone by the whims of erosion. A mid-size telephoto in the 200mm range will capture the Picasso Face perfectly. About 50 yards to the right of the Face, across the creek, you'll find a route going up. It's a bit of a scramble at first, but it quickly turns into a good trail as you slowly gain elevation onto the sagebrush-covered bench. You should be able to follow the trail along Pool Canyon's rim for a while, but it becomes less obvious as you reach two successive gullies to the left, which you have to cross before resuming the climb toward the bench top through dense Junipers. One good way to avoid getting lost if you lose the trail is to mark the top of the mesa directly south of Steamboat Rock on your topo map and aim for this point: 40°31'00'' 108°59'20". The walk is almost a mile one-way. Once you reach the top, you'll have a fantastic bird's eye view of

Steamboat Rock, surrounded by cliffs. This view is best captured with a moderate wide-angle lens.

Time permitting, continue along the rim in the direction of the Yampa. There is a trail, but don't worry if you occasionally lose it. As long as you keep following the rim, even from a short distance, you won't become disoriented. Another mile or so brings you close to the confluence of the Green and the Yampa, with the surprisingly long east face of Steamboat Rock in front of you. This is a fantastic shot

Picasso Face

with a panoramic camera. From here, you can bear southeast until you find a safe way to descend into previously-mentioned Sand Canyon or you can return the way you came.

Photo advice: Mid-morning and late afternoon offer wonderful views of Echo Park and Steamboat Rock from a variety of vantage points on the high talus close to the Ranger's residence, or from the rim accessed via the above-described hike. My preference goes to late afternoon as the sun rays strike the left face of Steamboat Rock until very late due to the perfect orientation of Pool Creek Canyon. There are also very nice views along the Mitten Park Trail.

Echo Park (photo by Bill Mitchem)

Getting there: Coming from Harpers Corner, you'll find the marked Echo Park Road to your left about 6 miles from the parking area. From the Visitor Center on US 40, drive 25 miles on Harpers Corner Road.

Time required: From Vernal or Dinosaur, it is possible to visit Harpers Corner Road and Echo Park in a long day, but my advice is to camp at Echo Park and enjoy this beautiful place at a leisurely pace. Doing so, you can exit the Monument the next day via the interesting Yampa Bench Road *(see next section)*. Water is usually shut off at the Echo Park campground in late September or mid-October; however; the pit toilets remain open. Note that during a few weeks in early summer, mosquitoes can make your life miserable at the campground.

Yampa Bench Road

The Yampa Bench road follows the Yampa River for much of 40 miles from the Echo Park Road to US 40 at Elk Springs, with some spectacular overlooks of its canyon along the way. It is a graded dirt road with relatively few rough spots, but a high-clearance vehicle is highly recommended. As usual, it is essential to inquire at the Visitor Center about the state of the road before embarking. This is one long road and you wouldn't want to get stuck on it, although you're likely to meet a few other vehicles from time to time.

Six and a half miles from the junction with Echo Park Road, after crossing the bench for a while far from the river, the road reaches the first overlook at a huge meander. This is Castle Park Overlook. A short walk from the car park brings you to the rim and the incredible view below. Exercise extreme caution here, especially while photographing. You can wander a bit along the rim to look for an inspiring location. Framing the entire meander and some of the rim in the foreground requires a super wide-angle lens or a panoramic shot, but there are excellent views of the eastern meander by itself alongside Castle Park.

Castle Park Panorama (photo by Philippe Schuler)

One mile further, as you near Hell's Canyon, you'll see the private Mantle Ranch Road to your left. Mantle Ranch used to be a working cattle operation within the borders of Dinosaur National Monument. The previous owners used to welcome visitors wanting to rough it for a week in a ranch still operating on "pioneer time", i.e. it had no electricity, no running water, no phone, and no mail. The ranch has now been sold and there is a dangling question mark on the future of the property, raising fears of private property development within the Monument. As of this writing, the ranch is still operating as usual.

Continuing for 1.5 miles, your next stop is the Harding Hole Overlook with a sweeping panorama of several smaller meanders, making another interesting photograph. The last direct view of the river is a little bit over a mile further at the Wagon Wheel Overlook, which has a slightly longer footpath to the overlook but provides similar views.

After that, the road moves inland passing the historic Baker Cabin to the right before approaching the river one last time at the Haystack Overlook, reached via a side road almost 12 miles from Wagon Wheel Overlook. From here, you can walk to the edge of the cliff and look down over the Yampa. The Haystack itself is an impressive formation jutting out of the landscape and vaguely reminiscent of Gunsight Butte on Lake Powell *(see Photographing the Southwest - Vol. 2)*. The road to the overlook is closed to visitation from April to mid-July to allow for an undisturbed nesting season of the Peregrine Falcons, whose eggs are seeded to other conservation areas around the country. A vast wooded area near the Monument's border was ravaged by wildfires in 2002 leaving a scarred landscape behind it. Hopefuly, if nature has its usual way, new growth may be underway by the time you read this.

Finally, you'll leave the Yampa Bench by climbing the east flank of Blue Mountain and rejoining US 40 at Elk Springs by way of roads 14N and 14.

Getting there: From Harpers Corner Road, take the above-mentioned Echo Park Road, continuing straight on at the Yampa Bench turnoff almost 8 miles from the beginning of the road. Coming from Echo Park, drive up-canyon for about 4 miles and turn left on the Yampa Bench Road. From US 40, take County Road 14 at Elk Springs and continue for 13.5 miles to the junction with 14N leading in 2 miles to the Monument's entrance. A useful NPS pamphlet entitled *Echo Park, Yampa Bench, and other unimproved Roads* is available. Although you won't have any difficulty finding your way without it, it's a nice thing to have.

Time required: 4 to 5 hours including stops at the viewpoints.

Nearby location: if you're coming to Dinosaur Nat'l Monument from the east and you're looking for a place to camp, consider the side trip to Deerlodge Park along the Yampa River. A small paved road leaves US 40 about 7 miles northeast of Elk Springs, leading to the campground in less than 14 miles. From May to July, you 're likely to meet rafting parties as it is the put-in for Yampa River trips. Outside this period, it's pleasant and quiet. The next morning, follow the footpath to where the Yampa enters a slickrock canyon, yielding a nice image.

The Gates of Lodore

The stunningly beautiful Gates of Lodore are located in the far north section of the National Monument, a long way from anywhere. It is the beginning of famed Lodore Canyon, which rises out of a completely flat area. The sudden emergence of the canyon is what makes Lodore so impressive. Most people who make it here are rafters intent on descending the rapids, but this spectacular location is for everybody, even non-photographers. So don't be rebuked by the mileage and motor to the Gates. You won't regret it.

Having said that, I must admit that I didn't visit Lodore on my first trip to Dinosaur Nat'l Monument many years ago and I was still hesitant on my subsequent visits. I'm glad I eventually did and I have since returned to enjoy this unique vista. One thing that proved an irresistible magnet was the Tolkienesque sounding name evoking an otherworldly setting of monumental proportions fit for heroic battle feats of great Kings of yore. And the reality... well with a little imagination and positive thinking, it is really not that far from this description.

Lodore is, quite literally, a one shot deal. A single entrance road leading to a single trail and a single viewpoint. That's it! If you come to Lodore for hiking and photography, you'll be tantalized by what lies ahead beyond the end of the trail. Unfortunately, you can't penetrate deeper into the canyon unless you take a raft trip. But, what a view from this vantage point located at the end of

Gates of Lodore

a 1.5-mile round-trip trail. You'll be able to admire and photograph the abundant waters of the Green River entering the deep canyon with its dramatic dark red walls. The place has a definite ominous feel not unlike the Black Canyon of the Gunnison *(see Chapter 4 - Western Colorado)*, except that the river is wider and you are closer to the water. For a more intimate look into this remote section of the park, a raft trip on the Green River is necessary. For the photographer, this is not a simple matter because of several rapids made infamous by Major Powell in his memoirs under the name of Hell's Half-Mile, Disaster Falls and Triplet Falls. Still, with adequate protection for your equipment, a 4-day/3-night raft trip from Lodore to Split Mountain will be a memorable experience.

Photo advice: The best light is in mid-morning, using a normal lens.

Getting there: Coming from the southern part of the Monument, heading northeast on US 40 toward the town of Maybell, turn northwest on CO 318 and drive 40 miles to a marked well-graded dirt road to the left. Continue westward another 10 miles to the Gates of Lodore Ranger Station and campground. The trailhead is another 0.3 mile past the river put-in.

   Alternatively, you can come directly from Flaming Gorge via Dutch John and a good all-weather graded road leading to Brown's Park or from Jones Hole Road on a very scenic 4WD road through Crouse Canyon (which requires crossing a narrow suspension bridge with a 3-ton limit as you reach the Green River in Brown's Park).

Nearby location: Brown's Park Wildlife Refuge borders the northern boundary of Dinosaur Nat'l Monument. The Refuge serves as a nesting area for migratory waterfowl, and approximately 200 species of birds can be found here. It offers outstanding opportunities for bird watching and solitude and includes two campgrounds alongside the Green River. Brown's Park didn't attract only birds: it used to be a hideout for outlaws such as Butch Cassidy and the Wild Bunch, due to its remoteness and proximity to the Utah and Wyoming state lines.

AROUND DINOSAUR

Canyon Pintado

Guess how Canyon Pintado got its name? Spanish sounding? Yes indeed, Dominguez and Escalante did pass through this canyon during their 1776 expedition and managed to find many of the petroglyphs and pictographs that can still be seen today along CO 139. They named it Canyon Pintado for the colorful paintings they saw along the way.

It will never cease to amaze me that the good friars came so far north and managed to find so many interesting spots in the course of their quest, on foot and almost a century before Powell. These were men of steely resolve and I'm in awe; more than that, I'm totally humbled. After a couple of weeks of roughing it in the area, knowing exactly where I'm going with maps, GPS, plenty of food and the comfort of my car, I invariably want to go back home to my family. And what about the Fremont who inhabited these canyons around a thousand years ago, so dependent on the whims of nature for their harvests, living a short and fragile existence constantly on the edge?

The Sun Dagger

Canyon Pintado is visited by few, yet it is rich in memories from those who came here before us. The pictographs, so conveniently marked along the road for our enjoyment, are just a few amongst a dense patchwork of Fremont sites spread around the numerous canyons forming the Canyon Pintado National Historic District.

As previously mentioned, most of the accessible rock art is located along CO 139, just south of the little community of Rangely, CO.

Coming from Douglas Pass and heading north, stop at the marker for some information on Canyon Pintado. The first site you'll see is the Waving Hands, about 0.5 miles past milepost 53 with several small Fremont paintings as well as more recent Ute paintings around the corner. The Waving Hands are quite elegant and their white color is very unusual.

The next site, right by the roadside at milepost 56, has a very large painted Kokopelli and some other pictographs to the left. The main painting is a bit

Carrot Man at the Moon Site

faded and it is encircled in its center by a steel cable preventing the sandstone slab from falling off.

Of the other sites to the north, the most spectacular is the Sun Dagger. This beautiful and still colorful painting is located 400 yards inside East Four Mile Draw, shortly past Milepost 61. The Sun Dagger is said to have been used as a sun dial by the Fremonts. There is an interpretive sign and an easy-to-follow trail to the pictograph and some less interesting petroglyphs. All the other sites along the road: Cow Canyon, State Bridge Draw and White Birds are worth seeing but photographically less rewarding. The Camel Ridge site, closest to Rangely, doesn't warrant a stop.

Among the sites not located inside the National Historic District per se, but nonetheless accessible and worth seeing, is the Reservoir site along the road to Meeker and the Shield, Fremont Ridge and Carrot Man sites on Dragon Road. The Carrot Man site, located in Moon Canyon, deserves a special mention. This fine pictograph panel is quite unique and easy to get to. At the Rangely traffic light, turn south and follow the street which becomes CR 23, aka Dragon Road. After about 11.5 miles, you'll come to a road to the right with a sign pointing toward Cottonwood Creek. Follow this road for 0.3 miles to a pullout on the left side. Park here and follow the very good path for 200 yards to the overhang harboring the Carrot Man panel. True to its name, the panel includes a bizarre anthropomorph in the shape of a carrot. Some of the humanoids next to it are actually even weirder. A normal lens to short telephoto is perfect for capturing the panel. Just below the panel, to the right, is a small bat cave.

Photo advice: The best time to photograph the Kokopelli, the White Birds and the Sun Dagger is early in the morning, before the sun is too high, causing the overhanging ledges to partially shade the figures. The Carrot Man site can be photographed throughout the day.

Getting there: 1¼ hour north of Fruita, CO and I-70 on beautiful CO 139 via Douglas Pass or just minutes south of Rangely, CO.

Time required: 1 to 3 hours to see the various sites long CO 139. Half a day if you add a foray onto Dragon Road. ❧

Snowmass Wilderness (photo by Ron Flickinger)

Chapter 4

WESTERN COLORADO

Split and Fallen Aspens (photo by Ron Flickinger)

WESTERN COLORADO

This chapter covers some of the most spectacular sites and mountains of western Colorado, with one exception: due to the specificity and overabundance of photogenic sites in the San Juan Mountains, the San Juans have their own chapter.

Many of the roads mentioned in this chapter are spectacular and highly suitable for photography. In most cases, no single feature makes a particular road stand out: each road is simply remarkable as a whole. While photographing in Western Colorado, you'll find that much depends on the quality of the light as you happen to drive by a particular spot. You'll often stop to photograph a scene that caught your eye because you were there at just the right moment. You'll find many such opportunities in all seasons.

The best time to visit Western Colorado is fall—usually the last week in September and/or the first week in October. Summer is also spectacular during the wildflower season—usually the last week in July and/or the first week in August—but there is more chance of rain and thunderstorms and more people on the roads. Winter is of course the busy skiing season and the Western Rockies look gorgeous in the snow.

Colorado National Monument

For the photographer, Colorado Nat'l Monument is a dream come true: few crowds, clean air, highly scenic vistas along the road, with great side light mornings and afternoons and wonderful hikes.

A brief daytime visit during your trip would not do it justice photographically and would almost certainly result in mediocre images as you'd miss the golden hour. Instead, I recommend that you spend the night in lovely Fruita or in Grand Junction and take one afternoon, as well as the next morning, to explore the monument. Another alternative, if you like camping, is to stay at the very nice Saddlehorn Campground in the western part of the park, which has spectacular views nearby. In recent years, the Monument has become a favorite of climbers from all over the world, so you may face a bit of competition at the campground in the spring or fall, but it is almost never full.

A 23-mile stretch of road called Rim Rock Drive crosses the Monument. Using South Camp Rd, South Broadway and CO 340, it forms a loop that can be started in either Fruita or Grand Junction. My recommendation is that you start in Fruita to concentrate on the western half of the road.

The road climbs the length of gigantic arms of sandstone, gradually rising to about 2,000 feet above Grand Valley. Spectacular views of the valley can be had from a large number of viewpoints on the rim. The gradient of the various canyon arms jutting down toward the valley floor forms extremely interesting perspectives, creating strong lines starting from the edges of your picture and leading the eye toward the center. There are limitless opportunities for creative, strong compositions involving perspective and you'll have a field day doing so, with very little walking involved.

Below is a list and short description of the viewpoints, as you will encounter them starting from Fruita.

Balanced Rock is a mid-to-late afternoon long telephoto shot. It is somewhat similar to the beacon rock you can see in Arches' Park Avenue (see *Photographing the Southwest - Volume 1*), but not quite as nice and easy to photograph. There is limited parking space at the turnoff and you will not be able to stop if you're coming from Fruita.

Fruita Canyon View offers an excellent morning and mid-afternoon view with a moderate wide-angle lens.

Monument Canyon

It is a good example of the strong compositions you can get playing with the arms of the canyon as they meet the valley floor.

Book Cliff View, located on the campground loop road, offers a fantastic sunrise view on Monument Canyon with a moderate wide-angle to short telephoto. If you want a slightly broader view, encompassing Sentinel Spire, walk all the way to the end of the Window Rock Trail. It's only a 5 to 10-minute walk between

Colorado Nat'l Monument in Winter

the two and you can easily visit both locations. These two locations will yield great photographs and are highly recommended.

Otto's Trail to Pipe Organ is a nice trail offering a good late afternoon view of Independence Monument, an isolated 450-foot high sandstone tower, but it is somewhat weak photographically.

Independence Monument View offers a splendid late afternoon shot of the huge monolith. This view is very interesting in winter or spring when the Entrada monolith cuts a striking profile on snow or green grass with Grand Junction in the background.

Grand View has a beautiful view looking toward Fruita Canyon with Independence Monument in the foreground. This view is equally as good during mornings and afternoons.

Monument Canyon View offers a superlative view of the spires of Monument Canyon, great for both sunrise and late afternoon.

A good view can be had from the Coke Ovens Overlook in both morning and late afternoon. There are also a couple of roadside spots, northeast of the overlook going toward Cleopatra's Couch, affording great, but distant, views over the ovens.

The Coke Ovens Trail is mildly interesting. It puts you almost on top of the softly rounded monoliths, but you're so close that it's difficult to take a picture from there. Likewise for the Coke Ovens Viewpoint, located south of the ovens, unless you want to catch the top of the ovens glowing in the early morning or late afternoon sun. I find the shape of the Coke Ovens less striking from Artist Point as from the Coke Ovens Overlook, but you may disagree with that.

The Monument Canyon Trail shares the same trailhead as the Coke Ovens Trail. If you have about three hours available and can arrange a car shuttle to the opposite trailhead on CO 340, this 6-mile trail is highly recommended as it goes past the major monoliths, providing a totally different perspective from the bottom. The walk is easy overall, beginning steeply—you'll lose 600 feet of elevation in less than a mile—before becoming gradual. You'll get a great view of the Coke Ovens at Mile 1. You can isolate them individually with a short telephoto for superb effects. Further down the trail, you'll pass at the base of the majestic monoliths, first the Kissing Couple, then Independence Monument.

As you continue east along the road, you'll encounter Ute Canyon and the very steep but beautiful trail of the same name. It offers solitude and plenty of intimate views, if you have time.

Your next stop is Red Canyon Overlook. Red Canyon is vast and long; it doesn't have the dramatic sloping of the smaller canyons to the west, but its long parallel walls are spectacular, albeit harder to photograph.

Past Cold Shivers Point, you'll catch a glimpse of the Serpent's Trail. The 2.2-mile trail, sporting more than 50 switchbacks, is actually the old road leading into the Monument. It's a fun walk down if you can arrange a car shuttle close to the Devil's Kitchen picnic area. Your visit will end up at the Devil's Kitchen Trail, a pleasant and popular 1.5-mile round-trip walk leading to huge upright boulders on a ledge, at the entrance of No Thoroughfare Canyon. This spot is very photogenic.

Getting there: The west entrance to the Monument is not far from the Utah State line. Coming west on I-70, take Exit 19 at Fruita and CO 340 to the west entrance. Coming east on I-70, take Exit 31 at Grand Junction to downtown, then Monument Road to the east entrance.

Time required: At least 2½ hours, with brief stops at

Coke Ovens

several viewpoints, if you are in a hurry. An overnight stay with mid- to late-afternoon and early morning drives is highly recommended to get good light.

Nearby location: If you find yourself with some time to kill near the east entrance to Colorado Nat'l Monument, you might consider a hike to the Mica Mine. Although this is more of a geological curiosity than a place of interest for photography, some may be interested in shooting close-ups of the mica. Mica was mined here in the 1950s and was used predominantly in the production of car windows. As the best spots of visible mica are inside an open-air grotto, use of an 81B filter or an equivalent white balance setting is recommended to avoid the strong blue cast when shooting in the shade under a bright blue sky.

The mine is located 1 mile from the Bangs Canyon Staging Area on a mostly flat trail following a pretty sandstone canyon. The hike itself takes a bit over an hour round-trip, however the trailhead is not easy to find. Coming from downtown Grand Junction, take Monument Road and turn left on D Road, which soon changes its name into Rosevale Drive. Follow Rosevale for 1.2 miles and turn right into Little Park Road. Drive for 5.5 miles on Little Park Road and make a sharp left on the dirt road to the Bangs Canyon Staging Area. A good map of the Bangs Canyon Recreation Area is available at the BLM office in Grand Junction.

The Rattlesnake Arches

Rattlesnake Canyon is located in the Black Ridge Canyon Wilderness just west of the Colorado Monument. The Black Ridge Wilderness, now part of the greater McInnis Canyons National Conservation Area, contains the second largest concentration of natural arches in the country and Rattlesnake Canyon is the most accessible canyon in that area. Even at that, it is a challenge to get to and I would only mention it in passing if the arches weren't so different from those found at Arches Nat'l Park (see *Photographing the Southwest - Vol. 1*). At Rattlesnake Canyon, arches are of the pothole variety, meaning that erosion has occurred from the top, with water trapped in a pothole, percolating through the porous sandstone until the pothole eventually collapsed.

The 13-mile track to Rattlesnake Canyon is not technically challenging and does not require any particular driving skills, just a reliable high-clearance vehicle with good tires. Under normal conditions, 4WD is a necessity but low-range 4WD adds a degree of control and confidence to your driving, especially during the first couple of miles of the Black Ridge Wilderness track (almost 3 miles past the Glade Park turnoff) and the steep 1.5 miles at the end of the track. This track is definitely not for passenger cars and cannot be driven when the ground is wet. There are long stretches of soft clay that would turn into a gooey mess during a rain and even a 4WD vehicle would get stuck, so inquire about recent conditions by calling the BLM Field Office in Grand Junction (see *Appendix*). Although it is not under their jurisdiction, the Rangers at the Colorado Monument Visitor Center might also be able to help you, if only by recalling recent rains.

The track roughly parallels the Grand Valley, traversing pleasant terrain of mostly high foothills in a northwestern direction. By the time you get to the trailhead, it's surprising how close you are from Fruita, as the crow flies. From the marked trailhead, the trail follows a closed portion of the track to the north for about 0.3 mile until you come to a marker. The trail to the left is the Upper Arches Trail, which leads to the top of the mesa above the arches and is less interesting photographically. The trail to the right is the Lower Arches Trail; this is your trail. After a short section of switchbacks, the trail levels off and follows the bottom of the mesa in a northwest direction, After a mile or so, the trail skirts the arrowhead-shaped tip of the mesa and doubles back on the southern side. You are now inside Rattlesnake Canyon proper. This part of the loop is where the arches are located; locals call it the Parade of Arches; it is 0.8-mile long and contains six interesting arches, some of which are quite different from what you've seen at Arches Nat'l Park. The most intriguing is the Hole-in-the-Bridge Arch, which sports a large pothole in the center of its span.

The total hiking distance is 2.2 miles from the trailhead to Rainbow Arch, the last arch on the parade. At that point, you're faced with a major decision: you either go back the way you came, or you attempt the escape route that climbs under the bridge to join the Upper Arches Trail on the mesa, in which case the distance back to your car is only 0.7-mile. Climbing under the arch requires a bit of class 4 scrambling on the slickrock, but is not really difficult for an agile person and the exposure isn't high. There are some well-placed moki steps on the left side and, if you feel uneasy about the climb, you can always sit on your behind and lift yourself up with your arms. The angle isn't steep enough for you to slide, so you'll eventually get there in a minute or so. Once on safe ground under the arch, you'll easily locate the way to the top of the mesa with no additional scrambling.

One of the Rattlesnake Arches

There is one additional arch in the area that is not on the Lower Arch Trail but can be visited with minimum effort. As you reach the bottom of the switchbacks on Lower Arch Trail, past the junction with the Upper Arch Trail, you'll come to a second junction with a trail bearing northeast on the right side. This is the Old Ute Indian Trail, which is featured on the USGS map. Follow this trail for about 0.3-mile and you should see some faint tracks going up in a south/southeast direction toward the mesa and a bit of routefinding should lead you there without too much effort. Although you can't see the arch from the trail, it becomes visible in the distance when looking back from further west on the Lower Arch Trail. This could help you get your bearings should you choose to take this side trip after visiting the main grouping.

I assume there are quite a few locals visiting Rattlesnake Canyon on weekends, but you may not encounter a single soul at other times. It would be wise to have a partner with you on this trip.

Photo advice: The trail and short footpaths come fairly close to the arches so a 28mm or wider angle is a must. The cliff is exposed to the southwest and is well lit almost all day, except for Rainbow Arch which is tucked into a small amphitheater facing east and is in shadow from mid-afternoon on.

Getting there: 11 miles from Colorado National Monument's west entrance near Fruita, go right at the Glade Park turnoff sign. Travel 0.2-mile and turn right toward the Black Ridge Wilderness Area, following the "public access" markers. There are two roads leading to the Rattlesnake Canyon trailhead, the Upper Road and the Lower Road. Use of these roads is seasonally rotated. The Upper Road is open from April 15 through August 15 and the Lower Road from August 15 through February 15. No motorized travel is allowed on either road from February 15 through April 15. Pick the one that is open and stay on it for 13 miles to the trailhead. Again, both of these roads shouldn't be attempted in inclement weather or if the surface appears wet.

Time required: At least 5 hours, including 2 hours just for the drive in and out.

Nearby location: Mee Canyon has a few interesting arches and a massive alcove. It is hard to reach from land, but easy for those who paddle down the Colorado River. Inquire at the BLM Field Office in Grand Junction.

Grand Mesa

Grand Mesa is a huge flat top mountain overlooking Grand Valley, east of Grand Junction. At an average elevation of over 10,000 feet, this vast mesa is in stark contrast with the surrounding desert. Rising quite abruptly from the valley floor, the mesa goes through several life zones, displaying a striking variety in vegetation: classic sagebrush plain on the northern valley floor, fruit orchards in the south, scrub oak, juniper & piñon pine, quaking aspen on the higher slopes, fir and spruce forest on top, interspersed with alpine meadows and many lakes and ponds. Scenic Byway 65 travels through these different zones in a relatively short time, making the trip across Grand Mesa all the more striking. The mesa offers mild temperatures in summer—while temperatures are sizzling in Grand Junction—making it a haven for all forms of outdoor recreation. Wildflowers in the meadows usually come out early in summer while fall colors peak in late September. The vastness and isolation of the mesa provides a safe habitat for a profusion of wildlife, including bobcats, mountain lions, bears and foxes. While it's doubtful that you'll ever be able to sight any of these rare species on a first trip, you'll likely encounter deer and perhaps elk while driving on the mesa at dawn or dusk. Drive slowly and be prepared to stop quickly. Wintertime brings abundant snowfalls to the mesa, which turns into a playground for the greater Grand Junction inhabitants. People come in droves for cross-country skiing, snow-mobiling and other winter activities. Many good camp-grounds and several lodges contribute to make things comfortable and appeal-ing year-round. The lit-erature you'll find on the mesa claims that it is the highest flat mountain in the world. One thing is for cer-tain, Grand Mesa is a unique and remarkable place, both ecologically and visually and deserves to be discovered and

Egglestone Wildflowers

enjoyed by many more people. We'll begin our discovery on the north side, at the town of Mesa, ending up at the lovely little community of Cedaredge, south of the mesa.

After ascending the north side of the mesa, your first stop will be the Skyway Overlook. The wide-open view of the valley below is quite striking. It is spec-tacular in the fall when the vast stands of aspens are turning color.

Past the Mesa Lakes area at mile marker 29, about halfway through the Scenic Byway, the well-graded Land's End gravel road leads west to an observatory with an even more open view extending as far as the Manti-La Sal mountains. This road follows the mesa rim much of the time; it was built by the Civilian Conservation Corps in 1933 to provide a shorter alternative from Grand Junction. After enjoy-ing the view from the Observatory Overlook, looking down 6000 feet to the valley floor, drive back the 12 miles to SB 65 and continue right.

Your next stop is the Land O'Lakes Overlook, which is marked on the road. From the car park, an easy 0.5-mile paved loop trail leads to the overlook. The view is so vast, you can only photograph two or three of the lakes with a wide-angle lens.

Continuing on SB 65, you come almost immediately to your left to the west-ern trailhead of the outstanding Crag Crest Trail. The 10-mile round-trip Crag Crest National Recreation Trail is the most famous and spectacular trail on the mesa. I consider it a "must see" of the Southwest and I highly recommend it. Despite the awesome elevation, it is surprisingly easy provided you're already accustomed to altitude and it can be through-hiked in only 5 to 6 hours.

The trail ascends steeply to Wolverine Lake where it splits into the so-called Loop portion to the south and the Crest portion to the north. The idea is to hike the Crest portion first and return via the leisurely Loop portion, hence the name.

The 6.5 mile long Crest portion is high-alpine and very exposed, straddling the crest of the mesa. Some narrow sections are flanked by sheer drop-offs, but the trail is so well constructed you'll seldom have to worry about your footing. At the highest point, you'll be close to 11,200 feet, The panoramic views all along the ridge are spectacular, ranging as far as the West Elk Mountains, the San Juans and the Uncompahgre Plateau. You'll be pulling out your camera often. The 3.4 mile Loop portion is a wider multi-use trail through beautiful forested terrain and some meadows with wildflowers in summer. It is mostly flat and easy to hike. The Loop Trail is as calming as the top trail is exhilarating; you stand a good chance of encountering deer on the Loop Trail, even in the middle of day.

If you don't feel like doing the entire loop and if you can arrange a car shuttle you could hike only the Crest Trail portion, exiting at the East trailhead near the Egglestone Lake campground. The most spectacular and highest part of the Crest portion is closest to the eastern trailhead. In summer, this is also where you'll find the best wildflowers, in the meadow just above Upper Egglestone Lake.

Outside of the potential risk of altitude sickness, hiking the Crag Crest Trail also requires some caution due to the vagaries of weather on the mesa. This is a place where the day can begin warm and sunny and very suddenly turn nasty cold and rainy by mid-day. Be sure to take warm layers and rain gear and don't be caught on the crest during a thunderstorm, especially with a tripod.

Back on SB 65, you'll soon come to the Forest Service Visitor Center located at the entrance of the main forest road (FR 121) heading east. There are excellent exhibits explaining the recent geology of the mesa. If you haven't had a chance to hike the Crag Crest Trail, you may want to take the short Discovery Nature Trail, starting just behind the building. It's a quick but pleasant 0.5-mile loop through the forest with a nice view of nearby Ward Lake.

Past the Visitor Center, continue on the forest road, turning right at the first opportunity and descending along the shore of Ward Lake for some nice views at lake level. Go back the way you came and continue east on the forest road, passing Spruce Lodge and Alexander Lake. Pushing further to Egglestone Lake, you can do all or part of the previously-mentioned Crag Crest hike from the eastern trailhead.

The descent on SB 65 towards Cedaredge through dense cedar and scrub oak forest looks and feels quite different from the northern

Highest Section of the Crag Crest Trail

side of the mesa. There are fewer aspens and a much thicker green belt.

Cedaredge is a pretty and dynamic little community at the foot of the mesa. Its 19th Century pioneer town has been entirely reconstructed or assembled from buildings originally in other locations. Of particular photographic interest are the three large wooden silos located at the entrance of the park. The project's architects and dedicated volunteers have done a masterful job of recreating the old town, although some may think that the structures look modern and a bit too "clean cut". Still, the place is fun and uncrowded and you could come out with some interesting shots, not only of the buildings but of the numerous authentic artifacts they contain. The village operates only from Memorial Day though late September, although a private visit could

Old Silos in Cedaredge Pioneer Town

be arranged by contacting the Surface Creek Valley Historical Society (see *Appendix*).

Getting there: From Grand Junction, follow I-70 east for about 20 miles and take CO 65 at exit 49 toward Mesa and Cedaredge. Coming from Montrose on US 50, bear right on CO 92, passing by Delta, then turn left on CO 65.

Time required: 3 hours to just drive though at a leisurely pace, stopping at the viewpoints, the Land O'Lakes Overlook and the Visitor Center. Count on at least a couple of days to discover and enjoy the mesa thoroughly, including the Crag Crest hike and a visit of the surrounding communities.

Rifle Falls

Rifle Falls State Park is a gem that you shouldn't pass up; in fact, I don't hesitate calling it a little photographer's paradise. Located in a gorgeous setting a stone throw away from the lush valleys and hogbacks of the Rifle Gap, it showcases a small but highly photogenic triple waterfall, as well as some very interesting limestone caves.

A short 0.2-mile trail leads from the car park to the bottom of the falls, set in a surprisingly lush area; the green vegetation has a quasi-tropical feel thanks to the constant spray emanating from the waterfalls. This is a place to linger, taking in the postcard-perfect view and capturing your own vision of the beautiful scene.

The trail continues to the top of the falls, passing by a small but very picturesque limestone grotto. A couple of platforms extending over the top of the falls allow you to catch a close view and feel the massive power of the water dropping down below; this is a mesmerizing view. The trail then splits, with the right path leading back to the car park and the left one descending toward a small grotto and another spectacular viewpoint very close to the base of the larger of the three waterfalls. As the trail forms a loop around the waterfalls, you can also go directly to this last viewpoint without climbing to the top of the waterfalls.

Photo advice: The trail brings you close to the bottom of the falls, allowing you to capture them from different sides using a moderate wide-angle lens. Although it is tempting to leave the trail and move closer to the vegetation in front of the falls, this area is off-limits and State Park rangers keep a watchful eye. On the other hand, there is no rule against wading closer to the falls to take pictures, but I'm not sure it's worth the trouble. If you do so, be sure to wear shoes to avoid stepping on hooks lost by fishermen. Also, watch out for sudden drifts of moisture from the falls that could damage your lens and camera; a filter of some kind is a must to protect your lens. Several filters could prove useful, depending on the circumstances: a 6-stop ND filter could help lengthen your exposure on a bright day; a polarizing filter could also make the falls look more dramatic and would help reduce glare from the green vegetation. If you shoot Velvia, a warming filter would reduce the tendency of that film to overemphasize the greens. Also, be sure to add a half stop to your exposure when the sun is out. To capture the triple falls from the viewpoint located near the base of the rightmost fall, you'll need a 17mm to 21mm lens to avoid having part of the platform show up in your shot. The falls are best visited in summer when the surrounding vegetation looks its best, but wintertime can lead to interesting shots of the frozen waterfalls.

Getting there: From the Rifle exit on I-70, go north on CO 13 for 3 miles then turn right onto CO 325 for another 10 miles to the car park. From Meeker

via Buford, take FR 245/17 (Buford to Newcastle); this road is dirt most of the way but is generally well maintained. It will lead you south to FR 246 (Buford road cutoff west). The road then intersects with Grass Valley Rd. To get to the falls go west for about 5 miles, then turn right (north) on CO 325 for 4 miles.

Time required: 1½ to 2 hours with ample time for photography; add 30 minutes of travel time each way to and from the Park from I-70.

The Rifle Falls

The Flat Tops

East of Meeker lies an outstanding wilderness area called the Flat Tops; it could be briefly described as a "wilder" version of Grand Mesa. If you've enjoyed Grand Mesa, I can almost guarantee you that you'll love the Flat Tops. The Flat Tops are crossed by the 81-mile Flat Tops Trail Scenic Byway, leading from Meeker to Yampa over 10,343 feet Ripple Creek Pass.

Meeker is an appealing little community with remarkably pristine surroundings and a famous, if tragic, past. In 1879, it was the scene of the infamous "Meeker Massacre", involving the killing of Nathan Meeker, the government's agent for the White River Ute Reservation. An avid proponent of communal farming, Meeker tried to impose his views on the Utes, whose way of life was of course incompatible. After calling in the army to force the recalcitrant Utes to bend to his views and become sedentary farmers, Meeker was slain by the

Utes along with seven other members of the agency. The Utes also attacked the troops headed for the reservation, killing nine, including their commander. This unfortunate episode resulted in the closure of the White River Reservation and the deportation of the Utes to their current reservation in southeastern Utah. The excellent Ute Museum of Montrose documents the incident and its consequences on the way of life of the Utes in the aftermath of the tragedy.

The Devil's Causeway

The Flat Tops Scenic Byway is open from June to late October or until the pass is closed by the first deep snow, but it remains open year-round to local traffic from Meeker to Buford. Most of the Flat Tops area is above 10,000 feet elevation. The paved road follows the White River to Buford. Past Buford, the route becomes gravel and follows the North Fork of the White River.

About 18 miles past Buford, an 8-mile side road leads along the North Fork of the White River to Trappers Lake, the first ever Wilderness area in the country. A 3-mile round-trip trail leads to Little Trappers Lake, with a sheer basalt wall rising 1,600 feet above the lake. From here, it's another 4 miles round-trip with a 1000-foot elevation gain to the top of the Chinese Wall. The forest along the last 3 miles of the road to Trappers Lake was extensively burnt in a wildfire in 2002 and now exhibits extraordinary expanses of fireweed.

Immediately after returning to the Byway, the road starts ascending Ripple

Creek Pass, reached at the end of a 5.5-mile climb. Another 17 miles brings you to Dunckley Pass before descending toward Yampa amongst views of grasslands, small lakes, golden aspen, fir and spruce-covered hillsides below the ubiquitous flat summits.

Yampa is the gateway to the Devil's Causeway, one of the Flat Tops' most popular hiking destinations. The Causeway is a narrow land bridge of volcanic origin; about 80 feet long and only a few feet wide in one place, it connects two flat top mesas, with 1,500-foot drop-offs on each side! The trailhead for the Devil's Causeway is located at the end of FR 900; the car park is adjacent to the large Stillwater Reservoir. From here, it's a 5.8-mile round-trip hike to the Devil's Causeway on a good trail; beware the elevation as the Causeway is at 11,800 feet. Most people choose to end their hike here; some prefer to marvel at the Causeway from the trail, but most actually cross over the narrow hump-backed bridge for sheer kicks. You may want to crawl on your hands and knees at the narrowest spot. As you retrace your steps, there are excellent views of Little Causeway Lake. A 10-mile loop can be also made by following the flat top and returning to your car via the south end of the Stillwater Reservoir. The section close to the reservoir is a fantastic location for shooting wildflowers in summer.

Fireweed at Trappers Lake

With a car shuttle, it is also possible to hike all the way to Trappers Lake.

One of the biggest draws of the Flat Tops Wilderness— and arguably one of the most compelling one from a photography standpoint—is the abundance of wildlife. There is a huge elk popula- tion (reportedly numbering in the tens of thousands in late summer) and large herds can be seen in forest clear- ings. This abundant wildlife draws large numbers of hunt- ers to the Flat Tops during the fall. The local economy is greatly dependent on money spent by hunters; the signs of this quasi-industry are everywhere in Meeker and it may not be to everyone's taste. If you are a wildlife enthusiast, take solace in the fact that a majority of the hunters who come to the Flat Tops want to keep the wilderness pristine and are against the opening of more land to mining and development.

Getting there: From Meeker, drive 2 miles north toward Craig on CO 13 and turn east on CR 8. From Rifle on I-70, a couple of forest roads lead north to Buford. In addition to the road described in the Rifle Falls section (CO 325), a more scenic route follows Little Box Canyon Road (FR 825) through Rifle Mountain Park to Triangle Park, then on to Buford on FR 245. This road can be muddy after rains and a 4WD vehicle is recommended.

Time required: 3 hours one-way to cross from Meeker to Yampa with the side trip to Trappers Lake; the better part of a day if you do the hike to the Devil's Causeway. Backpackers can easily spend a week here, as there are almost 300 miles of trails.

Black Canyon of the Gunnison – South Rim

The Black Canyon of the Gunnison is both superb and still relatively uncrowded, despite its recent National Park status—acquired in October of 1999. During many of my visits, I have managed to get wild and woolly weather, ending up in powerful evening thunderstorms. I feel that this is when the canyon is at its best, basked with spots of light filtering through a threatening dark gray sky. Unlike its southern neighbors running through a landscape of sandstone layers, the Gunnison River has carved its way through hard bedrock, resulting in a very steep, rugged gorge. The Black Canyon is in fact one of the rare canyons that is deeper than it is wide—much deeper in this case. The almost vertical walls are over 2,000 feet deep and at one point only 1,200 feet across; this makes the bottom of the canyon very dark, hence its name.

A dozen spectacular viewpoints dot the 7-mile South Rim road, all of which offer different views of the canyon from very short trails. My personal favorites are the Pulpit Rock Overlook, the Cross Fissures View, Chasm View and Painted Wall View, and most specially Cedar Point. Of course, it's all a matter of taste as the other viewpoints are all spectacular in their own way. Cedar Point offers an excellent view of the Painted Wall from two fenced areas at the end of a 0.7-mile round-trip trail. The western end of the road offers less dramatic views of the canyon despite its height at over 8,200 feet.

Hiking to the bottom of the canyon brings out a totally different perspective but is a challenging experience, which is not remarkably

Storm on the Black Canyon

rewarding from a photographic standpoint. If you feel the urge to do it, you'll need a backcountry permit, even for day use. Of the three very steep routes going down 1,800 feet to the river from the South Rim, the Gunnison Route is the least difficult and most popular one. Nevertheless, you must be in excellent physical condition and not be afraid of heights for this descent. Among other challenges, you'll have to contend with extreme steepness, very loose rock, much scrambling, an unwieldy 80-foot chain, and poison oak in the river area. The section with the chain and immediately below is particularly treacherous on the descent (a bit easier coming back up) because the long chain has a tendency to move from side to side and you're really just moving in a drainage with no firm footing. Be extremely careful, this is prime territory for twisting or breaking an ankle. I recommend that you wear sturdy hiking shoes with good ankle protection. Luckily, the chain section is located only one-third down from the top, so if you don't feel

Painted Wall Sunrise

like tackling this obstacle, you won't have wasted too much time. Conversely, if the chain hasn't scared you, you'll have no problem with the rest of the descent. Count on 3 to 4 hours for the round-trip.

Photo advice: A super wide angle is very useful to capture the depth of the canyon and the Gunnison River below. Pay particular attention to limiting the amount of sky in your photos, especially during the golden hour when there is a major risk of a blown sky; the problem is even more prominent on clear days. The contrast of the dark rock and the clear sky is way too much for any camera. I find this particularly exacerbated in digital cameras; this is a good place to use your ND Grad filter if you have one. Verticals obviously work well here, remember this in your composition. Late afternoon light works best on the South Rim.

Getting there: The South Rim is located 15 miles east of Montrose on US 50 and CO 347. The campground is very pleasant. Nearby Montrose has a large number of motels.

Time required: 2 to 3 hours to enjoy the viewpoints of the south rim.

Black Canyon of the Gunnison – North Rim

Few people bother to visit the North Rim of the Black Canyon; this is due in a large part to the fact that they believe it represents a substantial detour from the Ouray-Delta-Montrose axis between the San Juan Mountains and I-70. In reality, it is not such a long detour as long as you come in and out the same way on CO 92 and avoid driving around the Curecanti Reservoir—which has nothing to offer to the photographer anyway.

On a map, the North Rim doesn't appear to be substantially different from the South Rim. This may be so for most of the views along the rim; however, the view from Exclamation Point is totally unique.

On the Rim Drive, one particular spot stands out: the Narrows Viewpoint. It is the only viewpoint offering a continuous rectilinear view of the Gunnison River as it flows deep at the bottom of the extremely dark canyon. The Gunnison Narrows have some kind of foreboding quality under the right light and this view is really awesome.

At Island Peaks View you can photograph jagged rock spires on the south side of the viewpoint. At the south end of the road, the Kneeling Camel View shows the strikingly realistic shape of a camel, including head and hump.

On the north end of the road, close to the North Rim Visitor Center, the 0.3-mile round-trip Chasm Nature Trail offers great views of the Painted Wall from a very different angle than what you see on the South Rim. The canyon is at its narrowest here; it's a strange feeling to think that the folks on the other side are only 1,100 feet away as the crow flies but several hours away by car.

The 3-mile round trip hike to Exclamation Point is the highlight of a trip to the North Rim, offering the most scenic views of the inner canyon. It is part of the 7-mile round-trip North Vista Trail. You'll be surprised by the spectacular panoramic view of the South Rim cliffs from the overlook. This is a must see view, amply justifying the detour to the North Rim. I suggest that you do this hike in mid to late afternoon; it will be hot, but the trail is good and flat and the second half is partially shaded.

The North Vista Trail continues another 2 miles toward Green Mountain, leaving the rim, gaining elevation and providing spectacular bird's eye views of the deep fracture of the canyon, with the Uncompahgre Plateau and San Juan Mountains in the background. This is a very different perspective of the Black Canyon and one you can't have from the South Rim.

One of the three routes to the bottom of the canyon from the North Rim is S.O.B. Draw. It starts from near the North Rim Campground, descending down a steep gully visible from the North Vista Trail. Balanced Rock Overlook is the starting point of the Long Draw Trail and leads down into the canyon at its most interesting part, deep inside the Narrows.

Photo advice: Conditions are identical to those of the South Rim. The best way to come back with good pictures of the North Rim is to spend the night at the nice campground near Chasm View.

The main viewpoint at Chasm View has a view of the river but no foreground. Walk another hundred yards past it to find another good open view with some nice rocks and junipers in the foreground. For Chasm View, I suggest sunrise, but no later, otherwise there will be direct light on the top of the Painted Wall and some very strong shadows.

Exclamation Point, on the other hand, is best in late afternoon. There are two viewpoints located about halfway to Exclamation Point but they are not as good as the main viewpoint: so if you are pressed for time you can pass them. Consider a panoramic camera for Exclamation Point, or if you shoot digital you could easily stitch a couple of images together for a spectacular panorama.

Getting there: The North Rim is located 41 miles southeast of Delta and 11 miles south of Crawford on North Rim Road.

Use CO 92 from Delta via Hotchkiss and Crawford. In Crawford, follow the signs through a sparse residential area (a bit unusual for a National Park access) then on to the rim; this is the strangest approach of any National Park I know. I have seen elk and many deer on this road, so be very careful. North Rim Road is closed in winter

Time required: 3 to 4 hours from Delta for a brief visit just cruising the overlooks; up to a full day if you're going to hike, preferably spread over an afternoon and the next early morning.

Nearby location: 4 miles east of Crawford, Needle Rock abruptly rises 800 feet above the Smith Fork River valley. This striking volcanic monolith is somewhat reminiscent of Shiprock, NM and El Capitan in Monument Valley. It makes an awesome sight in the afternoon sun when driving north on Black Canyon Road. The view is especially outstanding from a distance with a long telephoto. The

Needle Rock

south entrance road to Crawford Lake State Park is a good place for such a shot. It is also possible to drive just below Needle Rock; while in Crawford, turn east at the sign announcing Nat'l Forest Access-Smith Fork and follow the good road, passing through small farms, to the base of the monolith. There are also several good vantage points along this road.

The Maroon Bells

The Maroon Bells are one of the most photographed locations in North America and although they've appeared in print again and again, every one of us is filled with a burning desire to capture our own version of this iconic photograph, cliché or not. On a crisp autumn morning, when aspen leaves are at their peak, it isn't rare to find between fifty and a hundred photographers lined up along the lake shore, intent on capturing this great American photograph.

The Bells are reached at the end of a splendid drive following the course of Maroon Creek. During summer, this road is closed to private vehicular traffic during the day and you must use the mandatory shuttle service. Coping with the crowds of hikers, climbers and casual visitors on shuttle buses—as well as with the heavy traffic in and around Aspen—can take its toll. In the early morning and late afternoon, things are much quieter and you are allowed to drive your own vehicle outside normal business hours and stop anywhere along Maroon Creek Road.

During fall color season you can drive your own vehicle, except Friday through Sunday. There is no fee if you enter before 8 AM and after 7 PM. Many photographers take advantage of this to drive up late in the day and spend the night on location. There is an overnight parking lot for this purpose, but most photographers tend to ignore it and spend the night in their vehicle at the Maroon Lake car park. Although the Forest Service frowns on this practice, it has a lenient attitude toward it. This is because

Maroon Bells Dawn (photo by Ron Flickinger)

the campgrounds along Maroon Creek Road are always full during summer and fall colors and you can't simply chase people away from a car park in the middle of the night, and perhaps more importantly because so many people do it that it has become unenforceable, short of closing the road at night.

Photo advice: Wherever you end up spending the night, be sure to arrive early at the lake—at least 20 minutes before sunrise—as you'll be competing for prime spots with many other photographers. Another reason to arrive early is to catch the beautiful alpenglow on the summit, which starts about 20 minutes before sunrise. First light on the peaks start about 10 minutes after sunrise.

Overleaf: Maroon Bells around 9 AM

Early arrivals rush to grab spots at the beginning of the lake, hoping to take advantage of the logs stuck in the inlet as a foreground for their shots. These are by no means the only good spots. In fact, it won't do you any good if the lake level is low; on the other hand, there are plenty of great locations along the shoreline, a hundred to two hundred feet from the inlet. Setting up your tripod along the bank, close to the water, opens up more terrain to the left of the Maroon Bells, somewhat reducing the large shadow area that mars so many pictures. It also allows capturing the best possible reflection of the twin peaks in the water. This is about the extent of the control you can exercise over your photograph, the rest is up to the weather.

The main factor that varies from year to year is color density and intensity. In some years, strong storms may blow away some of the aspen leaves, creating bald spots. In wet years, the leaves may become waterlogged and develop a fungus, which can render them dull. In dry years, the leaves may also lack shine and fizzle out early.

One major factor to get a great reflection in the lake is how calm the wind is: the slightest breeze will fuzzy up the reflection. This is obviously unpredictable, but there are always some lulls you can take advantage of. Also, the lake's volume has shrunk in an alarming way in recent years and the shoreline has receded tremendously; this reduces the potential reflection.

Finally, snow on the peaks and clouds in the sky—two lesser factors nonetheless contributing to a more dynamic photograph—are very unpredictable, at least when planning your trip.

My personal philosophy on the matter of less-than-optimum conditions runs along the lines of "don't worry, be happy". Even if you're here too early or a bit late in the season, there is always enough color for a pleasing image. Consider your first trip to the Maroon Bells as some enjoyable rite of passage, and don't take it too seriously. Relax and enjoy the camaraderie, the sharing of heroic past photographic experiences—that time you swerved at the last second to avoid the moose—and the inevitable gear talk. If you are not the mingling type, you can still have fun lending a distracted ear to the chatter. You'll have plenty of time to kill anyway.

I have to say I greatly enjoy the Maroon Bells during fall colors, although I wouldn't turn this into a compulsory yearly pilgrimage as some do (in their defense, most are Colorado-based photographers). Watching the early sunrise hit the top of the peaks and color them gold is

Autumn Reflection

a transcendental experience, which will make you forget the hundreds of noisy clicks from camera shutters...as well as your bitterly cold fingers and toes.

After the initial magic of sunrise fades away, the two summits become totally lit while the forested area at the base and to the left of the lake remains extremely dark for a long time. The contrast is too high for any film or sensor to handle and you'll need to wait about 1½ hour between your first sunrise shots and even illumination of the aspens—with the shadow area reduced to an acceptable level. Be patient, don't waste shots early on or you'll be disappointed. Mount an ND split or grad filter if you haven't already done so. While I usually recommend the less aggressive 2-stop graduated filter for most applications, a 3-stop split filter will not be overkill here.

Even basked in a lot of light, the view of the peaks and lake remains excellent well into mid-morning, allowing you to wander around and shoot from different angles. In the fall, once the golden aspens are in full sun, they'll cast a rich color on the lake's surface. To photograph the Maroon Bells from the lake, any moderately wide to normal lens will work well.

When you're done with your photography of the lake, it's time to hit the trail and explore the creek upstream. Crater Lake is only 1.5 miles from the trailhead and there is plenty to see and photograph in between. Free permits are needed to enter the Maroon Bells-Snowmass Wilderness area and hike any of the trails; you simply self-issue your permit at the trailhead and there is no fee to pay.

A final word about when to go to capture fall colors at their peak: although it varies slightly from year to year, you can be practically assured of having excellent color during the last week in September and the first few days in October. The variations will be a little bit more green early on, with more bold spots toward the end. If all else fails, you can try again the next morning... and there is always next year!

Getting there: Maroon Creek Road starts about a mile west of downtown Aspen on CO 82 and is well marked; it travels 10 miles to Maroon Lake, passing many spectacular overlooks. In recent years, visitation has drastically increased, impacting the growth of wildflowers and aspens and creating massive traffic jams. To fight this, the National Forest Service restricts vehicular access during summer and early fall. A mandatory bus service is in place from 9 AM to 5 PM every day during summer, as well as on week-ends during early fall. The road remains open to private vehicles every day outside of these hours, which is of course perfect for photography. There is a $10 fee per vehicle in the two-hour time frame before and after the mandatory shuttle hours, but it is free if you come sooner in the morning or later in the evening. Private vehicles are also allowed on weekdays during the fall season. Schedules, regulations and fees may change; be sure to contact the Aspen office of the White River Nat'l Forest (see *Appendix*).

Time required: As much as you feel like staying. The drive up in the early morning or late evening takes 30 minutes. Driving down, you'll want to stop a lot. A nice rewarding hike upstream toward Crater Lake takes 1 to 2 hours; a longer hike into the wilderness area can take the whole day or more.

Nearby locations: Castle Creek Road runs somewhat parallel to Maroon Creek, leaving from the same traffic circle downtown. The 13-mile paved road sees considerably less traffic than Maroon Creek Road, which makes it very enjoyable. Although it lacks the outstanding views of the Maroon Bells, it goes through similar groves of aspens, ending in a beautiful valley full of wildflowers in summer. There, you'll find the old mining town of Ashcroft, which has several remarkably well-preserved buildings. There is a small fee to visit the old town, which has good photographic potential.

The Snowmass Wilderness is an excellent location for photography. Snowmass Lake is a 20-mile backpacking trip, but a simple day hike on this trail is also very rewarding. To reach the Maroon Bells-Snowmass Trailhead, drive 14 miles northwest of Aspen on CO 82 and turn left at the sign for the Old Snowmass post office. The road follows Snowmass Creek for 12 miles, passing large aspen groves along the way.

Glenwood Springs is a busy resort town on a mission to help visitors relax in its mineral spas; I'm sure it's very pleasant, but the traffic is enough to chase you away. CO 82's character changes radically southeast of Aspen and you'll love the

Independence Pass

beautiful aspen groves along the way to Independence Pass. The very popular Grottos Trail is located 10 miles southeast of Aspen on CO 82. Look for the spur road just beyond mile marker 50. Several trails lead to waterfalls, a narrow granite slot canyon and a picnic site complete with a large fishing dock.

Shortly before reaching Independence Pass, you'll notice Independence Ghost Town on the south side of the road; it is worth a brief stop only if you haven't already visited Ashcroft. At the pass, a short trail leads to an overlook with stunning panoramic views. This road is usually closed from November through May, but it could be earlier or later depending on weather conditions. The eastern end of CO 82 along the shore of Twin Lakes and in the shadow of Mount Elbert—Colorado's highest "Fourteener"—is also a good photographic location.

Turn north (left) at the junction of CO 82 and US 24 and continue on to Leadville, a historic mining town located at over 10,000 feet elevation. Leadville offers lots of things to do and places to visit, both in and out of town. It is a must-see and a great base to continue your explorations of Colorado further north. For now, this is as far east as I'll take you in this book.

One very nice way to come back west toward Gunnison is to drive south on US 24 and turn west (right) on CR 306 at Buena Vista, crossing the Continental Divide at Cottonwood Pass. There are some great views and many aspens on both sides of the pass. The road is fairly steep before the pass then turns to a mostly well graded gravel road during the descent toward Taylor Park Reservoir. Another alternative is to continue south on US 24 and take US 50 over Monarch Pass to Gunnison. This is a much easier road, however it lacks the feeling of adventure and isolation you'll get at Cottonwood Pass.

The Crystal Mill

The quickest and most popular way to go southwest from Aspen is via CO 82 then CO 133 from Carbondale to Hotchkiss. Shortly after Carbondale, you'll come to the beehive-shaped Redstone Coke Ovens. The long string of ovens is definitely worthy of a photograph if you can find an interesting composition. CO 133 is spectacular, especially McClure Pass, which offers great views of the east face of Snowmass Mountain. Stunning fall colors can be seen at and around the pass and you'll often be out of your car photographing.

Just before McClure Pass, you'll come to FR 314 to Marble and its old quarry, which at one time produced vast quantities of marble used in hundreds of buildings and monuments across the country. The 6-mile drive to Marble has great scenery and fall color and the traffic is light in comparison to the highway. Marble proper is not a tight little community but stretches over a rather expansive forested area.

Marble is the gateway to the famous Crystal Mill, presented in some literature as the most photographed site in Colorado—a really outlandish claim. After passing Marble, continue past Beaver Lake on the 4WD road to Crystal, bearing right at the Y about a mile past the lake. From here, the distance to the mill is only 5.5 miles including 4 miles of non-technical but extremely rocky road, totally unsuitable for cars and people with fear of heights. The road is single-lane and very narrow in places. When you encounter oncoming traffic, one of you may be forced to backtrack in order to find a suitable passing location; fortunately there are many of these along the road. The drive includes a couple of exciting descents with serious side-exposure; it may be a bit scary for your

Aspen Candy at McClure Pass

passengers with no prior experience of this kind of terrain. Although there are no technical difficulties, you'll be using low-range all the way. Long-wheelbase SUVs and trucks are at an advantage on this rocky road; if you drive it in a short-wheelbase Jeep, be prepared for 45 minutes of relentless pounding each way.

Lizard Lake

About halfway through the drive, you'll encounter tiny Lizard Lake, set in a lovely forested area—a perfect spot for a lunch break or a relaxing moment.

Finally, you'll reach the site of the Old Mill at Crystal (actually a former power-house). The setting of the mill, built precariously over a 15-foot waterfall, is spectacular. It is surrounded by small aspens, looking gorgeous in the afternoon light. It is a highly esthetic and powerful symbol of Colorado's high country and mining heritage. Fall is of course the preferred season due to the added color; however, the waterfall is fuller during spring runoff and early summer.

Photo advice: The best time to photograph the mill is in mid-afternoon between 2 and 4 PM in summer. There are two obvious spots to capture a classic photograph of the mill. One is from the car park, just across and slightly above the mill; this calls for a 24mm to capture the entire structure and the waterfall. Another spot is the rough footpath to the right of the car park, which people use to descend to creek's level. A moderate wide-angle is sufficient from here.

Time required: Between 2 and 2½ hours round-trip from Marble, including time for photography; If you do not have a 4WD vehicle, you can book a 2½ hour tour from Marble during summer and early fall (see *Appendix*).

Around Crested Butte

Crested Butte is a lovely year-round resort, with one short but very busy main street surrounded by the cutest Victorian houses. The crowds are mostly yuppy-ish and young, definitely into outdoors activities and showing it. There is less wealth and sophistication than in Aspen and Telluride at the high end, but it's still a well-heeled crowd and the few hard-core jeepers and bikers who strayed from Silverton and Ouray look a bit out of place here.

Opposite page: the picturesque Crystal Mill

Mount Crested Butte, just north of town, is a world-class ski resort with many large hotels and restaurants; obviously a booming place in wintertime. Crested Butte calls itself the Wildflower Capital of Colorado and while other towns may cringe at that, there is no question that it is a wonderful place to spend a summer week hiking and photographing wildflowers. It seems to me that the peak season in Crested Butte happens a week before peak in the San Juans, say mid-July as opposed to the last week in July. This may be due to the slightly higher latitude, the lesser elevation, perhaps also a bit more sunshine. This is not a scientific observation, just a seat of the pants feeling. In any case, if you have a flexible schedule, be sure to call and find out how the flowers are coming. Crested Butte also offers a tremendous incentive to visit during the fall season: the area west of the Kebler Pass has one of the most outstanding stands of aspens in Colorado and is a favorite of knowledgeable leaf peepers and photographers.

The best way to get acquainted with the Crested Butte area is to drive the Gothic-Schofield-Slate River loop. This road is very good up to the Schofield Pass, but requires high-clearance on the upper Slate River side. From Crested Butte, drive north on Gothic Road past Mt. Crested Butte and continue on the excellent FR 317 dirt road, toward Gothic and Schofield Pass. The road follows a small creek through a soft alpine landscape of sheer beauty, intensely green and quite similar to the Engadine region of Switzerland—perhaps it should also claim the St. Moritz of America moniker? There are vast rolling meadows with wildflowers on both sides of the road; it's an absolute enchantment.

East River Meanders (photo by Denis Savouray)

The most popular hike along this road is the Rustler's Gulch Trail, 2 miles north of Gothic. Access to the trailhead is on FR 569 and is well-marked. This is a bumpy dirt road requiring high-clearance and there aren't too many parking spots at the trailhead. If there is no space, you can park close to FR 317 and walk from there; it would only add about 0.5 mile to the hike. Rustler's Gulch is an easy hike, but you'll need to get your feet wet several times, so come prepared. In mid-July, you'll be greeted by a festival of colors.

Continuing on FR 317, drive past Schofield Pass, bearing right at the Y. Descend for about 0.7 mile until you reach a vast and beautiful valley, ford the creek and pull out into the large East Fork Trail trailhead. This trail leads to Maroon Pass; it is an outstanding trail at any time throughout summer. The round-trip hike to West Maroon Pass is about 7.5 miles and you'll start seeing lots of wildflowers as soon as you gain elevation.

To continue on our loop, return to the Y and turn right, following the sign to Paradise. The road passes by the lovely meadow of Elko Park climbing gently toward Paradise Basin. This is a superlative high alpine valley. Pull out close to the lovely lake at Paradise Pass for an outstanding view of the Slate Valley. After Paradise Pass the road follows a hillside high above the Slate River Valley. Bear right at an unmarked Y to

Paradise Basin (photo by Jan Forseth)

descend the switchbacks leading to Slate River Road.

From the fairly steep switchbacks, there are also outstanding vistas of the Slate Valley and you'll want to stop to take pictures. Although quite steep, this portion of the road is never challenging.

About 3 miles south of the final switchback marking the beginning of the Slate River valley, you'll find a dirt road leading to another popular hike: the curiously-named Oh-Be-Joyful Trail. The road is signed when coming from Crested Butte, but unmarked coming from Paradise Valley. Just to be safe, you can reset your odometer at the sign for the old Pittsburgh site; the road is 2.7 miles from there. After fording the Slate River, the short road leads to the main trailhead. If you have high-clearance 4WD, you can continue for another mile but this is a rough road and it doesn't really save you that much compared to the trail shortcut. From there it is a 10-mile round trip to Democrat Basin.

Back on the Slate River Road, another 5 miles through private land brings you back to Crested Butte. You'll probably want to stop and photograph the beautiful little lake near the Alpine Meadows private community.

Needless to say the loop road I describe is closed in winter, nearly impassable during springtime because of the mud and extremely photogenic in summer and fall.

For the best fall colors,

Slate River Valley (photo by Philippe Schuler)

Aspen Groves at Kebler Pass

however, nothing in the area comes close to the outstanding sights on CR 12, west of Kebler Pass. Starting from Crested Butte, the paved road passes through a landscape consisting predominantly of conifers. A few miles before the pass, the road turns into an excellent unpaved all-weather road and the vegetation changes radically. This is a prime location to photograph aspens, definitely on a par with the best locations in the San Juan Mountains.

One good place for photography is by mile marker 20 near the Horse Ranch Park and Cliff Creek trails. Looking south, you'll be close to a spectacular stand of aspens forming a great foreground to the mountain behind. Just west of this point, the road enters a very old aspen grove with huge white trunks; this is a very impressive spot and you'll want to stop here to photograph or just enjoy the place. Further west, between mile markers 10 and 11, you'll come to an exceptional panoramic view of the West Elk Range with an immense aspen forest at its foot. This section of the road offers the largest unobstructed view of aspens and mountain scenery in Colorado; it is a perfect spot for a late afternoon shoot. CR 12 between Kebler Pass and the junction with CO 133 is best driven in the morning in the Crested Butte to Paonia direction and in late afternoon from Paonia. The best photography will definitely be in mid- to late-afternoon. ✿

Dream Lake Sunrise

Chapter 5

ROCKY MOUNTAIN NATIONAL PARK

Secret Tarn (photo by Ron Flickinger)

ROCKY MOUNTAIN NATIONAL PARK

Along with its northern siblings Grand Teton and Glacier, Rocky Mountain National Park protects some of the most outstanding and pristine sights of the Rockies. Although its location close to Denver's metropolitan area brings throngs of visitors on week-ends, the combination of an early start, visiting on weekdays and outside of the main holiday period allows for a wonderful hiking and photographic experience in a world-class setting.

To get an early start, you'll need to base yourself in Estes Park or at one of the campgrounds inside the park. Reservations are accepted at the main campgrounds and Golden Access or Golden Eagle cardholders enjoy a 50% discount.

Horseshoe Park & Falls

I suggest you begin your discovery by entering the park from Estes Park via US 34, aka Trail Ridge Road. Shortly after passing the Fall River entrance station, you reach Horseshoe Park, a stunningly beautiful meadow formed around small lakes and the innumerable meanders of the tiny Horseshoe River. Horseshoe Park is refreshingly peaceful and riparian, in stark contrast with the jagged peaks and barren tundra you'll discover later on Trail Ridge Road. Horseshoe Park is also a prime location to observe and photograph wildlife early and late in the day. In autumn, the elk "bugle" in the area, attracting a lot of people.

Just past the second Sheep Lake, you'll find the trailhead for the Lawn Lake Trail, a long and strenuous 12.4 mile round-trip trail leading to Lawn Lake and Crystal Lake. Crystal Lake is tucked in under a sheer cliff and more rugged and photogenic than Lawn Lake. Few people hike this trail, although it is very pleasant. The trail follows the spectacular Roaring River all the way, but the river is actually even more spectacular just above the Alluvial Fan.

Back on the road, leave US 34 and turn right at the sign for Old Fall River Road. The road continues along the north side of Horseshoe Park, passing below the aforementioned Alluvial Fan. The boulder-laden fan was created when the Lawn Lake dam gave way in 1982, killing three visitors and creating Horseshoe Falls. The cascades are quite spectacular. To photograph the final few hundred yards of the Roaring River as it becomes the Horseshoe Falls, you can simply climb to the right of the falls until you find a suitable location. Here, the steep river cascades inside a gully over rust-colored granite unearthed by the flood. The paved road ends 2 miles from US 34 at the lovely Endovalley picnic area.

Old Fall River Road

Past Endovalley, the road continues as a well-graded dirt/gravel road. This is Old Fall River Road, a 9-mile one-way road leading to the Alpine Visitor Center on Trail Ridge Road. It is a popular road and, on a good day, chances are you'll be with lots of other cars. Note that this road may be subject to temporary closure in case of bad weather.

Chasm Falls is reached after 1.2 miles. This is a spectacular waterfall offering excellent photographic potential; the trick is to avoid direct sunshine of the water. The falls are oriented east, but still get a substantial amount of direct sunlight in mid-afternoon. Late afternoon is your best bet for photography. Walk down to the bottom of the falls for the best views.

The Roaring River (photo by Jesse Speer)

At mile 5.7, you'll notice a private road with a locked gate. Park on the side of the road, walk past the cabin and follow one of the footpaths leading to a tiny stream running through the lovely park. You can follow it downstream for a while, just enjoying the peace and looking for wildlife.

Back on the road, continue on the switchbacks until you reach a good car park above the timberline with an expansive view of the cirque below the Alpine Visitor Center, which is also visible from here. Looking down the valley, you may be able to spot a large herd of elk that is often grazing here. Another mile brings you to the end of the road and huge crowds at the Alpine Visitor Center.

Trail Ridge Road

From the Alpine Visitor Center, take US 34 toward Estes Park to continue your exploration of the eastern side of the park. This section of the road is known as the Trail Ridge Road. It is usually open from June through mid-October. There is always a lot of traffic on this road and people tend to stop a lot so be extra cautious.

Your first stop is the large car park of the Gore Range Overlook. The view from here is breathtaking and is one of the best sunrise locations for grand scenics. Fog often shrouds the valley below during the night, providing a thick carpet of grey from which the snowy peaks of the Never Summer Mountains emerge majestically in glorious pink tones at sunrise. It is always very cold and windy out there, so come prepared. After reaching the highest point on the road at 12,183 ft., the road goes past Iceberg Lake, which warrants a stop for its perennial glacier. It then slowly winds its way down toward Iceberg Pass, making two wide curves through the barren tundra. Stop along the road for a telephoto shot of the winding road, with the massive silhouette of Longs Peak in the distance. The next overlook, called the Rock Cut, has a short paved trail called Tundra Communities Trail, with a nice hoodoo at the end and beautiful lichen patterns on the rocks. Forest Canyon Overlook, your next stop, also has a trail through the tundra. Although less grandiose than the Gore Range Overlook, Forest Canyon Overlook is also a good sunrise location, less distant and perhaps easier to squeeze inside a photograph. The overlook proper is surrounded by a short stone wall offering some protection against the fierce wind. This area is pika and marmot heaven and you'll want to spend some time watching the little critters busying themselves with their chores.

The next major stop is the Rainbow Curve. It offers a distant view of Horseshoe Park, clearly showing its meanders between large clusters of conifers. This can yield a nice telephoto shot when the light is right.

The final stop is the Many Parks Curve, offering good views of Horseshoe Park, Hidden Valley and Beaver Meadows.

Iceberg Pass

Moraine Park & Fern Lake

Moraine Park is a major stop along the paved road leading to the heart of Rocky Mountain National Park. It consists of a vast "park" located in an alluvial valley of the Big Thompson River—the river you've seen earlier from the Forest Canyon Overlook on Trail Ridge Road. To get here from Estes Park, enter the park at the Beaver Meadows entrance station on US 36. You are bound to pass by Moraine Park several times during your visit, going to the numerous trails leaving from the Bear Lake and Glacier Gorge trailheads. Moraine Park has a small Visitor Center and some good trails allowing you to hike to the heart of the "park" as well as around it. There are some beaver ponds at the western

Moraine Park (photo by Jesse Speer)

end of the park, which are easily reached from the Cub Lake trailhead on Fern Lake Road. The odds of spotting an elk from the trail (or even from your car) are very high, so be sure to have a telephoto handy. Observe and photograph from a distance that is comfortable to the elk; if the elk move, you're too close. From the trailhead, you can hike 4.6 miles round-trip with less than 600 ft. elevation gain to Cub Lake. This is an easy hike and one of the best locations to see elk in the park. Cub Lake also has some nice water lilies that are fun to photograph.

Moraine Park is also one of the two gateways for Fern Lake. The Fern Lake trailhead is located a little bit farther than the Cub Lake trailhead at the north end of the meadow. There isn't much parking space at both trailheads so unless you're having an early start, it is advisable to park at the Moraine Park Museum and catch the free shuttle bus.

It's a 7.6 miles round-trip with 1,400 feet of elevation gain to the very popular Fern Lake. The trail initially follows the Big Thompson River, going past formations called Arch Rocks and turbulent narrows called The Pool at mile 1.9, before ascending steeply to the Fern Falls and reaching the lake at mile 3.8. Another 0.9 mile one-way with 500 feet elevation gain past Fern Lake brings you to Odessa Lake, which is alpine in character and more photogenic than Fern Lake. Both lakes are also accessible from the Bear Lake trailhead; I'll discuss this in a later section.

Sprague Lake & Bear Lake

Your first stop along the central and very popular Bear Lake Road is Sprague Lake. Many people drive directly to Sprague Lake and the car park tends to be full very early on. Sprague is a large lake located at 8,700 feet and surrounded by forest. A short level hike from the car park brings you to many excellent locations along the north side of the lake, which is best for photography. The lake's waters are a deep blue, perfectly reflecting the spectacular alpenglow on Hallett Peak and Flattop Mountain at dawn, if you're lucky enough to have no wind.

You can get a good panoramic view from just before the pontoon on the north side, where a small bypass follows the lake offering nice shots of reflections. Most people go for the classic picture shot from the east end, with the round boulder protruding from the lake in the foreground.

As for Bear Lake itself, it is pleasant enough, but it lacks the "alpine look" and feels a little bit too ensconced for grand scenic photography. Save the shooting for the other lakes you'll hike to from the Bear Lake trail network.

Photo advice: A 35mm to 55mm is optimum to capture the classic Sprague Lake panorama. Sprague Lake is the easiest lake to photograph at sunrise, given

Sprague Sunrise

its location near the paved road. Sunrise is not necessarily the only time to photograph Sprague. Stay around for a while and watch the lake open up to the light; it's a wonderful show.

Getting there: Bear Lake Road winds off US 36 for 9 miles until it dead-ends at Bear Lake. At the peak of the season and on weekends, the parking lots become full very early and it is advisable to take the free shuttle buses, unless you are having an early start. The shuttle operates daily from 7 AM to 7 PM from mid-June to late-September between the Park & Ride car park (across from Glacier Basin Campground) and Bear Lake, conveniently connecting with the Fern Lake trailhead shuttle. Note that there is no stop at Sprague Lake.

Photographing in the Bear Lake area at sunrise requires that you drive all the way up to Bear Lake in your own vehicle. You'll have plenty of room to park at that time.

Time required: From Estes Park, allow 45 minutes to drive to the Bear Lake parking area.

Bear Lake to Fern Lake Trailhead Thru-hike

Doing this entire thru-hike one-way from Bear Lake to the Fern Lake trailhead is an excellent solution, thanks to the shuttle buses. The thru-hike is slightly above 10 miles and takes the better part of a day, without being too strenuous. Doing so, you'll be able to see not only fantastic Odessa Lake, but also a couple of smaller spectacular alpine lakes: Lake Helene and Two Rivers Lake. An early start is recommended for a better experience with less crowds.

Lake Helene

The first part of the hike is common with the Flattop Mountain Trail, a popular destination for high-altitude junkies—although not a highly photogenic destination. In the early season, the trail may be buried deep below snowfields, but this isn't a big challenge. Still you may want to have your 7'5 USGS map handy to make sure you stay on course. After about 2.5 miles, you'll catch a glimpse of Two Rivers Lake below. If you want to explore its shores, it's easier to backtrack a couple of hundred yards on the trail and look for a faint path leading southwest to the Marigold Pond. Two Rivers Lake offers an outstanding view of Notchtop Mountain. A bit further, just before the trail angles north, a large cairn signals the short detour to Lake Helene. It is much easier to reach and also extremely pretty, however its shores are densely vegetated, making it harder to catch a good picture.

Continuing north, the trail descends rapidly to Odessa Lake, a large, stunningly beautiful alpine lake, which makes a great resting spot. Due to its larger size, Odessa Lake is difficult to photograph without a super wide-angle. If you don't have one, just relax and soak in the beauty.

After Odessa Lake, the previously-described Fern Lake and its namesake trail are a bit of a letdown, lacking in grandiose alpine beauty. If you have enough energy left after you reach The Pool and don't mind adding another easy mile to your hike, I suggest finishing by way of Cub Lake to its namesake trailhead. It provides more scenery and a chance to see elk, and perhaps even moose along the way.

Dream Lake, Emerald Lake & Lake Haiyaha

Nymph Lake

Dream Lake and Emerald Lake are quintessential Rocky Mountain alpine lakes. It is said that Dream Lake is the most photographed lake in the park, a reputation that is well deserved.

Their close proximity to the Bear Lake trailhead adds to their popularity. If you want to photograph spectacular alpine lakes at dawn without hitting the trail at 3 AM, this is your chance. The trail is wide, partially paved and easy to follow. If you time your departure well, you'll use your headlamp only until about Nymph Lake, 0.6 mile from the trailhead.

Nymph Lake is partially covered with water lilies. You can photograph them on your way back to the trailhead when Hallett Peak has a better reflection.

Dream Lake is only 1.1 miles from the trailhead. It is best photographed from the outlet, close to where the trail arrives, as there is plenty of good foreground. This is where most people tend to concentrate, so arrive shortly before sunrise to secure a good spot. You'll need to wait about 10 to 15 minutes after sunrise for the sun to strike Hallett Peak and Flattop Mountain, so you'll be there a while. Dream Lake is also popular with snowshoers in winter, thanks to its easy access and low 425 feet elevation gain.

Lake Haiyaha

Emerald Lake is a short 0.7 mile past Dream Lake, with only 220 feet elevation gain. It's very idyllic, but it's a bit too close under Hallett Peak and doesn't offer the same encompassing view.

Return past Dream Lake and take the marked trail to Lake Haiyaha, 1.2 miles from Dream Lake with 380 feet elevation gain. There are some outstanding open views of the Loch Vale and Longs Peak from the switchbacks, as well as a nice spot by a little inlet just before the bridge. The lake, whose name means "rock" in the local native-American tongue, has a very different character, with interesting granite boulders and rock piles along its shores. There is a beautiful view of Chaos Canyon, with Hallet Peak to the right. Return to Bear Lake the way you came, or you can take the shortcut to The Loch if you want more hiking. Although the trail is infrequently maintained, it is in fairly good shape.

Photo advice: Dream Lake is at its best from its outlet on the east side, with Hallett Peak to the west and part of Flattop Mountain to the right in a portrait orientation, using a 35mm to 28mm focal length. Prime locations on the left side of the trail were closed for revegetation at the time of this writing and are likely to remain close for quite a few years. Emerald Lake yields a very tight, but workable shot with a 24mm. A super wide-angle works best to capture the lake, Hallett Peak and the Tyndall Glacier in portrait mode. There are some good photo spots a short distance along the north shore.

Time required: Under normal conditions, it takes less than 30 minutes to reach Dream Lake from the Bear Lake trailhead. The entire hike including Emerald Lake and Lake Haiyaha is about 3½ to 4 hours.

Alberta Falls

Alberta Falls is one of the most popular destinations in the park. The falls are easily accessed via a 1.2-mile round-trip walk on a broad trail, with only about 220 feet elevation gain. At the height of the season, the foot traffic to Alberta Falls can be astounding.

Photo advice: The falls proper are not very impressive from the viewpoint; they are better photographed from river level, before the light becomes too crude and the contrast too high. After midday, I suggest that you don't linger and, instead, concentrate on the next hikes to higher ground.

Getting there: The Alberta Falls are reached from the Glacier Gorge trailhead, located almost a mile before Bear Lake. This trailhead also provides access to several spectacular high-alpine lakes located just below the Continental Divide, which we will explore in the next couple of sections. The parking area is much smaller than Bear Lake's and fills up very early. It is usually full one hour after sunrise.

Alberta Falls (photo by Jesse Speer)

Glacier Gorge

Continuing your hike past Alberta Falls (*see previous section*) along the moderate trail takes you through the beginning of the Loch Vale, where the trail splits about 1.3 miles past the Alberta Falls viewpoint (or 1.9 mile from the Glacier Gorge trailhead). Take the left fork, following the sign to Mills Lake.

The trail follows Glacier Creek past the small Glacier Falls to Mills Lake, reached at mile 2.6 from the Glacier Gorge trailhead. You are greeted by an expansive view of the Glacier Gorge with the lake in the foreground, Storm Peak and Longs Peak towering over it.

A short and level 0.4 mile past the onset of Mills Lake brings you to the small Jewel Lake. From here, it is a moderate 1.7 miles with a 750-foot elevation gain along Glacier Creek to Black Lake, 4.7 miles from the trailhead.

Photo advice: There are good potential shots from the bridge above Glacier Falls. The best shots of Mills Lake are from several large granite outcroppings along the shore, just as you reach the lake. Just take your pick. A mild wide-angle is adequate for Black Lake. The area above Black Lake is very nice.

Time required: 3 to 4 hours round-trip to Mills Lake from the car park. The better part of a day to Black Lake.

The Loch Vale

Lake of Glass

This spectacular hike branches out from the previously-described trail to Mills Lake at mile 1.9 from the Glacier Gorge trailhead. At the junction, follow the sign to The Loch, Glass Lake, Andrews Glacier and Sky Pond for an exhilarating day in the high country.

The trail passes through a wooded area along the north shore of the Loch, reached at mile 2.7 with 940 feet elevation gain from the Glacier Gorge car park. Past the Loch, the trail climbs steadily under a partial canopy of trees. Your next destination, Glass Lake (aka Lake of Glass) is just above Timberline Falls, which you can spot in the distance. The last few hundred feet before Glass Lake are next to the Timberline Falls and require a bit of Class 3 scrambling on wet and slippery rock. Early and late in the season, you might find snowfields and icy spots here. Use caution when negotiating this short ascent (even more so on the way back). Glass Lake is 4.2 miles from the Glacier Gorge trailhead. By contrast, the trail from Glass Lake to Sky Pond, at mile 4.5, is quite tame. There are few people here and in any case there is plenty of space to stretch and take in the view in relative solitude.

Be sure you get an early start for this 9 miles round-trip hike from the car park. Clouds form early in the afternoon and getting caught above Glass Lake during a thunderstorm can be a terrifying experience.

Photo advice: You'll reach the best spots by following the trail to the left. To get a better view of the jagged needles of Sharktooth, to your right, you need to detour around the lakes outlet and climb on the east side of Sky Pond. A 24mm or wider is necessary to capture the lake and Sharktooth in portrait mode. There is also an excellent view of Glass Lake from a long granite promontory to the northeast.

Time required: 5 to 6 hours to Sky Pond and back.

Chasm Lake

The last alpine lake hike I recommend to photographers starts from the Longs Peak trailhead, located on the eastern border of the park. It leads to Chasm Lake, a beautiful, stark, high alpine lake, located at the foot of Longs Peak, Rocky Mountain Nat'l Park's tallest summit at 14,255 feet.

The 8.4-mile round-trip trail to Chasm Lake is more strenuous for its altitude than for its actual steepness. Although the total elevation gain is about 2,400 feet, the grade is relatively consistent and the trail is well-maintained with no obstacles until the final ascent. Still, this is not a trail that should be undertaken without adequate preparation and acclimation. It is not necessarily harder than the other trails described earlier, but almost half of the hike is above timberline, which makes it very exposed. It's a good idea to garner a little bit of experience on other park trails before tackling this one.

After climbing through thick forest for about 2 miles, the trail emerges above timberline, continuing on the open tundra. At about mile 3 and 11,500 feet elevation, it reaches the Mills Moraine

Chasm Lake Dawn (photo by Ron Flickinger)

and crosses on the other side. From here, the trail continues almost level above a beautiful meadow. At mile 3.6, you pass the Columbine Falls, which feed the tiny Peacock Pond below. Soon after a second set of falls, you start the final scramble to Chasm Lake. The Class 3 route is rough, climbing over the characteristic jumble of rocks below alpine lakes. It is normally well cairned and there is little chance of straying off course. The rocks can be slippery or there may even be snow. Take your time to avoid slipping, especially on the way back.

Photo advice: Chasm Lake is a fantastic location: Longs Peak's diamond-like east face towers almost half a vertical mile above the lake. The view is best at dawn during August, as illustrated in Ron Flickinger's superb photograph on the previous page. However, the logistics can be daunting, as you need to be on the trail by 3 AM at the latest.

Getting there: The Longs Peak trailhead is accessed from CO 7, about 8 miles south of Estes Park on CO 7.

Time required: It will take you up between 2½ and 3 hours to reach the lake from the trailhead.

The Wild Basin

The Wild Basin area offers hikers a trio of falls packed on the 5.4-mile round-trip Thunder Lake Trail. Don't expect any grand vistas here, but it's a pleasant, moderate hike with wildflowers in July and colorful aspens in late September. The trail constantly follows flowing water: North St. Vrain Creek and a small portion of Cony Creek and Ouzel Creek, which adds to the enjoyment. This is a relaxing hike which doesn't call for a pre-sunrise departure. In fact, I'd recommend doing this hike in the afternoon. Leave the morning for the alpine lakes and grand scenics; here you have an opportunity to take advantage of the usually cloudy afternoons, as creeks and falls do not photograph well in the sun, which creates way too much contrast.

Copeland Falls

You'll encounter the first set of falls after only 0.3 mile. A short spur leaves to the left, leading to the twin Copeland Falls. Both have very short drops. The upper falls have a little more water action because they are tightly squeezed between rocks. I tend to prefer the lower falls, which are wider and have nicer surroundings below.

About 1.2 miles past the Copeland Falls, the trail crosses the St. Vrain, continuing South toward the Calypso Cascades. The trail splits after 0.3 mile, with three successive bridges spanning the base of the surprisingly wide falls. With the falls being so wide, the photographic potential here is more in abstract and intimate landscapes of the water cascading over the rocks.

Continue on the marked trail leading to the Ouzel Falls, 0.8 mile further to the northwest. The trail climbs a bit more steadily in the last 0.4 mile and you hear the roar of the falls before you see them. There is almost no view from the bridge and most people climb the obvious, but unofficial, footpath just before the bridge to get to the base of the falls. If you decide to follow it, use caution as it can be quite slippery.

Getting there: The Wild Basin entrance station is located 12 miles south of Estes Park off CO 7. Take the paved turnoff to Copeland Lake, then follow the graded dirt road west for another 2 miles to find the trailhead.

Time required: 2½ to 3 hours from the car park.

Kawuneeche Valley

The Kawuneeche Valley is often referred to as the "West side", as it sits on the west side of the Continental Divide. Except for a chunk of the Never Summer Range, it doesn't have any of the spectacular vistas seen on the east side, nor does it have any alpine lakes. What it has, however, is the Colorado River set in a beautiful valley with large numbers of wildlife, including moose, easily seen from the road. I have never traveled this road without seeing at least one elk.

For the purpose of this chapter, I'll describe the West Side from the Alpine Visitor Center down to Shadow Mountain Lake along US 34. Your first stop is Medicine Bow Curve, which is very similar to the Gore Range overlook described in the Trail Ridge Road section. The peaks are a bit closer, but not quite as spectacular. From here, the road descends along the Cache la Poudre river on your right. It's also known for being a frequent grazing spot for elk herds. The road then descends steadily, traversing the Continental Divide at Milner Pass. This is major elk country, watch for cars stopped on the road.

At Farview Curve, you catch your first very good glimpse of the Kawuneeche Valley below. This is also a good spot for a panoramic shot of the Never Summer Range. We would see more sunrise shots of the range taken from here if it wasn't so far from everything. There is also a good view of Mt. Ida to the southeast. After going down the switchbacks, the road enters the valley proper. At the Colorado River trailhead, you can hike to the old mining town of Lulu City, but there isn't much left there. Instead, I recommend stopping at the Beaver ponds picnic area and to the south of the historic Holzwarth Trout Lodge (formerly Never Summer Ranch) to look for nice shots of the Colorado River and beaver ponds meandering in the grassy valley. The Holzwarth Homestead itself consists of the old lodge buildings and has strictly a historic value. The old farm equipment sitting on the grassy field is of limited interest.

The Timber Creek trailhead provides access to Timber Lake, just below Mt. Ida, a 9.6-mile round-trip hike, with about 2,000 feet elevation gain. This is a nice semi-alpine lake and the trail sees little traffic compared to its east side counterparts, but it is hard to get an early start unless you are camping and most of the trail is in dense forest with no views.

Bull Elk in the Kawunechee

If you are looking for an easy hike on the West Side, a good choice is the Green Mountain Trail, less than 6 miles to the south. From the trailhead, it's only 3.6 miles round-trip with 600 feet elevation gain to the vast Big Meadows, which definitely deserves its name. This is a great place to photograph elk and moose. There are few crowds and, if you feel like more hiking, you can follow the trail north on the western edge of the meadows to link with the Tonahutu Creek Trail, a favorite of backpackers going to Bear Lake. One of the highlights of the Tonahutu is actually within reach on a day hike: The superb Granite Falls require a 10.4-mile round-trip with only 1,100 feet elevation gain. A short walk past the falls brings you to a really lovely meadow where you'll want to linger a while before retracing your steps. This hike is admittedly better done as a backpack, especially for photography, but it's definitely worth it as a day hike too.

One last hike I recommend to photographers is the East Inlet Trail out of the far end of Grand Lake. Grand Lake is the northernmost of the three large lakes at the southwestern edge of the park, just south of the Kawuneeche Visitor Center and Grand Lake entrance station. Grand Lake is also a sizeable community along the north shore of the lake. From the East Inlet trailhead, it's only 0.3 miles to the popular Adams Falls, which are of minor interest to photographers. Continuing past the falls, you reach a large, photogenic meadow about a mile into the trail. This is such a short hike, it's a must-see. The East Inlet Trail continues toward Lone Pine Lake, Lake Verna and Spirit Lake. I admit sheepishly that I totally ignored this area for many years, concentrating exclusively on the east side of the park. I was stunned to discover the beauty of the West Side on the East Inlet Trail. Granted, this hike as well as the previously-mentioned Green Mountain/Tonahutu Creek Trail combo are much better done as backpacks, but they can also bring great enjoyment as day hikes. If you can spare enough days to Rocky Mountain Nat'l Park, by all means spend at least a day, or better yet a couple of days, on the West Side.

AROUND DENVER

Mt. Evans

Mt. Evans boasts the highest paved road in the U.S, dropping you at the 14,130-foot summit parking area, a mere 134 feet below the summit. The Scenic Byway is actually more fun to drive than it is scenic. Nevertheless, there are some good photographic opportunities, especially of wildlife.

The first good spot is the Mt. Goliath Natural Area, reached shortly past Echo Lake. It has a fairly good stand of bristlecone pines and is worth the short walk. Shortly after leaving the Goliath area, the road emerges above the timberline and you can see Mt. Evans far above and Echo Lake, far below.

About 7 miles past Goliath, you reach Summit Lake. This is perhaps my favorite place on Mt. Evans. It's a desolate area, and it has some minimalist kind of beauty, enhanced by lots of wildflowers and small lichens clinging to rocks.

Past Summit Lake, the grade gets as steep as 15%. As you attack the numerous switchbacks leading to the summit, your car will really feel the rarefied atmosphere. There are many mountain goats, usually in small groups, along the switchbacks; it's almost impossible not to see them as you get closer to the top. Look up and down on both sides of the road to spot them.

Once on top, be sure to put several layers on as well as sun protection on your face if you hike the short 0.3 mile trail to the summit or even just the remains of the Crest House. The latter was destroyed in 1979 by a propane explosion and never rebuilt, so there is no shelter. It is cold and extremely windy. You've gained over 7,000 feet elevation since you left I-70. At 3°F per 1,000 feet, that's at least 21°F less. Add to this the wind-chill factor and it will be easily 35°F less than when you started the ascent. Many people are prone to minor headaches at such elevation, but it will pass as you drive down.

The view from the top is what you would expect: peak after peak as far as the eye can see, and the flat land far below. This is way too big, of course, for interesting photographs, so just enjoy the feeling.

Photo advice: Mt. Evans' main interest is its wildlife, specifically the mountain goats. It is best to visit during a week day as too many cars make it more difficult to pull off for an impromptu shot of mountain goats or bighorn sheep. Although the road is open 24 hours—allowing an early start—it

Woolly Creature

doesn't seem to make a difference whether you drive early in the morning or later in the day: the goats are always there. A long telephoto is essential to capture interesting close-ups of the woolly mountain creatures.

Getting there: West of Denver on I-70, take exit 240 in Idaho Springs and drive about 15 miles southwest on CO 103 to the Mt. Evans Entrance at Echo Lake. From here, it is a 15 mile drive to the summit. The $10 fee is waived for Golden Eagle Pass holders. The road is open from Memorial Day till the first significant snowfall in September. Call the Clear Creek Ranger District of Arapaho Nat'l Forest for up-to-date information (see *Appendix*).

Time required: About 3 hours from Idaho Springs.

Georgetown & Guanella Pass

Georgetown makes an excellent stop along I-70 (Exit 228). It has retained much of its old Victorian charm and it is not overly touristy. You can easily stroll the small historic district on foot looking for interesting subjects. Most of Georgetown's streets are still unpaved. The Hotel de Paris Museum is a little jewel and definitely worth a visit. Also well worth a stop is Gary Haines' very nice Grizzly Creek photography gallery on 6th Street.

Georgetown is also home to the Georgetown Loop Railroad (see *Appendix*). The Loop takes you from Georgetown to the old Silver Plume mining town over a 3-mile narrow gauge track with an elevation gain of 640 feet. The train doubles back on a tight loop toward the end of the track, offering an opportunity for riders to photograph the engine and the scenery. The ride takes about 1 hour.

Just south of Georgetown is the Guanella Pass Scenic Byway (CR 381), a popular destination for wildflowers and fall colors. The pass, at 11,669 feet, offers great views of Mt. Bierstadt to the east. The Georgetown/Guanella Pass area is famous for winter sightings of bighorn sheep. The road is rather narrow and not recommended for large RVs.

The Peak-to-Peak Byway

Traveling from Mt. Evans to Rocky Mountain National Park, your natural route is the Peak-to-Peak Byway, combining CO 119, CO 72 and CO 7 to reach Estes Park. The route is at its best on the stretch between lovely Nederland and Ward when it finally opens up to the west, revealing exceptional views of the Indian Peaks Wilderness and its high peaks. A quarter mile past Ward, take the first road leading west to Brainard Lake. The 10-mile round-trip road takes you to a great view of Mt. Audubon and the other Indian Peaks with the lake in the foreground. This road is plowed to Red Rock Lake in winter and is extremely popular with snowshoers. After meeting with CO 7, the Peak-to-Peak Byway passes through some outstanding aspen groves. About 3 miles past the junction, a large scenic overlook on the right offers good views of Mount Meeker and

Mirror on the Edge (photo by Ron Flickinger)

Rocky Mountain National Park. As you drive toward Allenspark, Longs Peak comes into view to the west. About 6 miles past Allenspark, you'll pass the previously mentioned spur road to the Longs Peak trailhead and Chasm Lake.

Nearby location: From CO 119, about 5 miles north of Black Hawk, it's only a 5-mile one-way detour to Golden Gate Canyon State Park's Visitor Center on CO 46. Take the Gap Road to the left shortly after the park entrance. The steep, windy dirt road takes you in less than 4 miles to the Panorama Point scenic overlook, which has a great panoramic view of the Rockies.

The Cache La Poudre Scenic Byway

I suggest driving this outstanding road from east to west. At 100 miles long, it's a fairly long drive and it will be less fatiguing with the sun in your back rather than in your eyes. Starting from Ft. Collins on CO 14, the first 20 miles of the scenic byway follow the rapids of the Cache La Poudre River. This portion of the road is hugely popular with rafters, especially on summer week-ends, when you're likely to see dozens of rafts braving the non-stop Class III and IV rapids.

Nokhu Crags

The river eventually shrinks down at the Narrows, which have beautiful pink granite walls. After leveling off a bit, the road passes a succession of beautiful meadows and small hamlets

Just past the Joe Wright Reservoir, which offers outstanding open views of the lower Medicine Bow Mountains, the road tops at Cameron Pass then drops down inside a beautiful valley with views of the spectacular Nokhu Crags across the highway. The Crags form the northern tip of the Never Summer Mountains. From the highway, you are only 2 miles from Rocky Mountain Nat'l Park, as the crow flies, but one hundred miles from the nearest park entrance.

To stretch your legs after all these miles, consider an easy 1.7-mile round-trip jaunt through dense forest to Lake Agnes. From here on, the road follows the wider valley of the Michigan River though hauntingly remote and beautiful North Park to Walden.

If you drive the entire loop from Estes Park via Ft. Collins, Walden and the southwestern entrance of the Rocky Mountain NP, it will be a cool 260 miles.

Getting there: From Ft. Collins, follow the signs to US 287 N/CO-14 W.

Roxborough State Park

Roxborough State Park, southwest of Denver, contains spectacular red-rock formations similar to the much more famous Garden of the Gods (see *Southern Colorado chapter*), albeit in a somewhat less dramatic setting. It is much quieter, however, and there is a larger diversity of flora and fauna.

There is a good network of trails, but the best one to see the hogback at close range is the easy 2.2-mile Fountain Valley loop which leaves from the parking area. From the trailhead, a short hike brings you to the Fountain Valley Overlook, which has good views to the northwest and southwest. Continuing along the trail, take the right fork. At 0.7 mile from the car park, a short spur trail leads

up in about 200 yards to the scenic Lyons Overlook from which you gain an outstanding view of the jagged monocline to the west. From here, you can either retrace your steps to the car park or do a full loop around the ridge on which you're standing. The trail continues down and around the hogback, close to the formations, providing good views from below.

Getting there: From I-25 south of Denver, take Freeway C-470 west to CO 85 south

Roxborough

(Santa Fe Hwy). About 4 miles south, turn right (west) on Titan Road, which becomes North Rampart Range Road, then left on Roxborough Park Road.

Time required: 1½ to 2 hours at a relaxed pace.

Nearby location: Red Rocks Park, 15 miles west of Denver, is also geologically similar to the Garden of the Gods. In fact, it was even named Garden of the Angels and Garden of the Titans, before acquiring the simpler Red Rocks moniker. Who can compete against Gods?

The fabulous 10,000-seat Red Rock amphitheater is located within its grounds. The location is fantastic, set between two large sandstone monoliths: Ship Rock and Creation Rock. Another formation forms a backdrop to the stage. The Red Rocks Amphitheater can easily be visited after your hike in Roxborough State Park—except, of course, when a concert is scheduled.

The pleasant 1.4-mile Trading Post Loop Trail goes past sandstone formations, but it's nowhere near as spectacular as Roxborough. The trail closes 30 minutes before sunset, but the park and the amphitheater remain open until 11:00 PM.

The park can be reached from the same C-470 freeway you took for Roxborough. Continue to the Morrison exit, turn west and follow the signs.

The Devil's Backbone

On the western outskirts of Loveland is a spectacular hogback called the Devil's Backbone. It is now part of a vast recreational/preservation complex formed by the Coyote Ridge Natural Area, the Horsetooth Mountain Park and the Devil's Backbone Open Space. It's hard not to be impressed by the huge opportunities offered to hikers, horseback riders and mountain bikers by the 7-mile trail corridor (sometimes separate trails) traversing the area. Photographers will want to access the Open Space from the south to be closest to the Devil's Backbone.

The shortest hike of interest is the 2.1-mile round-trip Wild Loop passing by a large opening in the hogback called the Keyhole. Unfortunately, the Keyhole is most spectacular from the west side, which no longer has public access. Also, the spur trail to the Keyhole is usually closed during springtime and until mid-June to allow raptors to roost in peace. Nevertheless, there is good potential along the way as you follow the hogback from below. One particular spot has many little holes in the hogback making the latter look like fine lace.

From the end of the Wild Loop, you can continue for

The Devil's Backbone

another 1.5 miles to the end of the Hunter Loop. It gets a little closer to the Backbone, but one can never get to the Backbone itself. Still, it's worth hiking inside the park. Despite the fact that there are quite a few people on the trails, there is a feeling of wide open spaces and solitude.

Photo advice: Be there at sunrise, when the park opens, as only the east side of the Backbone can be photographed.

Getting there: On CO 34, about 25 miles east of Estes Park or about 8 miles west of Exit 257 (Loveland) off I-25, turn left (north) onto Hidden Valley Drive, where a sign points to the park.

Pawnee National Grassland

For a day away from the Rocky Mountain NP and a radical change in scenery, I recommend a drive through the Pawnee National Grasslands. Finding yourself engulfed in this immense expanse of Colorado prairie with limitless views on all sides after days amongst the highest peaks offers an interesting contrast. At 50 miles from the Rockies as the crow flies just for the western border of the grasslands, it's admittedly a bit of a drive, but it's well worth it.

Deep in the middle of the prairie are the Pawnee Buttes—the star attraction of the grasslands—consisting of two pale-colored sandstone buttes rising 250 feet above the prairie floor. From The Pawnee Buttes trailhead, a short walk leads to an overlook with a distant view of the buttes. The trail continues for a 3-mile round-trip to the base of West Butte.

Pawnee Buttes (photo by Jan Forseth)

Photo advice: Late afternoon in springtime is the best time to photograph the grasslands, with the golden stems rhythmically animated by the wind, like kelp beds in the ocean. Thunderstorms are frequent in late afternoon, adding drama to the scene. If you'd rather be here at sunrise, your best option is to stay at the Crow Valley Recreation Area, just outside Briggsdale.

Getting there: From I-25 at Fort Collins, drive east on CO 14 for almost 50 miles. Turn left (north) on CR 103 and follow the signs to the Pawnee Buttes along the various county roads to the trailhead. The 7.5' USGS map is of limited use here. Use the Forest Service's "Pawnee National Grassland" map. ❀

In a Garden of Eden

Chapter 6

SOUTHERN COLORADO

Garden of the Gods at Sunset

SOUTHERN COLORADO

Garden of the Gods

The Garden of the Gods is a public park, owned and managed by the city of Colorado Springs. This little gem is so exceptionally beautiful, it's a wonder why it is not a National Monument. On second thought, however, it is clear that it was developed early on by Colorado Springs and that it is a great source of income for the city, which is doing a great job managing it anyway. If it was administered by the National Park Service, more people would know about it and it could put a lot of stress on the little park's ecosystem.

The Garden of the Gods consists of several dramatically shaped ridges of red sandstone emerging from a landscape of beautiful tallgrass and very green vegetation. It is extremely photogenic at all times of the day and in all seasons, but it shines even more during the golden hour and during wintertime after a fresh snowfall. It is set in front a majestic background, which is itself world-class scenery: Pikes Peak.

The ridge is running north/south, which is great for photographers. You can photograph on the main east side at sunrise, and again on the west side in late afternoon. The park is accessible by car from both sides and the views from the viewpoints established along the paved roads are so open that many visitors are just as happy to see it from their car. A loop road runs around the main ridge, making it easy and convenient to scout the park during your first visit and decide where you want to shoot from. The road is shared by a bike lane, providing the most exhilarating circuit to cyclists. Drive very cautiously; don't stray and don't park inside the bike lane.

The park also has an outstanding network of trails, some paved and some dirt, which makes it a jogger's and hiker's paradise. And if this weren't enough, climbers can also get their kicks in the park; there are many popular routes just above the trails. Despite the close proximity of the urban population, it has a large amount of wildlife: deer, rabbits, coyotes, and numerous species of birds can be observed in the park.

Photo advice: The park is open from 5 AM to 11 PM from May to October and 5 AM to 9 PM from November to April. These generous hours are perfect for photographers.

For your afternoon shoot, I recommend spending mid afternoon wandering along the Central Garden trails on the west side, looking for creative shots amongst the rocks around you. About 1½ hour before sunset, move into position at the upper car pullout or just below the car pullout located at the latitude of the Tower of Babel. The Tower of Babel is the uppermost (also northernmost) side of the largest hogback. You can park there on the loop road, but spots are very limited and there is no guarantee that you'll find one. You can also park at the main west side car park providing access to the Central Garden and walk along the loop road to the car pullout. From this spot you'll have the perfect, but classic, perspective of Pulpit Rock to the left and the serrated Cathedral Spires and Three Graces with Gray Rock in the back. Be in position on the backside at least 1 hour before sunset, otherwise the scene will be in shadow. You'll need at least a 3-stop ND Grad filter to bring out detail in the lovely green vegetation below which is gradually in shadow from mid-afternoon on. If you don't do that, your fore-ground will be totally black, or worse, the formations will be overexposed.

For your morning shoot, you should be in position at your pre-scouted location at least a few minutes before sunrise. You have several choices. The easiest is to park at the Visitor Center and shoot a large panoramic view of the two uppermost (and largest) monoliths. This is a very good spot for general observation, but it is a bit static photographically due

Garden on the Gods at Dawn

Garden of the Gods Sunrise

to the lack of foreground. A remedy for that would be to shoot from along 30th street, a bit south of the park entrance, with the lake in the foreground. Yet, this is still a bit static and you've lost the elevation and have to include more sky which is not very good.

A much better possibility is to park at the large north parking lot below the Tower of Babel and to shoot from along the Susan Bretag Trail. There are many good spots along this trail, which let you include the White Rock monolith for a touch of contrast with the overwhelming red rock. One excellent possibility is to climb one of the social trails (unofficial) close to the intersection of the Gateway and Susan Bretag trails. You can find a good foreground of juniper trees on top. Perhaps the very best possibility is to take the Dakota Trail and follow one of the numerous (but unofficial) footpaths leading up the hill to your left. From the top of the hill you have an awesome bird's-eye view of the entire ridge, with an excellent foreground.

Needless to say, sunrise on the Garden of the Gods is an incredible sight, with the entire ridge turning an intense glowing red in the first couple of minutes, assuming the air is haze-free.

After sunrise, you'll have about an hour of good light to work with. There are many good possibilities. One is along the paved trail between the north parking lot and the Gateway Trail. Another is along the Chambers Trail and the trail leading south from the Gateway Trail to the mountain bike area.

As you can see, there are many excellent locations and they are not limited to what I just described as my personal favorites. The Palmer Trail is also very nice in the afternoon, although I find it a bit less open than the road below and you have to hike about 0.7 mile one-way before finding a very good view. I also like the Siamese Twins Trail in afternoon and the Ridge Trail in mid-morning. In the Balanced Rock area, near the south entrance, Balanced Rock proper isn't very interesting, but there is a good telephoto shot of the Toadstools from the road in the morning. The bottom line is that you can't be everywhere at the same time, so you'll need at least a couple of morning shoots to do the park justice.

You can use a whole gamut of lenses at Garden of the Gods, although you'll primarily use a wide-angle.

Getting there: Coming from the north on I-25, take Exit 146 and head west, toward the mountains, on Garden of the Gods Road. Turn left (south) onto

30th Street and go 1.4 miles. The Visitor Center is on the left, on a small hill, and the park road is on the right. Coming from the south on I-25, get off on US 24 (Exit 141) to the Garden of the Gods Road/Manitou Springs exit.

Manitou Springs Cliff Dwellings

Time required: At least one afternoon and the next morning at dawn.

Nearby Locations: Manitou Springs is a hugely popular town for Colorado Springs visitors. Many would call it a tourist trap, but I personally think it's a very convenient base as long as you're not there on a week-end. Manitou Springs is the gateway to hugely popular Pikes Peak, without a doubt one of the most visited summits in the world with more than 500,000 visitors per year. You can reach the summit by car or using the wonderful Pikes Peak Cog Railway. The 19-mile Pikes Peak Highway is paved part of the way and open year round, except when temporarily closed by snow. It's world-famous for the yearly Pikes Peak Auto Hill Climb, run each June on the unpaved portion to the summit. The railway is the highest and oldest cog railway in the world, having been in operation since 1891. It is incredibly cute and fun.

Some of the many other Manitou Springs destinations have questionable merits. I'll just mention the heavily-advertised Manitou Cliff Dwellings as you may be wondering about them. Although built from scratch in the early 1900s as a competing attraction to Mesa Verde—in part from authentic dwellings acquired elsewhere from private landowners—the fact is there is some potential for amateur photography here. If you can avoid the massive crowds and signs plastered on almost every wall, you could come back with a few decent pictures. There, I said it, and I'm even including a photograph to illustrate the point.

Florissant Fossil Beds National Monument

Beneath the ground of Florissant Fossil Beds Nat'l Monument lies one of the richest and most diverse fossil deposits in the world. Trapped in a layer of volcanic sediments at the bottom of an ancient lake, insects, animals, plants, and trees became fossilized and ultimately revealed by uplift and erosion. The most spectacular fossils are of course the giant Sequoias. The petrified stumps are really massive—about the size of the largest living Sequoias. It's a bit strange to see them protruding here and there from the semi-alpine hills and meadow. The largest one, appropriately named Big Stump, is 14 feet tall and 74 feet in circumference.

There are a number of trails you can hike inside the monument. The most popular are the two short self-guided loops in the vicinity of the Visitor Center: the 0.5-mile Walk Thru Time/Ponderosa Loop and the 1 mile Petrified Forest Loop. Both are flat and very easy and can be done one after the other in less than an hour at a relaxed pace.

The Visitor Center has displays of some exceptionally well preserved fossils of small plants and insects, but this is of course out of the scope of this book.

Just 0.7 mile north of the Visitor Center road, the historic barns of the Hornbek Homestead strike a very pretty picture in the middle of the verdant meadow.

Photo advice: Although the petrified trunks are fascinating, they are clumpy and static and don't make a particularly good subject. It's fair to say that it falls in the documentary photography category. A mid wide-angle is the lens of choice.

Giant Fossilized Trunk

Getting there: Heading northwest from Colorado Springs on US 24, turn south on CR 1 in the town of Florissant and drive 2 miles to the Visitor Center. From Cripple Creek, follow CR 1 north for 16 miles.

Time required: 1½ hour for a short visit.

Gold Belt Scenic Byway

If through some fateful event or family obligation, you got suckered into the tourist traps abounding in and around Cañon City, know that there is one great redeeming feature to this area: The drive between Cañon City, Victor and Florissant. This popular drive, known as the Gold Belt Scenic Byway, consists of several roads, mostly dirt and gravel, located west/southwest of Colorado Springs. The two most popular roads are the Phantom Canyon Road and the Shelf Road, which can be driven as a loop.

The 22-mile long Phantom Canyon Road follows the path of the now defunct Florence and Cripple Creek Railroad. It is a good, wide, graded dirt and gravel road, normally passable by passenger cars in good weather. Although visually attractive and interesting with its narrow sections, tunnels and bridges, it is hard to find features suitable for photography.

The same goes from its western counterpart, the Shelf Road, linking Cripple Creek to Cañon City. My preference nonetheless goes to the Shelf Road for both sheer kicks and variety; however, it is not suitable for passenger cars. The Shelf Road was used by stagecoach and is more sub-alpine in character than the Phantom Canyon Road, which is more ensconced. If you choose to drive only the Shelf Road, you should not miss the old mining town of Victor, which has tremendous character and authenticity, as well as good potential for photography. Surprisingly, there is still a large, and ugly, gold mine apparently thriving on the outskirts of town.

Time required: 4 to 4½ hours for the full loop using both roads, with a short drive through Victor. Allow more time to soak in Victor's atmosphere.

Nearby Locations: The hugely popular attraction of the Royal Gorge Bridge draws hordes of visitors. The view from the overlook next to the parking area is quite distant. The best photographic potential is from the bridge proper.

The Royal Gorge Railroad is also very popular. It runs for two hours inside the Royal Gorge portion of the former Denver & Rio Grande Western line. The train has an open-air observation car to view and photograph the gorge.

The western branch of the Top of the Rockies Scenic Byway follows the Arkansas River from Leadville to Salida and is quite pleasant. I mention it here in passing due to the numerous rafting opportunities on the Arkansas River.

Highway of Legends

If you are driving east after visiting the Great Sand Dunes, or if you're traveling on I-25 between Santa Fe and Colorado Springs or Denver, don't miss CO 12, aka the Highway of Legends National Forest Byway. It begins off US 160, just north of La Veta, with a superb view of the Spanish Peaks. Goemmer Butte, a striking volcanic plug with several extensive dikes similar to Shiprock, towers 800 feet above the Cuchara Valley floor, south of La Veta. The section between La Veta and Cuchara Pass is extremely scenic, especially when you can catch a glimpse of the Devil's Stairstep, which is part of the Dakota Wall. If you don't have time for the entire road, you might consider driving only this 22-mile round-trip portion. South of Cuchara Pass and its large stands of aspens, you'll finally have a close encounter with the Dakota Wall in the small town of Stonewall. The Dakota Wall is not a dike but a gigantic sandstone wall stretching hundreds of miles, parallel to the Rocky Mountains but surfacing only here and there. This is the same wall formation as the Garden of the Gods. In Stonewall, you can actually touch it.

Time required: About 2 hours for the entire 82-mile drive.

Capulin Volcano

Although Capulin Volcano National Monument is located in New Mexico, you are more likely to visit it during a trip through Southern Colorado than from Santa Fe or Taos which are quite a ways away. This is why it is included in the present chapter.

This elegant little volcano rises more than 1,200 feet above the surrounding plain. The monument is very tiny, just large enough to encompass the base, which is about 0.5 mile wide. A 2-mile road spirals steeply along the side of the near-perfect cinder cone to a platform on the west side. From here, you can either hike up on the rim or down 0.2 mile to the bottom of the crater.

The Rim Trail around the 1,500-foot wide crater and its bottom is about 1 mile long and takes about 45 minutes to hike. It has magnificent views of the entire area, with numerous small craters emerging here and there from the vast plain. The most spec-

Capulin Volcano Sunset

tacular view is to the southeast, looking toward the 15-mile wide Sierra Grande stratovolcano.

Photo advice: I have seen a great picture of the volcano's shadow projected on the plain, at or near sunset. The monument opens at 7:30 AM and closes at 6:30 PM from Memorial Day to Labor Day. This makes it impossible to catch the shadow of the volcano from the rim in summer, as sunset occurs much after the closing time. Such a picture would have to be taken in winter, when the closing time is 4 PM.

To get a good shot of the volcano itself, you'll have to exit the monument to put some distance between you and the cone. Driving 1.5 miles on CO 325 toward Folsom, you'll find a dirt road to the right. This good dirt road skirts the north side of the volcano. You might like this location, but I find it a bit too close. Instead, I recommend the grassy flats on the west side of the road during the next 0.5 to 1.5 mile. Just pull off the road and walk a bit away from it. With plenty of nice tallgrass and lava rocks in the foreground, it yields a decent picture close to sunset.

Another excellent evening spot is about 0.5 mile south of the monument junction on CO 325.

Getting there: From Raton on I-25, just south of the Colorado border, drive 33 miles east on US 64/87. The park entrance is off NM 325, 3 miles north of the town of Capulin.

Time required: 2½ to 3 hours.

Great Sand Dunes National Park

The Great Sand Dunes of south-central Colorado are the tallest dunes in North America, reaching heights of nearly 750 feet. I am extremely fond of sand dunes and I have had the good fortune of seeing many on all continents, but one thing sets the Great Sand Dunes apart from the rest: The presence of a creek at their very base during springtime and the beginning of summer. This somewhat incongruous factor creates a unique ecosystem that is unlike any other dune system in the world.

The Great Sand Dunes offer a majestic sight both from afar and at close range. From afar, the tall dunes strike a fantastic profile in front of the oft snow capped peaks of the Sangre de Cristo Mountains and lend themselves to superb telephoto photography. From a short distance, the rich brown sand creates a fantastic contrast with the abundant foliage of Medano Creek's riparian area, which turns golden in early fall. On top of the dunes, you'll be rewarded with the view of a vast field of sand with superb crests and ripples, stretching for what seems forever at the foot of the mountains.

There is one drawback to these dunes, as far as photography is concerned: the crowds. This is an extremely popular place for families with kids, particularly on weekends. You'll find kids climbing and rolling down all over the dunes. Fortunately, there are almost 40 sq. miles of dunes so if you climb high and walk on the dune field, you're guaranteed to find solitude and lack of tracks. Talking about tracks, the Great Sand Dunes usually don't keep them for long. The wind is often blowing and will erase yesterday's tracks as easily as they came.

Arriving at the Dunes (photo by QT Luong)

To climb the dunes, you'll have to be in excellent physical shape, as it is fairly strenuous exertion at an elevation of 8,000 feet. Dunes are never easy to climb in general, but these can be lethal and if you don't pick your way carefully and climb on ridge lines, where the sand is more solid, it will be one step forward, half a step back. Previous climbers' footsteps usually—but not always—reflect the easiest way to climb. Remember that distances are deceiving on the dunes and that your destination is often farther away than it looks. If you hike during hot afternoons, you'll need to drink lots of water.

If you want to be on top of the tallest dune—aptly named High Dune—for sunrise, plan on an early start, allowing about one hour from the Medano Creek crossing. Although it feels good to walk barefoot on the cool sand in the early morning, be sure to use tennis shoes or you'll burn your feet later on when the surface temperature of the sand can reach 140°F.

From the top of the dune you'll enjoy an awesome 360° view. It's also a great spot for sunset.

There are plenty of photographic opportunities walking upstream in the Medano Creek riverbed. The creek is wide at the crossing but gets progressively narrower. The water flows in strange waves of varying intensity. Sometimes it stops flowing where you are and the current starts building up just a few feet away. This is due to the

Sunflowers among the Dunes (photo by Ron Flickinger)

sand forming small dams, which periodically give way, causing the water to flow in waves along new paths. Just standing there in the shallow water is a wonderfully relaxing experience.

Beginning at Mosca Creek near the Dunes parking lot, follow the creek for a tad over 2 miles until you reach Castle Creek, passing a ghost forest of dead trees suffocated by newly formed dunes. There, the dunes rise abruptly from the creek bed at impossibly steep angles. To return, follow the Medano Pass 4WD road to the Point of No Return car park and take the Little Medano Trail heading to the Pinyon Flats campground. You'll have great views of the dunes from the trail, especially if you take the spur trail to Dunes Overlook, about half way. From the campground, take the 1-mile Pinyon Flats Trail to return to your car.

If you have limited time, walking downstream at the base of the dunes is also very rewarding. There are few people going in that direction and excellent views of the dunes. During summer, moonlight walks on the dunes are pleasant and you can watch some small animals not visible during the day.

Photographers who don't want to walk or carry heavy or fragile equipment can drive their 4WD vehicle on the 12-mile long Medano Pass primitive road.

A Sea of Sand

Medano Pass affords spectacular views of the dunes. Check road conditions at the Visitor Center before going, as deep sand is often present past Point of No Return (it may be necessary to reduce the air pressure in you tires) and creek crossing could be hazardous during snowmelt.

Although the park is open year-round, the best time to visit Great Sand Dunes is from mid-May through mid-June and mid-September through mid-October. Winter and early spring are very cold and sometimes windy. Summer is very hot and brings a high danger of lightning during afternoon thunderstorms, making photography on the dunes hazardous with a tripod. June can be made unpleasant by the myriads of aggressive mosquitoes and biting gnats.

Photo advice: A medium telephoto will work wonders to compress the perspective between the dunes and the Sangre de Cristo. Stop anywhere on the road

High Dune (photo by Adam Schallau)

leading to the park; I suggest about a mile past the private lodge and campground on CO 150. On the dunes, anything goes from extreme wide-angle to short telephoto. In early morning, late afternoon and early evening, the dunes have much better color and interesting shadows. Protect your camera when walking and exercise caution when you shoot, as sand penetrates everything in this often-windy area.

Getting there: Most people come from Alamosa, which is 35 miles southwest of the monument and has numerous motels. Unless you take US 160 and CO 150 to the north, I recommend coming on US 17 via Mosca and turning east into 6 Mile Lane—which is actually 16 miles long. This is a more scenic road and the San Luis Lakes State Park is an excellent riparian area with good bird watching during the high season. The Pinyon Flats campground is pleasant and convenient and makes a good base for photographers. The private Great Sand Dunes Lodge, just outside the park, is very nice. They have very few rooms available, so be sure to reserve well in advance.

Time required: At least half a day. If you have limited time and stay at the campground or at the lodge just before the entrance, you can arrive in mid-afternoon and leave in mid-morning the next day.

Nearby locations: The turnoff to Zapata Falls is on CO 150, less than 8 miles south of the entrance to the monument. Take the 3.5-mile well-graded road up to the parking lot and picnic area. From there, you'll have great views of the San Luis Valley and the distant dune field at the foot of the Sangre de Cristo Mountains. It's a good spot for pan-

Red Dune

oramic shots. Walk about 0.5-mile uphill, with good views along the way, to a creek leading to the falls, which are somewhat hidden from view inside a cavern-shaped narrow gorge. To see the waterfall, you need to wade in the gushing water, with the risk of slipping and falling in the water, so I don't recommend crossing with your camera. Photographically, it's not particularly rewarding in summer, but it can be worth it in winter when the waterfall freezes over, creating a beautiful icy-blue sculpture.

The Cumbres & Toltec Scenic Railroad

Built 126 years ago, the Cumbres & Toltec Scenic Railroad is the highest narrow gauge railway in the U.S. Less heralded than its Durango-Silverton counterpart (see *Chapter 7*), the Cumbres and Toltec railroad passes through landscape almost as beautiful and is worthy of a stop (see *Appendix*).

From late May to mid-October two trains run every day. One leaves from Chama, New Mexico and the other from Antonito in Colorado. They meet in the middle at Osier, where passengers eat lunch. People can either ride to Osier and then return to their point of origin or continue on, riding a bus back.

The trip from Chama to Osier over Cumbres Pass is definitely the most photogenic. For most of this part, the railroad follows CO 17/NM 17 closely and you can essentially see the same sights from the road. I have actually followed the train and even crossed path with it while driving.

Coming from Antonito, your first encounter with the railway is at Los Pinos, where the train does a 180° turn in the valley. When you first discover this scene with the small narrow-gauge railroad making the turn, you're left wondering whether you're looking at a train set built by a 6-year old. But soon enough,

after a stop at the water tank, the train is on its way, huffing and puffing on the 2.5% grade toward Cumbres Pass. Shortly before the pass, the train makes yet another impossible turn, called the Tanglefoot Curve.

The 10,022-foot Cumbres Pass is narrow and spectacular and it's worth stopping to look at the snow shed and water pipe. Shortly after the pass, the railway crosses the road. If you are driving, wait for the train to catch up and you'll be rewarded with a most unusual sight, especially

Summer Wildflowers near Antonito

if the train emerges from the clouds. After the pass, the train goes through yet another horseshoe turn before starting the 4% grade descent inside Wolf Creek, in close proximity to the road. This part of the trip is the most rewarding, with spectacular sub-alpine scenery and colorful stands of aspens in the fall. As the road approaches the Chama Valley, you can catch a good view of the train on the tall Lobato Trestle.

Wheeler Geologic Area

The Wheeler Geologic Area is a unique area of eroded badlands high in the La Garita mountains. The material consists of tuff, blown 30 million years ago by the nearby La Garita Volcano. Because it is the top layer, there is no compaction and the tuff remains extremely soft. Given the high elevation and harsh winter conditions, it is constantly subjected to erosion, forming remarkable pinnacles and crevasses. The area is highly reminiscent of Bryce Canyon (see *Chapter 4* of *Photographing the Southwest - Volume 1*) except for the color. The Wheeler pinnacles are essentially whitish, with a touch of blue when it's sunny, and brown under shady skies. Another comparison could be made with the Tent Rocks (see the *Around Albuquerque* chapter in this volume).

Wheeler, as I will call it, was once known as the Wheeler Monument. Following glowing reports of the area's beauty, it was proclaimed a National Monument in 1908 by President Theodore Roosevelt. In fact, it was the very first National Monument ever created in the U.S.

So why is it, you ask, no longer a Monument? The short answer is: Nobody showed up!

Wheeler was so remote and so difficult to reach that it was shunned by most visitors, save a few adventurous souls.

A slightly longer explanation is that the Monument fell victim to bureaucratic red tape and lack of funding, having been transferred back and forth between the National Forest Service and

Spires

the National Park Service. A road project never materialized and eventually the Monument was abolished in 1950 and returned to the National Forest fold. Whatever the status is and will be in the future, it is a spectacular area that will delight hoodoo aficionados. As you'll soon discover, it takes a bit of work to reach Wheeler, but the landscape you traverse in the process is just as beautiful and interesting as Wheeler itself.

You can either hike or drive (4WD) to Wheeler. At this point, I must stop and debunk a myth. You hear and read that the 28-mile round-trip drive takes about the same time as the 16-mile round-trip walk. The trailhead marker even goes as far as to say that hiking parties leaving at the same time as 4WD vehicles may arrive first. This is absolutely astounding to me, considering how different

it is from my own experience. I started driving for Wheeler about 30 minutes before sunrise after camping at the Hanson Mill, which is the trailhead for both the hiking trail and the 4WD roads. I didn't really pay attention to how long it took as I was totally immersed in the beautiful terrain I was traversing. Still, I was surprised that it had felt considerably much faster than I thought to get there. On the way back, I decided to time how long it took and I deliberately drove

Wheeler Pinnacles

very conservatively. I was back at the Hanson Mill in 1 hour and 25 minutes, around mid-morning. I am at a loss to understand why the marker says that it is a 3 to 4-hour drive one-way, equal to the 8-mile hike with 1,000 feet of elevation gain. This has nothing to do with the track conditions either, because they were actually quite bad during my visit.

The 4WD track alternatively traverses a landscape of forest and meadows. It doesn't present any major technical difficulty and it is within the capabilities of ordinary 4WD SUVs. There are 4 stream crossings altogether. The first one, at mile 4.1, would be the hardest in case of rain. At mile 11.5, you cross the vast, spectacular meadow of Canyon Nieve; it's a good place to look for elk.

I have not done the hike but I have been told that it is not very difficult despite the 1,200 ft elevation gain and 12,000-foot elevation on top of the formations. Besides, the superlative landscape contributes to make the time feel short.

There is ample parking and excellent signage at Wheeler. From the car park, a good trail ascends on the southwest side of the formations, bringing you in 0.5 mile to a platform from where you have a great side view of the main pinnacles, forming the Enchanted City. This is probably the best place for photography. It is well worth continuing this trail to reach the top, from where you can actually wander on the white tuff material. The trail forms a 2.1 mile loop around Wheeler.

Getting there: From South Fork on US 160, take CO 149 and turn right just past Wagon Wheel Gap on well-graded CR 600 (aka Pool Table Road). Proceed about 10 miles to the Hanson Mill trailhead. The graded 2WD road ends here. From here you either walk 16 miles or drive 28 miles, both round-trip.

Time required: From the Hanson Mill, 7 to 9 hours round-trip if you hike, 4 to 6 hours if you drive—assuming the track is in normal condition—depending on how long you stay at Wheeler. Most people probably stay only about an hour, but 1½ hour to 2 hours would allow for more exploration and photography along the top and the east side of the formations.

Nearby location: The Silver Thread Scenic Byway (CO 149) links South Fork to Lake City. This beautiful 75-mile drive takes 2 hours, plus a bit more if you stop in Creede. The highlights along the byway are: Creede, a well-preserved Colorado mining town, with a Forest Service Visitor Center which has up-to-date information on the Wheeler road condition; South

North Clear Creek Falls (photo by A. Schallau)   Clear Creek and its many lakes with good campgrounds; the spectacular North Clear Creek Falls, which you can photograph from an overlook reached by driving 0.6 mile on FR 510; views of the 13,821-foot Rio Grande Pyramid; two high passes: Spring Creek Pass and Slumgullion Pass with views of many peaks of the Continental Divide; and to finish, the interesting Slumgullion Earthflow, a still moving gigantic mud slide, which created Lake San Cristobal (see the *Alpine Loop* section in the *San Juan Mountains chapter*).

Chimney Rock

Chimney Rock used to be an "outlier" of Chaco Canyon (see the *Chaco Canyon* section in the *Northwest New Mexico chapter)*, one of the population centers known to have been part of the political, economical and spiritual sphere of influence of the powerful Chacoan civilization. Chimney Rock was of special importance, however, because it was the most isolated and remote of all the outliers, and also the most unique. Being 85 miles northwest as the crow flies— considerably more on foot—it was quite distant compared to the others. More puzzling was the fact that it was located in a very different ecosystem, far and above the deserty plains of northwest New Mexico. So why did the Chacoans maintain such a remote outpost? The answer lies in Chimney Rock's own name and topology: The tall chimneys, called the Twin Warrior Gods, had a special spiritual significance. It was only recently that the reason for this particular location was discovered: The "lunar standstill" phenomenon. Much like in the case of many of the great Mesoamerican centers, astronomy was the single most important factor in Chimney Rock's *raison d'être*. During a 3-year cycle occurring every 18.6 years, the moon rises between the two striking stone chimneys, when seen from the ruins of the Great House Pueblo atop the mesa. The year 2007 is the last year of the current cycle and Chimney Rock has a special program allowing visitors to observe and photograph this spectacular sight, independently of the regular tour schedule. The glow occurring during the moon's passing between the chimneys lasts from five to fifteen minutes, not counting a short moon glow prior to rising. This is a moment of beauty, awakening a strong spiritual connection with the past and the Ancestral Puebloans among the lucky participants.

Great House Pueblo (photo by Jerry Sadler)

The rest of the time, the visit is also very worth it. It begins with a loop around the west side leading to the Great Kiva, continuing on the Pueblo Trail to the Ridge House, then climbing steadily along the narrow ridge to the Great House Pueblo and finishing at the Forest Service's fire tower. The view from there is outstanding and you are able to peer down the mesa several hundred feet on both sides. The San Juan Mountains/Continental Divide can be seen to the east, the Piedra River valley down to New Mexico to the south, and the La Plata Mountains around Durango to the west.

Chimney Rock can only be visited on a guided walking tour most of the time. There are four of them everyday from mid-May through the end of September at 9:30 AM, 10:30 AM, 1:00 PM, and 2:00 PM. There is an additional tour at 12 PM from June 15 through August 31. The tours leave promptly. Be sure to arrive on time for the tour that fits your schedule or you'd have to wait a long time. Midday tours can get full early, so I recommend the 9:30 AM tour, which also offers better light.

The tour begins at the upper car park, 2.5 miles from the Visitor Center, after you caravan behind your tour leader. The tour leaders are almost all volunteers and a very knowledgeable bunch of people. For more information, check out their excellent publication: *Mysterious Chimney Rock - The Land, The Sky, The People* (see *Appendix*).

There is also a full moon program each month during the season, the Fall Equinox and Summer Solstice programs, as well as the Native American cultural gathering and dances, and Life at Chimney Rock: A Festival of Crafts and Culture which are both weekend events.

Getting there: Drive 17 miles west of Pagosa Springs or 44 miles east of Durango on US 160, turn south on CO 151 and drive 3 miles to the Archaeological area's entrance. The parking area and Visitor Center is 0.5 mile up the entrance road.

Time required: The guided tour averages 2½ hours.

Nearby location: Pagosa Springs is the main gateway into the eastern part of the Weminuche Wilderness, the largest wilderness area in Colorado and a world onto itself. If you intend to explore the Weminuche, get yourself a copy of *Hiking Colorado's Weminuche Wilderness* by Donna Ikenberry (see *Appendix*). ✿

Yankee Girl Mine

Chapter 7

THE SAN JUAN MOUNTAINS

Fall Color Patchwork near Red Mountain Pass

THE SAN JUAN MOUNTAINS

Having had the good fortune to see, trek and climb many of the great mountain ranges of the world, I can say with a degree of confidence that the San Juan Mountains offer some of the most outstanding mountain scenery you'll ever see. Even if you are on a mission to see "red rocks", ancient dwellings, or rock art, leave some time for a short detour to the San Juans just to get a taste of these highly photogenic mountains. I can assure you that you'll want to return for more. After all, from Mesa Verde or Canyonlands Nat'l Parks you are just a couple of hours away from the San Juans. An example: From Mesa Verde, you are less than 90 minutes away from the Purgatory Ski Area or the Lizard Head Wilderness. It's a short distance, but a world away!

If you have your choice of season to visit the San Juans, early fall is the most spectacular and what sets it apart from many other mountains. Leaves start turning in mid-September at higher elevations and generally peak at the end of the month, with some residual color well into the first part of October at lower elevations. Timing and color intensity changes from year to year, depending on several factors, with moisture during the earlier part of the year playing the most significant part.

If you have a chance to stay around for a while, in a good year, you'll go through an incredible palette of yellows and oranges, later turning into ambers and reds and contrasting with the green perennials, the blue sky... and hopefully some clouds and snow. The result is magical. Each time I visit the San Juans in the fall, I find it almost impossible to leave: I once was leaving with a heavy heart after an extended visit. After a couple of hours of flatland driving, I couldn't resist the urge to return and spend another couple of days.

Summer is also a wonderful time to enjoy the San Juans: A time of green meadows and colorful wildflowers, streams coming alive from residual snow, deep blue skies and fluffy clouds. All the passes and trails are usually open. This is definitely the best time for outdoor activities.

As for winter, it blankets the landscape with fluffy snow, transforming it into a fantastic wonderland perfect for winter sports or for those seeking a quiet and cozy retreat by the fireplace.

Having shared my enthusiasm for these mountains, I'll now take you on a journey to some of the most spectacular and photogenic spots of the San Juans by following the famous San Juan Skyway counter-clockwise, starting from the north.

Across the Dallas Divide

The Dallas Divide is by all accounts one of the most spectacular stretches of asphalted road in the San Juans. The feeling of vastness of its high-alpine vistas is what sets it apart from other locations. There is perhaps less mountain, but all the more room for vegetation, in particular those wonderful aspens! In summer, wildflowers abound, creating exquisite foregrounds to the high peaks. In early fall, large groves of quaking aspen turn gold and amber everywhere. But if you don't stray from the main road, you'll only scratch the surface of all this beauty. In this section, I'll describe several side roads providing access to the best photographic spots near the Dallas Divide.

Our trip starts at Ridgway, a tiny community on US 550, at the northern end of the San Juan Skyway loop. It has plenty of camping and affordable accommodations (and the wonderful Orvis Hot Springs), making it a good base for exploring the northern part of the San Juans.

Some of the best photographic locations for fall colors can be found on several county roads just a few miles southwest of Ridgway. The closest is CR 5. Going west on CO 62 while still in town, turn left on South Amelia then make a sharp right on CR 5 and proceed on this well-maintained county road, passing through private property. Shortly after 5 miles you'll come to a fork, with the road to the left marked "Restricted access". Bear right and continue for another 1.8 miles until the road opens up to your right, revealing magnificent panoramic views of the Sneffels Range. What makes it so spectacular is the foreground of golden fields (most often with cattle) and tremendous aspen groves perfectly located down below. This provides a very dynamic composition, perfect for panoramic shots. There are several good spots for the next 0.5 mile so be sure to scout the road and locate a few of these so you can come back later. There is also one very good opening on the left side at Mile 8, with a weather-beaten ranch fence making a nice foreground and a vast expanse of aspens in front of the Sneffels. Late afternoon offers better light, and the fence is lit by the sun; morning light is also nice but the angles are more limited. You can stop and photograph from any-

Aspens & Fence

where on the side of the road, but respect the posted signs signaling private property and do not trespass. The road continues for several miles, entering Uncompahgre Nat'l Forest and driving deep into the aspen forest as the track climbs toward the Sneffels.

After returning to Ridgway, turn left on CO 62. After a little over 4 miles, you'll come to CR 7 (aka East Dallas Creek Road), heading south. Again you'll be traversing private property before reaching great views of the Sneffels

Range. There are rolling hills alternating with gold fields in the foreground. This is another prime location for fall colors. The road eventually reaches the forest boundary, continuing to the Sneffels Wilderness and the Blue Lakes trailhead, about 9 miles from CO 62. This is the easiest trail to reach the Blue Lakes; it's a 6.6-mile round-trip hike from the trailhead to the lower lake. The Blue Lakes are also accessible from Yankee Boy Basin (see the *Around Ouray* section).

Another great location in this area is West Dallas Creek. Return to CO 62 and again turn left. Drive for about 1.3 miles and make a left onto CR 9 (aka West Dallas Creek Road). There is a small sign on the south side of CO 62 indicating the road, followed by a large gate marking the entrance to the Double RL Ranch. Should you find the gate closed, read the instructions and proceed on the CR 9 easement though the private property. The road through the RL ranch is in very good condition and the views of the Sneffels Range are superb. The best viewpoint along the road is located on the plateau less than a hundred yards past a cabin located on the left side of the road. This point provides an excellent perspective, with layers of aspens leading to the Sneffels Range. Remember, however, that the land on either side of the road is private property. Continue until you reach the boundary of Uncompahgre National Forest and Forest Road 850. Shortly thereafter, the good dirt road turns into a track and a high-clearance vehicle is a must. Another 1.5 miles past the National Forest sign brings you to Box Factory Park, a lovely meadow surrounded by aspens close to Mount Sneffels. West Dallas Creek Road is a wonderful drive even if you can't make it all the way to Box Factory Park.

CO 62 also has its own worthy overlook, located near the Dallas Divide summit, from where you can enjoy the Sneffels Range. However, the views are more distant; also, traffic noise and the many vehicles stopping here doesn't make this viewpoint as good a spot for photography, by comparison with the three above-mentioned roads. This overlook yields a better photograph in the morning if you walk back toward the fence and shoot the well-lit fence in the foreground.

About 1 mile west past the Dallas Divide summit on CO 62, you'll find the Last Dollar Road to your left. This is an extremely popular unpaved road, cutting 20 miles through plateau, mountain slopes and valleys toward Telluride. This outstanding road offers very diverse views and should not be missed; of course, it is just as nice coming from Telluride. A high-clearance vehicle is sufficient in dry weather, but don't attempt to drive it on a rainy day as there is a long and steep clay section in the middle where you would have no traction. I experienced this first hand once and even with low-range 4WD and all-terrain tires, it was a scary experience due to the steep drop-off on the southeast side.

There are great views from the high plateau traversed by the northern part of the road, especially so in the vicinity of the Silver Dollar Ranch's massive gate. The southern half of the road is even better. About 9 miles from the start, the previously mentioned steep descent offers an outstanding composition with hills and valleys covered with aspens and the Wilson Range in the background.

Last Dollar Road

At the end of the descent, you'll find a large overlook offering a stunning, albeit distant, panorama. You can see Mount Wilson in the distance—one of Colorado's top "Fourteeners"—and there are huge stands of aspens as far as the eye can see.

Past the overlook, the road continues for another 10 miles toward CO 145. It is extremely photogenic, passing through superb stands of aspens and skirting a lovely valley reminiscent of the European Alps. In recent years, some large residences have sprung up along this portion of the road. If this trend continues, it may negatively affect not only the beauty of the area but also the views of the Wilson Range.

The road eventually passes by the Telluride airport before joining CO 145, about 3 miles west of downtown Telluride.

Around Telluride

When it's time to return to civilization, you'll naturally gravitate toward Telluride. Set amidst an incredible valley surrounded by high peaks, this former mining town turned tourist Mecca has a lot going for itself... as well as all the trappings you would expect: Boutiques and art galleries, espresso bars, luxury hotels and expensive restaurants, summer festivals, the best winter sports facilities you can imagine, an unmistakable atmosphere of worldly sophistication... and the prices to go with it.

Telluride will delight affluent shoppers and casual visitors, but nature enthusiasts seeking a less hectic pace may not find it to their taste. It is definitely not the place for people on a budget.

Sneffels Range Sunset (photo by Ron Flickinger)

Don't expect to just drive to the middle of town, park your car and take a walk; it doesn't work that way! Parking is highly restricted during the season and you must leave your car at one of three large car parks at the edge of town and take a free shuttle, or walk. Many people seem to resent this, although I think it's a very sensible solution. If you have plenty of time, there is actually a better alternative to parking in Telluride: Drive a little over a mile south on CO 145 to the Mountain Village entrance. Go across this ultra-affluent community and leave your car at the Station Village Parking. Ride the first gondola to the Station Mountain Village, change gondolas and get ready for the climb to the Station San Sophia followed by the exhilarating descent toward Telluride. This is an extraordinary ride in a world-class setting, and it's free!

After photographing Main Street in its exquisite valley surroundings, continue toward the Pandora Mill and follow the road up to the bottom of Bridal Veil Falls. It's a 2.4-mile round-trip hike, plus another 1.2 miles if you decide to continue to the top of the falls. It can also be driven by 4WD if you don't want to walk through town or if the 1,200-foot elevation gain is too much for you.

For a great bird's eye view of Telluride below with Mountain Village in the background, take the 2.7-mile Jud Wiebe Loop Trail, starting at the north end of Aspen Street; this trail also provides access to the longer and higher Sneffels Highline Trail.

Later in this chapter, I'll describe the Imogene Pass Road in the Around Ouray section. You can drive this remarkable road in both directions.

West of Telluride on CO 145 toward Placerville, you can take a fine drive on Wilson Mesa, seeing Mount Wilson from a very different angle. Take the Silver Pick Road in Vanadium, 5.5 miles west of the junction of CO 145 with the Telluride Road or 6.9 miles from the junction of CO 62 and CO 145. Drive a little over 3 miles up Big Bear Creek, turn left at the fork, then right 0.7 mile further, and continue about 2 miles until you find the Wilson Mesa trailhead.

The Western Skyway – Telluride to Cortez

We continue our trip south toward Dolores and Cortez, picking up CO 145 about 3 miles west of Telluride.

Our first stop is the Alta Lakes, reached by turning east (left) on FR 632 (Alta Road). The road is 0.5 mile south of the Sunshine Campground turnoff and about 5.5 miles from the Telluride turnoff on CO 145. It winds up 4.5 miles through an aspen forest to the tiny ghost town of Alta and on to the lakes. This is a good dirt road, suitable to passenger cars in good weather, but high clearance is recommended for the last mile to the lakes due to some rocky stretches.

The two lakes are very scenic; they are separated by a narrow passage that also serves for cars to reach the other side. Next to the Alta Lakes is the Gold King Basin. Follow the sign on the dirt road, just before reaching the lakes; the Gold King Basin is less than 0.5 mile from this junction. Despite the private house located a short distance from the lake shore, Gold King Basin is a very scenic location; it has very nice wildflowers in summer and it is one of the rare high elevation basins that can be reached without a long walk or a 4WD vehicle.

Back on CO 145, about 2 more miles bring you to Ophir Road (at the Post Office sign). Ophir proper is located about 2 miles up the road. It's a tiny community with a somewhat bohemian atmosphere and

Summer Shower at the Alta Lakes

Crossing Ophir Pass

charm. Continuing up this road leads to Ophir Pass, the easiest of the passes leading to the east section of the San Juan Skyway on CO 550. The last 0.5 mile before the pass on the west side is the only challenge it poses. Under normal dry conditions, any 2WD pick-up or high-clearance vehicle equipped with proper tires should be able to cross Ophir Pass, but this is definitively not for passenger cars. This Class 2 pass may not be technically challenging, but it is nonetheless exhilarating if you've never driven on this kind of terrain. The aspen stands and beaver ponds just a mile past Ophir are spectacular and so is the rugged and colorful scenery near the top. It is possibly the best location to shoot a typical San Juan high mountain road dramatically cutting through yellow and red vertical slopes. The east side of the Ophir Pass is easier but not quite as scenic. As this is the first 4WD high pass I describe, a brief word of caution is in order: Drive very slowly and carefully. Stop if you want to take pictures or admire the scenery, but never take your eyes off the road while you're driving. Watch for changing weather conditions; even in summer, it could be snowing at the top.

Leaving aside Ophir Pass for now and continuing south on CO 145, the road begins a steady climb and about 0.8 mile from the Ophir Road junction you'll come to a large overlook with a spectacular bird's eye view of the San Miguel River, stretching out for miles in the valley. This is a highly photogenic spot offering a rich palette of colors in early autumn.

The road levels off at Lizard Head Pass with its vast meadows and nearby Troutlake. The rest-stop on the right side of the road serves as a trailhead to the Lizard Head Trail, leading to the Lizard Head Wilderness and the Wilson Range. This spot is very scenic in all seasons. Winter is especially beautiful here.

From the pass, the road winds down slowly toward Rico, a cute little community with nice Victorian buildings, making a good stop along the way. From Rico on, the road descends slowly and steadily toward Dolores, losing its high-mountain character, but gaining a special kind of sub-alpine beauty. The road follows the headwaters of the Dolores River down a lovely valley and the fall color display along this particular stretch of road is awesome; you'll likely be out of your car many times to take pictures. About 3 miles past Stoner, look on the west side for a long red sandstone wall. The colorful sandstone looks strangely out of place in this mountainous environment.

Dolores is a nice little town, with some great old buildings on the old main street running parallel to the highway. The town has wisely opted to leave the old street unpaved, giving it additional cachet. Close to Dolores, on CO 184, you'll find the Anasazi Heritage Center (see *Chapter 8 – Mesa Verde Nat'l Park*).

This section of the San Juan Skyway ends up in Cortez, arguably the most strategic location for visiting the Four Corners area, with plenty of lodging. Check out your map and you'll be surprised how close Cortez is from so many incredible locations in the Southwest.

The Southern Skyway – Cortez to Durango

While by no means rivaling the beauty and interest of the other sections of the San Juan Skyway, there are a few places along US 160 that are worth a detour.

The first one starts just north of Mancos off CO 184. Take CR 42, which turns into FR 561 past Jackson Gulch Reservoir and continue for 10 miles past the West Mancos Overlook to the Transfer Park campground. This campground is exceptionally nice, with beautiful views of the Mancos River. Continue on for 4 miles, passing FR 560 on your left and FR 350 on your right until you reach the Jersey Jim Fire Lookout Tower. The tower can be rented from the Forest Service for 1 or 2-night stays during summer and makes a good base camp for photographers to explore the surrounding area (see Mancos Ranger District, San Juan Nat'l Forest in *Appendix* for rental information). All you have to bring is food, water, a sleeping bag, and some basic necessities.

Back on US 160, you'll see a sign for Echo Park, about 2.5 miles east of Mancos. This is CR 44, turning into FR 566 after Weber Reservoir. There are good views of Mesa Verde and Ute Mountain as you gain elevation past the reservoir. After that, it's a long haul to Echo Basin and the road turns really nasty as it changes to FR 556 after 7.5 miles.

The next interesting road is La Plata Canyon Road, about 13.5 miles further. This road follows the La Plata River, providing access to Cumberland Basin, with its nice wildflowers displays and beautiful high-mountain scenery.

The Durango & Silverton Railroad

Continuing along the southern section of the San Juan Skyway, you'll soon arrive in Durango, gateway to the eastern San Juan Mountains. Durango is a fairly big and busy town, otherwise quite pleasant with its decidedly "mountain" atmosphere.

Durango offers just that with the extremely popular Durango & Silverton Narrow Gauge Railroad. The railroad was originally built to transport ore from local mines, but has been successfully converted into a tourist venture. But make no mistake; this is definitely the greatest little train ride in the West. Each morning, from May through October, the vintage steam-powered train climbs the highly scenic Animas River Canyon on its narrow track, crossing mountainous country along steep cliffs and above sheer drops, passing on spectacular wooden trestles, huffing and puffing its way at the foot of snowy peaks, and following the river so close that you can hear it. Three and a half hours later, you reach the little mining town of Silverton. After a 2-hour visit of scenic Silverton, you can re-board the train for the return trip. Instead, I suggest that you return by bus, which will give you a preview of the road for later. The drive, via Molas Divide, saves you 1½ hours, allowing you to spend time in Durango later in the day.

Photo advice: Reserve your train seats long in advance (see *Resources* in *Appendix*). The best seats are the very last on the right side—going toward Silverton—in the last car of the train; the bench seats are like being in an open-air Gondola, with no windows. Be sure to take warm clothes, because it can get very cold, even in summer. You'll see the best side of the landscape, far from the smoke and smut of the engine and you'll be able to take striking pictures of the locomotive negotiating curves and bridges, as well as panoramic shots through the three open sides at the back of the rear car.

In late September and early October, it will almost certainly be cold in the open carriage; it's a small price to pay for being able to admire and photograph the incredible fall colors of the high-country. Given the jolting and vibrations generated by the old train, choose a fast ISO and don't shoot below 1/250 sec. to avoid blurred images. A gyro-stabilized zoom or camera, or a monopod, could be useful.

The wonderful D&SNGRR (photo Philippe Schuler)

If you want to photograph the moving train, pulled by its picturesque engine spewing black smoke on a background of mountain peaks, you can do so easily without even taking the trip. Simply note the departure time from Durango and look for a good spot on the east side of the tracks on any of the numerous spur roads you'll find along the first 10 miles of US 550, just north of Durango.

Nearby location: Back in Durango after the train ride, a great place to relax is the Animas Overlook Trail, where you can enjoy panoramic views of the North Animas Valley and the high summits north of Durango. To get there from US 550 (Main Street in Durango), turn west on Junction Creek Rd. (25th Street) and follow it for 3.5 miles until the pavement ends. There, take the well-graded FR 171 for 7.5 miles, passing by the Junction Creek campground and ascending to the Animas Overlook car park.

The Eastern Skyway – Durango to Ouray

The most popular section of the San Juan Skyway is without doubt US 550 between Durango and Ouray. If you've already been to Silverton with the nar-row gauge railroad and have returned by bus, you'll be able to get directly to the spots that caught your attention. However, there is one worthy side road that you cannot see from the train or bus: Old Lime Creek Road is a lovely 11-mile dirt road running parallel to US 550 and a good place to take your time and photograph aspens without being pushed by traffic. The south access is located about 25 miles north of Durango on the right side of the road and is very well marked. The north access is

The Grenadier Range (photo by Ron Flickinger)

about 4 miles south of Molas Pass, also well marked. This good unpaved road is a favorite of mountain bikers as well as kayakers and canoeists descending Lime Creek, so be alert.

Next comes Molas Pass. At slightly over 10,000 feet, Molas can be considered a fairly low pass in the context of the San Juans. The scenic viewpoint has a nice panoramic view.

Of the three lakes in the vicinity of Molas Pass, I tend to prefer Little Molas, on the west side, which feels more isolated and serene. Andrews Lake is also very pretty and you can take a short hike from the Upper viewpoint to the shore and back. There are a lot of fishermen but the place is quiet. Molas Lake looks a bit trashed in comparison, because it has not only fishermen but picnickers who bring their cars up to the shore. Except during wintertime, the potential for photography isn't that great.

Molas Pass is also the entry point for the Weminuche Wilderness and the spectacular Grenadier Range.

Another 4 miles brings you to a spectacular view of Silverton, set in a deep ample valley. Although Silverton appears somewhat spread out, it is actually a small town with none of the constant buzz of activity of Telluride or Ouray, even more so after the departure of the last train. There are some nice Victorian buildings on Main Street as well as on the picturesque unpaved streets in the back. The high elevation (over 9,000 feet) and the large valley contribute to give Silverton its own special flavor, quite different from its larger and more crowded neighbors.

Silverton is one of the three gateways to the Alpine Loop National Scenic Byway, a 65-mile high-country road described below in its own section. If you don't have the time or confidence to tackle the entire Alpine Loop, consider the Silverton-Animas Forks loop as an alternative. This trip is much shorter and ideal for those with minimal 4WD driving skills. It leads to spectacular high-mountain scenery on a narrow and moderately difficult road, that any prudent driver should be able to drive with a 4WD vehicle, assuming the road is in good condition and the weather is cooperating (check first with the Visitor Center in Silverton). From the north end of Silverton, drive about 7 miles north on a good gravel road to the Gladstone Mine; along the way, check out Cement Creek and its surprising rust colored rock for potential abstracts. Just before the mine, take CR 110 toward Hurricane and California Pass. This narrow but decent 4WD road ascends gradually and without too much difficulty to Hurricane Pass, followed a mile further by California Pass at about 12,900 feet elevation. There is one very tight switchback to negotiate just before the top of California Pass, but there is plenty of room to maneuver. At California Pass, a short trail brings you to an overlook with a spectacular view of Lake Como and many summits all around. Some of them are red or snow-capped, which of course looks terrific in photographs. It takes approximately 1 hour to reach California Pass from Silverton. Follow the track going down California Gulch until you reach Animas Forks, a photogenic ghost town along the creek. Animas Forks is also one of the main attractions on the Alpine Loop. Return to Silverton via a 12-mile long well-graded gravel road following the Animas River. If you prefer continuing to Ouray, return the way you came, passing Hurricane Pass again and take the track

leading to Corkscrew Pass. This road is very good until the pass but tends to deteriorate later on. Still, it is within the capabilities of any 4WD SUV. It will take you about 1 to 1½ hours to reach Ouray from Corkscrew Pass. Unlike Hurricane and California Pass, Corkscrew Pass itself is not so spectacular but the highlight of this road is to see Red Mountain from the back side. This is best done in the morning, while Hurricane and California are best in late afternoon.

Lower Ice Lake Basin

Silverton marks the beginning of the Million Dollar Highway, which derives its name from the low grade gold ore present in its roadbed. This stretch of US 550 offers many hiking, 4-wheel driving and photographic opportunities.

First and foremost is what I consider the most spectacular basin in all of the San Juan Mountains: Ice Lake Basin.

About 2 miles north of Silverton, take the well-marked FR 585 leading to the South Mineral Campground. Drive 6 miles on this excellent dirt road to the trailhead for Ice Lake Basin, located next to the campground. From here it is 9 miles round-trip to Upper Ice Lake with 2,400 feet of elevation gain. This is a moderate, but long, hike on a good trail so be sure to pace yourself if you attempt it without prior altitude acclimation. After about 3 miles you reach a vast meadow near Lower Ice Lake. This is one of the top locations for wildflowers in the San Juans. The upper section of the meadow usually has plenty of columbines. The upper basin has many tarns, as well as two major lakes, dominated by the Golden Horn. It is also very photogenic.

Ice Lake Basin (photo by Ron Flickinger)

If you are unable to hike but want to see a similar high altitude lake, take the 4WD road ascending to Clear Lake. You'll find it marked on your left as you return toward US 550. This is a fairly decent road, except for some nasty spots in the last 0.5 mile.

Back on US 550, about 5 miles from Silverton, you'll find the west end of previously-mentioned Ophir Pass Road. After 5 more miles comes aptly-named Red Mountain Pass, just below the three incredibly colorful summits of Red Mountain to the east. While descending Red Mountain Pass, stop on your right at the Mining Reclamation Project to observe the old Guston mining district in the distance. You can see several old mining structures that are extremely picturesque, surrounded as they are by forested slopes and towering colorful summits. This will be our next stop.

In summer and fall, the contrast between the green forest, the colorful tailings on the slopes and the astonishing red summits comes out markedly better in late afternoon; I suggest that you do most of your photography at that time.

About 1 mile past the Reclamation Project, turn right onto CR 31. This is a well-maintained dirt road, suitable for passenger cars in good weather. The road follows a creek to the left with banks colored an extraordinary rust color. Continue for 1 mile past some old private mines to reach the spectacular Yankee Girl Mine, built in 1882 when silver was discovered here. This is one of the best preserved mining structures in the San Juans and it makes a terrific photo.

Back on US 550, the road now descends to Ironton Park. Take the short road on your right to the historic Ironton site, which has quite a few old houses still standing.

Your next stop will be on the west side of the road, at Mile Marker 87; you'll see a sign for Red Mountain Creek, Hayden Trailhead. Crystal Lake couldn't be closer from the road and it's an outstanding location for early morning photography. For about one hour after sunrise, the Red Mountain peaks reflect in deep blue waters of this lake, creating a beautiful scene. If you come here in the fall, you'll be able to add glowing yellow aspens from the east shore to your composition; if you're lucky, you may even have a little bit of fog hovering above the lake's surface just after sunrise.

Soon after passing Bear Creek Falls, you'll drive through a short tunnel. Make a mental note of it, as it is the trailhead for Bear Creek Trail, which I'll describe in the following section.

About 0.5 mile before reaching Ouray, a large pullout on the left side offers a great view of Ouray, tightly nestled in its valley. Just before reaching town, you'll pass FR 361 (aka Camp Bird Road) on your left, leading to some of the most awesome vistas in the San Juans. More on this in the next section.

Around Ouray

Ouray is a historic mining town with great character and atmosphere. It has very well preserved buildings, including some interesting traditional hotels. You may notice a striking contrast with Telluride, its neighbor and competitor across the mountain. Whereas Telluride wears its air of sophistication like a badge (particularly during wintertime), and is amply patronized by an affluent "in" crowd, Ouray has a more casual, no-nonsense, play-hard, sometimes even a little rough, atmosphere. This description may sound like a caricature—it's true that both towns share each other's characteristics to some extent—but I think it's accurate. To tell you the truth, I have always been puzzled by Ouray's "Switzerland of America" moniker. I see more similarities between Telluride and famous Swiss resorts such as Gstaad, Interlaken, Davos and St. Moritz. Regardless, both towns have their own individuality and charm.

Yankee Boy Basin

Ouray definitely rules when it comes to summer outdoor activities; it is the gateway of choice for an eclectic mix of 4-wheel driving, hiking, backpacking and mountain biking.

If you are not afraid of heights, are sure-footed and there is no chance of rain in the forecast to make the ground slippery, I recommend one particular hiking trail, perhaps more for enjoyment (and exercise) than for photography. Its trailhead is located alongside US 550, only 2 miles south of Ouray, at the southern end of the tunnel mentioned in the previous section. The 9-mile round-trip Bear Creek National Recreation Trail follows an old pack trail, gaining elevation via a series of steep switchbacks with good views of Ouray. After about a mile, the trail levels off as it follows Bear Creek Canyon on a ledge overlooking a sheer cliff. In places, the trail has been carved directly into the rock, several hundred feet above the creek. When you reach what is left of the Grizzly Bear Mine at mile 2.4, you'll ask yourself how the miners were able to carry their heavy and bulky equipment over this trail. The trail continues along Bear Creek Canyon passing by several cascades before reaching the Yellow Jacket Mine at mile 4.5. Count on about 2½ hours round-trip to Grizzly and 5 hours to Yellow Jacket.

After your hike, you can drive to the north end of town, toward Ridgway, and soak in the inviting open-air Ouray Hot Springs.

Ouray is only second to Moab as a 4WD Mecca, with one notable difference: The vast majority of 4-wheelers in Moab are hard-core enthusiast who bring their own rigs to tackle highly-technical slickrock trails. While this crowd also patronizes Ouray, a large number of visitors come to Ouray in passenger cars and rent jeeps to drive the local mountain roads. Renting 4WD vehicles is a thriving business in Ouray, for one good reason: Several local roads offer grandiose scenery without requiring any particular 4WD skills.

There are several remarkable high-altitude roads within a short distance of Ouray, allowing 4-wheelers to reach quickly and with only moderate difficulty a wonderful alpine world of mountain slopes and open meadows brimming with wildflowers in July and early August.

I have mentioned Ophir Pass previously. Let me say again how nice this road is on its west side! It is an easy 4WD road in comparison to other passes but it is highly rewarding for photography.

Twin Falls

Governor Basin

By far the most popular road is CR 361 (aka Camp Bird Road), which provides access to one of the jewels of the San Juans: the popular Yankee Boy Basin. We'll make this our first destination.

From the south end of town, take the well-marked Forest Access road and follow it for about 5 miles along Canyon Creek. There is a spectacular rock outcropping along the way, where everyone stops for the obligatory picture. Many people with passenger cars park in the vicinity of Camp Bird and below. About 0.6 mile past Camp Bird, you'll leave the Imogene Road to the left (more on this later). Less than 1 mile past the Imogene Road, you'll come to a fork, with the road to the left leading to Governor Basin. Continue straight on toward Yankee Boy Basin. The road becomes steep and rough but is within the capacity of any high-clearance 4WD SUV; just take your time in low-range and you'll be fine. In July and August, you'll find a multitude of tour jeeps and trucks here. The most outstanding location to photograph flowers is the stretch of road between the two signs marking the Walker Ruby Mining property. You are allowed to walk and take photographs along the trails leaving from the two pullouts. One of the highlights of a trip to Yankee Boy Basin is also to photograph Twin Falls, which are at their best in late spring, during peak runoff. The

Red Mountain Reflection

falls are located just a couple of hundred yards from the first Walker Ruby pullout. Get as close as possible to the falls to make them really stand out and, of course, use a long exposure and possibly a polarizer. The basin will hopefully be covered with wildflowers when you get there in late spring and early summer. Some years are better than others and the best time can vary considerably. Rainfall is probably the most significant factor; in a dry year, there may be a scarcity of flowers. Some flexibility is critical to capture wildflowers at their best.

You can continue driving above timberline to the Blue Lakes trailhead and a bit beyond that. If you're going to hike to Blue Lakes Pass or Mt. Sneffels, you can save yourself 0.5 mile by continuing to the little tarn lake just above the trailhead. The hike to Blue Lakes Pass is very rewarding and not too difficult once you're past the initial talus slope leading to the pass. You have great views of Yankee Boy Basin below, an exhilarating high-alpine landscape and a rewarding view of the Blue Lakes on the other side. The best way to go to the Blue Lakes proper is from the East Dallas Creek Road trailhead (see *Across the Dallas Divide* section). Climbing Mt. Sneffels is beyond the scope of this book.

Governor Basin is also one of the top basins for wildflowers. It is a little bit higher than Yankee Boy Basin and the road is quite a bit harder with many switchbacks. As a result, few jeep tours venture there and most Jeep rental companies prohibit their customers from tackling Governor Basin; yet this road is still within the capabilities of a high-clearance 4WD SUV with an experienced driver at the wheel. The road leads to a vast amphitheater with colorful tailings and the interesting remains of the Mountain Top mine just above 12,000 ft elevation, During the descent, you'll have spectacular views of Lower Yankee Boy Basin far below.

The other terrific road for sheer kicks is the 18-mile Imogene Pass road to Telluride. This fantastic road is technically challenging in places and will keep even experienced 4-wheelers on their toes. I have driven this Class 3.5 to 4 road in both directions in two different SUVs over the years. The occasional Class 4 sections definitely test the limits of a stock SUV, but with good tires and some patience and prudence you should be able to do it without incident.

Desolate Imogene Pass

Take the road marked Imogene Pass, which you can see on the way to Yankee Boy Basin. The Ouray side of the road is considerably longer and rougher than the Telluride side, except perhaps around the Tomboy mine. The pass is at 13,114 ft. and your car will be gasping for air in 1st gear along the last stretch. The weather on top can be anything. Be prepared for the worst; I have seen fog and ice even in summer. After straddling the top for a couple of hundred feet, the road descends steeply on the Telluride side.

About 2 miles below the pass, you'll come to the numerous dilapidated structures of the Tomboy Mine at 11,500 ft. This site is remarkably extensive compared to most other mines in the area; however, all the buildings are fairly run down and will not yield interesting pictures. The road levels off a bit and becomes less rough past Tomboy. There are some great views of Bridal Veil Falls and the Black Bear Pass switchbacks to the southeast and of Telluride to the southwest in the last couple of miles before reaching town.

The Alpine Loop

The Alpine Loop National Scenic Backway is an exhilarating 65-mile joyride through the east side of the San Juan Mountains on a well-signed and well-maintained 4WD road, with pit toilets strategically located along the way. It crosses two major passes above 12,000 ft, providing access to three Colorado "Fourteeners", and passing by a number of ghost towns, mines and other relics from the past along the way. The loop is generally open from June to October and can be started from either Ouray, Silverton or Lake City. A fair portion of this road is well-graded 2WD, but the two high passes make the loop 4WD territory. All in all, this is one of the finest mini-adventures you can experience in the San Juan Mountains. With time for photography and at least one short hike, it will take you one full summer day to accomplish. During wildflower season, an extra day would offer more flexibility to photograph American Basin and to hike one of the summits; there are plenty of nice places to camp along the way.

American Basin

Before leaving, be sure you have enough water and food, a good spare tire and a full tank of gas. A sunny morning can easily turn into a cold and stormy afternoon at this elevation; be sure you have some warm clothes too. Check the weather forecast; rain or snow is not uncommon, even in summer. There could be fog at the two passes, even when there is none in the valleys! From Ouray, you'll find the well-marked beginning of the Alpine Loop by driving 3 miles south of town on US 550. The road ascends steadily along the Uncompahgre River for the first 2 miles to reach the Poughkeepsie Gulch Road to the right. If you have made it safely up to here, you won't have any problem with the rest of the loop.

Continue left for about 3 miles to the Mineral Point junction. A rough 2-mile round-trip side road to the right leads to the old Mineral Point mining site and the San Juan Chief Mill. This road requires some 4-wheeling experience.

Less than a mile further on the main loop, you'll come to the junction with the Animas Forks Road, linking the road you're on to the southern portion of the loop. This connector road allows you to return to Ouray on the way back, without going all the way to Silverton and US 550.

The road climbs steadily toward Engineer Pass, reached after another 2.3 miles from the Animas Forks junction. This section of road to the pass is well-graded and doesn't present any major problem. About 0.3 mile before the pass, take the side road leading to an overlook on a narrow ridge. From here you have an exceptional panoramic view of the area and surrounding summits. The pass itself is at 12,800 ft. In early summer, you may still find walls of snow along the pass.

Columbine (photo by Philippe Schuler)

As you descend on the east side, you'll pass the privately-owned "Thoreau's Rest"—a modern log cabin with a remarkable view—and the meager remains of Rose's Cabin, an inn which used to serve travelers and miners. The road then descends gradually along Henson Creek with plenty to see and photograph along the way to Lake City.

Lake City is a surprising little town. It has an incredible old-time charm. There is almost nothing modern here; all the houses, shops, properties along the lake, and everything else looks remarkably quaint and from another era. I personally find this very refreshing.

After visiting Lake City, you're ready for the second leg of the trip; follow CO 149 south for 2 miles to the sign indicating the Alpine loop and continuing along the shore of Lake San Cristobal. Past the lake, the well-graded road follows the Gunnison River, passing through outstanding scenery and continuing toward the old Sherman town site, a mining camp destroyed by a flash flood. Not much remains from the site today.

After Sherman, you ascend a spectacular shelf road carved into the rock 300 feet above the Gunnison River, before leveling with the river at Burrows Park. This is the trailhead for three "Fourteeners": The Grizzly Gulch Trail leads to Handies Peak in a gradual and extremely scenic 4.2 miles while the Silver Creek Trail leads to Redcloud and Sunshine Peaks. You can also climb Handies Peak on a shorter route from yet to come American Basin.

View from Engineer Pass

At the next fork, the loop continues to the right, up toward Cinnamon Pass; for now continue south toward American Basin, a highly photogenic high-alpine cirque known for its spectacular wildflower displays. From the fork, it is about a mile to the Handies Peak trailhead. There is a car park shortly after the fork and many people choose to park here thinking that the track ahead is too tough; this is not really the case as there is only a short 300-foot section of non-technical rough track on the way to the trailhead, which has ample parking. Also, there is a deep stream crossing soon after the first car park, so if you decide to walk you'll have to get your feet wet. From the real trailhead, the Handies Peak Trail is relatively level to Sloan Lake, reached in 2.2 miles; from there it's only 1 mile to Handies Peak—a great opportunity to climb a Colorado "Fourteener".

The best wildflower displays are located near the end of the old closed road, about 2/3rd of the way between the lower car park and the trailhead. Flowers are also spectacular in the meadow just above the trailhead. Walking on the trail for about 25 minutes, you'll find a very photogenic spot to your left, with a waterfall surrounded by wildflowers.

Allow plenty of time to hike, climb, stroll, roll in the grass, and relax at American Basin. Oh, and you want to take pictures too? Just find a pleasant place to camp and spend some time here. Minimum impact camping is permitted along the road, including at the trailhead. American Basin is one of the jewels of the San Juans, so don't pass up this opportunity.

When it's time to say goodbye, return to the fork for the 2-mile ascent to Cinnamon Pass, where you cross the Continental Divide at 12,600 ft. The east side of the pass is a little rough in places, but within the range of a high-clearance 4WD SUV. The view from the top is expansive, but not as spectacular as Engineer Pass.

From Cinnamon Pass, it's an easy 3 miles down to the Animas Forks ghost town, with just a few short rocky stretches. From here, you can either continue toward Silverton via the good road described in the Eastern San Juan Skyway section, or you can return to the northern section of the loop and Ouray, using the previously mentioned connector road. ✿

Balcony House Fortress (photo by Philippe Schuler)

Chapter 8

MESA VERDE NATIONAL PARK

Spruce Tree House from the Chapin Mesa Museum

MESA VERDE NATIONAL PARK

Mesa Verde National Park is the crown jewel of cliff dwellings of the National Park System. Located on a high plateau towering more than a thousand feet over the surrounding area, the park preserves an extraordinary array of pit and cliff dwelling, spanning several centuries of occupation by the native inhabitants.

There are three areas of interest in the park: the vast rim area from the entrance to Morefield and Far View; Chapin Mesa, which has the most popular ruins, as well as the Museum; and Wetherill Mesa, which preserves another set of Puebloan ruins, also spectacular but more remote and accessible only in summer.

Since the summer of 2000, several great fires have occurred in Mesa Verde, resulting in over 50 percent of the park being burnt. Most of the park was affected, including Wetherill Mesa and Chapin Mesa, but fire crews managed to save the vast majority of the ruins. These fires coming in rapid succession have made recovery much more difficult than in previous decades and large tracts of the mesa still appear devastated as the time of this writing.

Photo advice: While visiting the main ruins on a mandatory ranger-led tour, consider that your enjoyment of the tour and the quality of the photos you'll bring back are greatly dependent on two human factors: the ranger leading the tour and the crowds. Most rangers give great tours, but they don't all move at the same pace and there is no guarantee that the previous group will have left the area when you arrive. Large crowds are best avoided by booking an early or late tour. Tripods are not allowed on ranger-led tours.

Getting there: About 8 miles east of Cortez and 35 miles west of Durango on US 160 to the park entrance turnoff. From there, it is 15 winding miles to the Far View Visitor Center and almost 6 more miles to the Chapin Mesa Museum. Count on approximately 45 minutes from US 160.

Time required: At least a half-day for basic car-based viewing, including a tour of Cliff Palace; a full day to visit a couple of sites on the main mesa at a relaxed pace. In summer, a day and a half is necessary to include Wetherill Mesa and the three ranger-led visits: The first afternoon you'd visit Cliff Palace, the next morning you'd see Balcony House, and the next afternoon Long House; this scenario affords the best compromise between lighting conditions and park regulations.

The Rim

As it winds its way south into the heart of the park, the rim road offers many superlative views of the surrounding area. This road looks even more beautiful on the way back, especially under the golden light of early evening. It is in excellent condition, but it's also long and winding as well as quite crowded, so take advantage of the four overlooks to get out of the car, stretch your legs and admire the distant views.

Mancos Valley Overlook offers a great view to the northeast looking down into the colorful fields of the Mancos Valley. If you are camping, you'll want to settle in at the Morefield Campground before proceeding. This vast campground has lots of spaces, so it is not essential to arrive early.

After the Montezuma Valley Overlook, looking down into Cortez, a stop at Park Point is a must. A short trail leads to a fire lookout, located at 8,750 feet, with incredibly distant views in all four directions. The last viewpoint before the Far View Visitor Center is the North Rim Overlook. All these viewpoints are better seen with the naked eye than photographed.

If you are spending the night at the Far View Lodge, you'll probably be eager to settle in first, but don't do so before stopping at the nearby Visitor Center.

During the high season, a stop at the Far View Visitor Center is essential to organize your visit, as reservations are required to visit the three most popular sites: Cliff Palace and Balcony House on

Far View Ruins (photo by Tom Till)

Chapin Mesa, and Long House on Wetherill Mesa. Tickets can be purchased on a first-come first-served basis; expect long lines during holidays and busy weekends. At the Visitor Center you will also find helpful trail guides and other booklets that will make your visit of the major ruins much more informative and enjoyable.

If you can afford to spend the night in the Park, take the time to stroll through the Far View ruins complex at sunrise.

Introduction to Chapin Mesa

Chapin Mesa has the highest concentration of cliff dwellings in the park. It also has the highest concentration of visitors. On some summer days, it can be bumper-to-bumper traffic along the roads, particularly in mid-afternoon. There is a minor caveat to visiting the Chapin area cliff dwellings, which I personally find non-objectionable, but which any visitor should be aware of. The main dwellings you will be visiting have been reconstructed to some extent. Most of the work has consisted in stabilizing the structures and the Civilian Conservation Corps have done a masterful job of it, but you don't quite get the same feeling of awe and spiritual awareness as with some less restored and less visited Puebloan sites of the Southwest. If you don't let this bother you, you'll enjoy a fantastic photographic experience at Mesa Verde.

Sun Temple (photo by Philippe Schuler)

The excellent Chapin Mesa Museum is a good place to start your visit and get acquainted with Mesa Verde and its human and natural history. It can be visited year-round and so can the magnificent Spruce Tree House a short distance from it. Just past the museum turnoff, you'll find two 6-mile loop roads. The road to the right—called Mesa Top Drive—takes you to some recently excavated pit houses from the Basketmaker era but, while they are interesting to visit, they don't make for spectacular photography. However, there are also two good viewpoints along this road. The first one overlooks Square Tower House, and the second one—located at the Sun Temple pullout—has a distant view of Cliff Palace (a 300mm telephoto is necessary to capture detail). The loop road to the left leads to the main sites of Cliff Palace and Balcony House. Cliff Palace is usually open from early April to early November and Balcony House from

Opposite page: Kiva Ladder

mid-May to mid-October. If you do not intend to visit Wetherill Mesa, which is only open from late May to early September, the Chapin Mesa area is best seen during early autumn or late spring.

There are plenty of excellent and widely available sources to help you visit Chapin Mesa, starting with the National Park Service's own excellent maps and numerous brochures, so let's examine the subject from a photographic perspective. I find the following game plan to be the most effective for someone with limited time. It is based on the best lighting conditions at the sites and the fact that, during busy times, the Park Service may not allow you to visit both Cliff Palace and Balcony House on the same day. At the time of this writing, the system has a measure of flexibility; if you come early to the Visitor Center (9 AM), the staff may let you reserve both tours on the same day.

Start with the Chapin Mesa Museum in early afternoon, when light isn't too good for photography, then proceed to the guide tour of Cliff Palace before returning to the Museum to photograph Spruce Tree House. Finish on Mesa Top Drive to photograph Square Tower Ruin.

If you're still in the park the following day, visit Balcony House in the morning and, during the high season, Wetherill Mesa in the afternoon.

Cliff Palace

Cliff Palace is the largest cliff dwelling in the park with 217 rooms and 23 kivas. I recommend that you visit this grandiose site on a pre-reserved ranger-led tour in mid-afternoon. Waiting for the beginning of the tour at the Cliff Palace Overlook, you'll want to photograph the ruins, but save most of your shots for later as the light will only get better and strong shadows will be minimized. The tour lasts approximately 1 hour and allows for plenty of opportunities to photograph the ruins. After going down some steep stairs, you'll be seated in the shade with Cliff Palace in full view while the ranger gives you some general but informative explanations about the Ancestral Puebloans.

Get your equipment ready. The previous group will still be visible amongst the dwellings, but as everybody moves as a group, they'll soon disappear toward the next spot, freeing more ground to photograph without people intrusion. With a bit of luck and timing, you should be able to get some great pictures from

Cliff Palace

this spot, before you begin your own walkthrough of the cliff house. A graduated neutral density filter is a must if you want to limit the damage from the strong shadow areas that will obscure the top of the structures.

During the walkthrough, you'll want to switch to a wide-angle lens. Almost anything goes. This is the perfect time to use this super wide-angle lens you've been aching to try. Even though you are not allowed to leave your group, you can easily move about and get creative with your angles and bring back some excellent shots. Stay at the tail end of your group so you can shoot the entire complex from its southern end unencumbered, just before exiting.

Back at the Cliff Palace parking after your tour, return to the overlook and take your pictures in the better light. You can photograph from the overlook with a variety of lenses going from wide-angle—to include the entire alcove as well as the overhang and a bit of sky—to medium telephoto to isolate a structure that catches your eye. During a brief moment, the ruins should be empty of people; you can shoot just as the first group is exiting while the second group is preparing to enter after the ranger's explanation. Don't linger, however, because you should now move to you next destination, the magnificent Spruce Tree House.

Spruce Tree House

Located just below the Chapin Mesa Archeological Museum, Spruce Tree House is the third largest dwelling in the park, with 114 rooms and 8 kivas. It's normally a self-guided tour, except in winter when you have to join a free ranger-led tour (there are only three tours per day).

By late afternoon, Spruce Tree House becomes basked in beautiful warm light and it's easy to photograph it from the side and get great depth and definition. You are allowed to move along the various structures of the cliff house, as long as you don't step on low walls. Thus, with a little bit of care, you can easily exclude fences, signs or other visitors from your images.

There is a reconstructed kiva you can climb into and photograph with the afternoon light falling on the wooden ladder. It requires a tripod and very wide-angle lens.

There is an excellent view of the entire Spruce Tree House complex from behind the Park Headquarters building, immediately to the right of

Spruce Tree House

the Museum. There, you'll find an open-air viewing area, sheltered by the roof of the Park Headquarters building. There are benches enticing you to stay and admire the ruin complex while waiting for the best afternoon light. A mid-range zoom is perfect for framing various parts of the structure.

As soon as the warm late-afternoon light begins fading, go back to your car and drive to your next destination: Square Tower Ruin.

If you have a couple of hours available during the afternoon—for instance, if you couldn't get a reservation for Cliff Palace—don't miss the Petroglyph Point Trail, a rewarding 2.8-mile loop beginning between the Chapin Mesa Museum and Spruce Tree House. This mostly flat and shady trail winds under a mesa ledge to an interesting petroglyph panel before returning to the plateau through a piñon juniper forest. This uncrowded and pleasant trail is a good introduction to the natural environment of Mesa Verde and provides beautiful views of Navajo and Spruce Canyons. It's better hiked counterclockwise—beginning near Spruce Tree House and ending on the plateau above the ruins—especially if you do it in late afternoon when the lower access gate is locked after Spruce Tree House's visiting hours, as there is no gate for the upper access on the plateau.

Balcony House

Facing east, Balcony House is still partially in shadow in the early morning, so take a mid-morning pre-reserved tour if you can. The fun factor is high during the 1-hour Balcony House tour. Not only do you have the ladders to climb, but you also have to crawl on your hands and knees through a 12-foot long dark tunnel before exiting the dwellings. Exercise caution if you are carrying a large photo backpack. Also, to exit the alcove, you have to climb a fairly steep ladder and it may not be advisable for people with a heart condition or a fear of heights.

The space in front of Balcony House is cramped, so a wide-angle lens is mandatory. Try to take advantage of the fact that people in your group will be waiting in line to pass through the tunnel to stay behind and shoot unencumbered.

Planning your visit, remember that your window of opportunity for Balcony House (mid-May to mid-October) is a full two months shorter than for Cliff Palace. Also, as previously mentioned, you may not be

Balcony House (photo by Philippe Schuler)

allowed to visit both on the same day when things are in full swing.

The only viewpoint on Balcony House is a very distant one, close to Soda Canyon Overlook, on a 1.2-mile round-trip trail beginning less than a mile past Balcony House's parking lot.

Square Tower House

Beautiful Square Tower House (*see front cover picture*) contained up to eighty rooms in its heyday. You can only observe it from above, from an overview located a few hundred yards from Mesa Top Drive. Outside summer, Square Tower ruin remains fully illuminated until the last rays of the sun have disappeared, so you do not need to hurry. Just don't waste time and you'll arrive right in time for an exceptionally rich, warm sunset light basking this beautiful structure; it is best photographed with a standard lens to medium telephoto.

If you can't stay long enough to photograph Square Tower House in the evening, you can also photograph it in mid-afternoon, prior to your Cliff Palace tour. The light won't be quite as spectacular but will be decent enough.

Wetherill Mesa

Wetherill Mesa is only accessible from Memorial Day to Labor Day, so you'll have to plan accordingly. If you can make the trip to this less crowded area, it is definitely worthwhile especially for the superb Long House Ruin. It is the second largest cliff dwelling in the park, with about one hundred and fifty rooms and twenty kivas.

Consider visiting Long House in the afternoon of your second day. Contrast is high in the morning and the House is in shadows later in the afternoon, so mid-afternoon is best. Bear in mind, however, that the last visit starts at 4 PM.

To visit Long House, you must first make your reservation at the Far View Visitor Center. Upon arrival at the Ranger Contact Station, check-in for the 1½ hour ranger-led walk to the ruin. Take the free tram to the ruin and leave it at the Long House stop. From here, it's a short 0.7-mile walk to the cliff dwelling, on a slightly downhill path. Unlike the heavily

Balcony Ladder (photo by QT Luong)

Step House

consolidated Chapin Mesa dwellings, Long House is almost 80% intact. A few walls have been stabilized here and there for the safety of visitors and the roof of the kivas have been rebuilt, but all the structures at the back of the alcove are pretty much untouched. Ladders provide access to a work area and Long House's fresh water spring toward the back.

After visiting Long House, you can walk to the nearby Badger House complex and visit it on your own. It consists of four different exhibits encompassing various stages of human settlement at Mesa Verde: Basketmaker pit houses, which have been dated at around 650 AD, and Puebloan ruins from the thirteenth century. It is very unusual to find sites from both eras concentrated in one location.

Step House is another Wetherill Mesa site you can visit on your own before or after the Long House tour. It is close to both the car park and the tram station. A 1-mile round-trip trail leads to a group of dwellings under a tall alcove. It is not as large as Long House, but there are relatively few visitors, so it's easy to photograph.

Getting there: You'll find the road to Wetherill Mesa just past the Far View Visitor Center. It is a narrower and more winding version of the rim road and it takes at least 35 minutes to negotiate the 12 miles to the Ranger contact station, where you park. You must walk or take one of the frequent free trams leaving for the 4-mile loop tour leading to the ruins.

Time required: Half a day.

Nearby location: Ute Mountain Tribal Park contains a large number of Ancestral Puebloan cliff dwellings and other ruins, although on a smaller scale than at Mesa Verde. The ruins can be seen by joining a half-day or full-day guided tour with a Ute guide. The full-day tour involves an 80-mile drive (in your own car), a 3-mile walk on trails and scaling some steep ladders. It's a very nice tour but the price is quite steep. The half-day tour doesn't visit any of the cliff dwellings and is not a very good value. If you've just come from Mesa Verde, you may be taken aback by the fact that the ruins here do not appear as pristine, due to the fact that they haven't been as extensively reconstructed. Note that "professional" photography is not allowed.

AROUND MESA VERDE

Canyons of the Ancients

Canyons of the Ancients is a relatively new National Monument protecting a large number of Puebloan archeological sites—the great majority of which are still unexcavated. The very first thing you should do to get acquainted with the vast new Monument is head north of Cortez to the Anasazi Heritage Center. The center has remarkable exhibits and is a great introduction to Ancestral Puebloan civilization; even if you don't intend to visit ruins in the area, you shouldn't miss the short detour. If you'd like to see some of the major ruins, I also suggest that you stop by the center for orientation and to check on road conditions.

Arguably the most interesting location in the Monument—in its current stage of excavation—is the Sand Canyon Trail. The trail leaves from CR G (McElmo Canyon Road) heading northeast for 6.5 miles to the Sand Canyon Pueblo and passing by several cliff dwellings along the way. At about Mile 4, the trail climbs out of the canyon and onto the broad mesa in a series of switchbacks, gaining about 700 feet in 0.5 mile.

The Sand Canyon Pueblo was partially excavated, then refilled so it could be preserved for future generations of archaeologists. At the present time, only a few structures remain excavated; they can be seen along a 0.25-mile interpretive trail. Esthetically, the Pueblo itself is far from remarkable, so if you want to hike the Sand Canyon Trail, I suggest you do it from the south trailhead and follow the trail for up to 3 miles before returning the same way; this will allow you to see most of the cliff dwellings. On the other hand, if you can organize a shuttle from Sand Canyon Pueblo to the south trailhead, it is probably worth hiking down the entire trail from the Pueblo to the trailhead.

Lowry Pueblo is currently the largest and most accessible of the excavated structures and can be visited on

Lowry Pueblo (photo by Tom Till)

your way to Hovenweep. Unless you are a die-hard aficionado of Puebloan ruins, you will be disappointed by Lowry. The pueblo is completely covered by a permanent roof that makes photography almost impossible and it has none of the towers, fortified houses and canyons that make nearby Hovenweep so attractive. Also, be aware that you will be traveling great distances on clay roads that quickly become a quagmire after a rain. I have been to Lowry when the road hadn't completely dried up and it was not a pleasant experience.

Ruin Perched on Rock (photo by Tom Till)

Getting there: The Anasazi Heritage Center is located 11 miles north of Cortez via CO 145 and CO 184 west of Dolores. Driving to Sand Canyon Pueblo involves taking a succession of dirt roads that is too complex to describe here. Just get the easy to follow map and directions from the Anasazi Center. It's a 22-mile drive from the Center to the Pueblo.

To find the Sand Canyon Trail southern trailhead, drive 3 miles south of Cortez on CO 491 (formerly CO 666) and turn right on CR G (McElmo Canyon Road). Continue for 12 miles and you'll find the marked trailhead to your right. This road is also the main access road to go to Hovenweep from the east. People tend to go too fast on this narrow, curvy road, so please be careful.

Time required: Allow at least 1 hour for a quick visit of the Anasazi Heritage Center; more if you want to go through some of their remarkable artifact collections. A 3 to 4 hour hike on the Sand Canyon Trail will let you see almost all the ruins. Allow 1 hour for the drive to Lowry and another hour from Lowry to Hovenweep, road conditions permitting.

Hovenweep National Monument

Located on the expansive Cajon Mesa, which is part of the Great Sage Plain of Southwestern Colorado and Southeastern Utah, Hovenweep National Monument protects some of the most interesting examples of pre-Columbian stone architecture in the Southwest. If you are in the Cortez, Mesa Verde, Farmington area, you should consider the short detour through Hovenweep to photograph its unique "towers".

Hovenweep's photographic interest lies primarily in the rich colors of the sandstone walls of its towers, contrasting with pure blue skies, beautiful fluffy clouds during the Monsoon season, and the snow-capped peaks of Sleeping Ute Mountain in winter. Although the remaining structures are only partially standing—Hovenweep was abandoned circa AD1300—they are all very interesting and well worth photographing.

Hovenweep Nat'l Monument consists of five distinct groups of ruins. The Square Tower group, is the largest and most easily accessible and we will concentrate on this one. It is located a stone's throw away from the tiny ranger station and museum. There is a very easy 1-mile loop around a shallow canyon, appropriately named Tower Point loop. A shortcut in the trail allows you to cut a half mile off the walk if you have had enough of ruins or are in a big hurry. The first part of the walk takes you past some interesting structures resting atop the canyon walls; these are easily photographed from various vantage points.

Hovenweep Castle is the most visible and photographed landmark, not only because of its proximity to the parking lot, but also for the outstanding masonry work of its remaining walls. The "Castle" was actually part of a larger structure bordering the canyon rim, which is now totally gone.

As you turn around the bend of the canyon, Hovenweep House ruins come into view under an alcove. Further up on the trail is Square Tower. This three-story high tower rests upon a large boulder, which makes it quite unique.

At the Twin Towers, you'll have to decide whether to return to the visitor center or continue on. The Twin Towers loop adds another mile and a half to the walk and leads to quite a few more structures around both sides of the canyon. It is an easy and pleasant stroll, mostly on the canyon rim. The most outstanding landmark on this trail is Stronghold House, so named for its lack of an easy entrance, leading archaeologists to believe that it may have been used for defensive purposes.

On the Eastern side of the monument is the Holly Group, once home to an estimated 150 people. This group contains five structures; the most noticeable of which is the two-storied Holly Tower, built on a tall, narrow boulder.

Raven & Ruin

Photo advice: You'll get plenty of good angles by moving around the structures in mid-morning or mid-afternoon and by concentrating on the strong detail of the masonry work. I have gotten better pictures this way, rather than by blasting the towers in strong evening light and losing much of the detail to the intense color. I also encourage you to seek snow or clouds to add more interest to your images.

Stronghold House

Getting there: Hovenweep is located 28 miles east of US 191, via CO 262, just south of White Mesa. From US 191, there are a couple of intersections, so be sure to follow the signs. Hovenweep can also be reached in about 44 miles from Cortez via the CR G (McElmo Canyon Rd), as mentioned in the previous section. If you are traveling between Cortez and Monticello, you can also take CR 10 from Pleasant View on US 491. This dirt road is usually passable by passenger cars, but call ahead to inquire on its condition. This road gives you access to Hovenweep's lesser visited groups of Holly, Horseshoe and Hackberry. A small campground is located inside the monument.

Time required: The detour from US 191 will take you a minimum of 2 hours; this will give you just enough time to stroll down the Tower Point Nature Trail at a brisk pace and photograph the main structures. Add another hour if you want to take your time and walk the 1.5-mile Twin Towers loop. ✿

Shiprock at Dusk

Chapter 9

NORTHWEST NEW MEXICO

The Great Kiva at Aztec Ruins

NORTHWEST NEW MEXICO

Aztec Ruins

Almost smack in between Mesa Verde and Chaco Canyon lie the outstanding ruins of Aztec, a misnomer originated by Anglo settlers, thinking that Aztecs built the pueblos. In fact this wonderful pueblo was built and occupied centuries before the days of Cortez and Montezuma.

Aztec Ruins Nat'l Monument is well worth a visit, especially if you travel to or from Mesa Verde and do not intend to visit Chaco Canyon, of which it is architecturally reminiscent. One thing I particularly appreciate at Aztec is the long perspective of low doors forming an almost 100-foot of continuous passageway between rooms. You'll find this feature at the western entrance of the West Ruin. Although the main passageway is too dark for good photography, there is a shorter perpendicular passageway to the right, shortly after you enter the West Ruin; it is well lit and offers some good photography. It is protected by glass windows, so be careful to avoid reflections.

Another nice feature of Aztec Ruins is the Great Kiva, reconstructed in the 30s by the Civilian Conservation Corps. It is an outstanding testimonial to the skills of the Puebloan architects and builders. The west wall also contains some fine examples of masonry.

Photo advice: The complex is open daily 8 AM to 5 PM (6 PM from Memorial Day through Labor Day), so don't expect to do golden hour photography in spring and summer. A wide angle, 28mm or less, is preferable inside the Great Kiva, and so is a tripod as the kiva has a ceiling and is quite dark. Photography of the masonry and of the passageways is also best done with a wide angle.

Getting there: The monument is located inside the confines of the town of Aztec northwest of the junction of Aztec Boulevard and US 550. Signs in town make it easy to find, but drive slowly as it's easy to miss the left turn when coming from Farmington.

Time required: About 1 hour, preferably 2 to see the Museum, watch the outstanding video on the Ancestral Puebloans and photograph without rushing.

Nearby location: Cox Canyon Arch is a seldom-seen but photogenic arch with an elegant shape and 35-foot wide span standing out from its surroundings. To get there, drive on US 550 for about 10.8 miles past its junction with Aztec Boulevard and turn left on CR 2300 just past Cedar Hill. Follow it northwest for 1.25 mile and turn right on CR 2310, continuing north for about 2.6 mile to a gas well compressor site. Turn right and head northeast for 0.4 mile on the dirt track and the unmarked trail leading to the arch. It is featured as "Natural Arch" on the Cedar Hill 7.5' USGS map.

Aztec Ruins Masonry

Shiprock (Tsé Bit' A'í)

I find Shiprock fascinating, and almost equally as striking as Uluru (Ayers Rock) in Australia, except for its color. Shiprock—meaning Rock With Wings—is sacred to the Navajos, which at least on paper reassures us that it is not going to turn into a commercial attraction, unlike its down-under counterpart. On a clear day, you can see Shiprock forever... well, not quite, but I have seen it clearly from 50 miles away and friends have reported seeing it from almost 80 miles away. You need to come to its base, however, to fully appreciate its magnificence; you'll be awestruck at the formidable power emanating from this larger-than-life diatreme, or volcanic plug, towering 1700 feet above the valley floor.

Getting there: The easiest way to reach Shiprock is from the south side; from the town of Shiprock, drive about 6 miles south on US 491 and turn west on Red

The Golden Wall

Valley Road. From the intersection, it's 6.7 miles to the first dirt road leading toward Shiprock. A slightly better road, suitable for passenger cars can be found almost a mile further, right before the spectacular serrated volcanic ridge that runs north toward Shiprock. From either of these two dirt roads, it's less than 4 miles to the base of Shiprock. You'll need high clearance if you want to drive through to US 64, as the track deteriorates badly near the base of the monolith. To reach Shiprock from the north side, follow US 64 about 4.7 miles from the town of Shiprock, then drive on N 571 going south, past the Rattlesnake pumping station and on toward the eastern side of Shiprock, where you'll meet the dirt roads coming from Red Valley Road.

Photo advice: Light is generally better in late afternoon from the north side, however the most pleasing views are from the south, either directly from the side of Red Valley Road or from the aforementioned dirt roads. A great sunset view can also be had from the south side, with some lovely rocks adding interest on both sides of Shiprock. If you don't mind doing a little bit of scrambling, you can also get a very interesting shot of Shiprock by climbing on the "neck", the volcanic ridge that runs north toward the monolith from Red Valley Road. There

is a notch a few hundred yards north of the road from where you can climb relatively easily on the ridge. You can then include the neck in the foreground of your image to convey depth. You can take interesting shots from the base of Shiprock with a 20 to 24mm lens. There are also good views from the west side of US 491 as you reach the Shiprock airfield. A zoom in the 70-200mm range is perfect to frame Shiprock in a variety of ways.

Shiprock Fire Sunset (photo by Barry Haynes)

If you want to get a sunrise shot of Shiprock, you'll have to get up very early, because there is no accommodation in the town of Shiprock. Your closest base will be Farmington, a little less than an hour drive.

Chaco Canyon

Chaco Canyon is without contest one of the premier archaeological destination of the Southwest. It is also a wonderful destination, even if you are not particularly interested in Puebloan culture. Granted, it is a bit out of the way of the trappings of civilization, but you'll be rewarded with the sight of the largest of all north-American pueblos, tucked in a lovely canyon. Chaco has relatively few crowds and good opportunities for spotting wildlife. Much of the Pueblo's masonry is reconstructed, but it is tastefully done. I can't say that you'll come out of your visit with a good idea of what life was for the inhabitants—all the rooms are bare and there a few clues to how they were used—but the vastness of the complex conveys a great sense of presence and power. Chaco was a major hub for trade, administrative and ceremonial life from AD 850 until about 1250. It was without a doubt a meeting place where native north-American cultures came into contact with their more developed neighbors from the south.

From a photographic standpoint, the highlight of Chaco Canyon is Pueblo Bonito and its immediate neighbor, Chetro Ketl. From the parking lot, a short walk leads to the pueblo, where you can stroll and get lost to your heart's content through a network of rooms, stairways, kivas, rooftops and more. You will most

certainly find angles and composi-
tions that will attract your eye. One of
the joys of Chaco is in photographing
the various styles of masonry. There
are several types, progressively more
intricate as the builders became more
skilled, and it can be quite fun to
observe and record, even if you are
not intent on becoming an expert in
Puebloan culture. If you are not in a
hurry—and you shouldn't be if you
went through the effort to come to
Chaco—take the time to hike to the
Pueblo Bonito Overlook. The trail is
a 2-mile round-trip from the parking lot. From the back end of the
pueblo, it ascends steeply through
a narrow passage to the top of the
cliff and follows the contour of the
canyon over hard slickrock for about
0.75 mile. All in all a very easy walk.

Storm on Pueblo Bonito

The bird's eye view from the overlook encompasses the hundreds of rooms and kivas of the complex. It's a classic view.

Pueblo Alto is only 0.6 mile from the Pueblo Bonito Overlook and definitely worthy of a visit. Once you get there and see the view in both directions, you'll understand why the Ancient Ones chose this location for a settlement. There are two Great Houses and the New Alto is by far the most striking, with its tall walls reaching out from the verdant plateau.

If you are looking for a nice hike without major difficulty and the temperature is pleasant, the 5.2-mile loop trail is for you. It is mostly level except for a very short and steep section through a narrow crack in the rock about midway. There is nothing too remarkable along the trail except for the Jackson ladder, a series of wide steps carved into the rock by the Ancient Ones and forming an almost vertical ladder from the canyon below. The view along the rim down Chetro Ketl is also very nice. The best part of the loop, however, is the area around Pueblo Alto, so you won't miss too much if you go straight to it.

Chetro Ketl

Just behind the Visitor Center, Una Vida has some faint petroglyphs at the end of an easy 1-mile round-trip walk that also passes through a Great House.

Photo advice: Use a tripod-mounted wide-angle lens with a very small aperture to ensure maximum depth of field when photographing the masonry, particularly for the classic perspective shot of doors connecting several rooms. A wide-angle to normal lens is needed to photograph the pueblo from the top of the cliff. On your way back toward the Visitor Center, stop at Casa Rinconada to photograph the Great Kiva. It is a bit of a challenge due to its large size, but a good way to do it is to position yourself behind the "Do not enter" sign and photograph through the wooden bars using a wide-angle lens and including some of the staircase.

I recommend finishing the day at the Pueblo Bonito Overlook, where you can photograph the Great House almost until sunset. Park regulations specify that you must finish hiking at sunset and it takes about twenty minutes at a normal pace to return to your car.

If you can camp at Chaco (49 sites on a first come-first serve basis) I suggest that you begin your day at Pueblo Bonito. The walls are higher on the east side and therefore, there is no harsh light inside the rooms which have no ceiling,

Opposite page: Classic Chacoan Doors

unlike in the afternoon. You can photograph the enfilade of doors from room 14 soon after sunrise or from the opposite site an hour after sunrise or in late afternoon.

Getting there: Coming from Bloomfield on US 550, turn off at the Nageezi trading post and follow the well-marked road for 21 miles. This road is paved at the beginning, but turns into a well-graded dirt most of the way; it could become impassable when wet. The loop inside the park is paved. There is also access from the south from NM 57, on a rough dirt road that is best tackled with a high-clearance vehicle.

Time required: A half-day, preferably an overnighter.

Nearby location: Coming from or returning to Farmington on US 550, you can stop at Angel Peak Recreation Site. It has beautiful badlands, which you can photograph from a rim road inside the park during the golden hour. The turnoff to Angel Peak is 14 miles south of Bloomfield on US 550.

El Morro

El Morro is a cuesta—a long rocky formation that drops off abruptly at one end. There are many similar cuestas around the Southwest, but one thing sets El Morro apart: The sheer vertical drop at its end providing a great source of shade and a permanent pool of water at its base, fed by runoff and snowmelt. The two factors combined to make it a natural rest stop for generations of travelers,

Puebloans, Spanish explorers and Anglo settlers. As they rested in the shadow of El Morro, these travelers started leaving messages in the rock to record their passage. The oldest of these inscriptions dates back from 1583, when a passing Spaniard carved the first of many inscriptions, most including the name of the traveler and the date of his passage.

Coming from Zuni, you'll be looking down at El Morro and it appears rather unimpressive, but as you drive past it and into the park road, it suddenly reveals itself. Coming from Grants, you'll get a better first impression. There are two good viewpoints on the road to the Visitor Center inside this National Monument from which you can capture the cuesta with a medium telephoto. The rocky outcrop is neither large nor tall, but it's quite pretty under the right angle and a bit of good light. But here lies

El Morro Pool

the trouble. It's hard to get good light because the monument opens at 8 AM and closes at 7 PM in summer (9 AM to 5 PM the rest of the year), either too late or too early for golden hour photography. Still, you can get good shots from the side of El Morro on NM 53 by walking up to the fence with a normal to moderate wide-angle lens; however, you are no longer able to park on the side of the road, so you'd need to walk to this point from the park turnoff.

El Morro Dawn

The 0.5-mile Inscription Rock Loop Trail is a must, if only to look up the inscriptions and ponder what causes people to carve their names on rock everywhere they go. Ancestral Puebloans, modern native Americans, Spaniards, railroad crews, gold rush emigrants, passing U.S. army soldiers, all have left their names or a sign of their presence in what must be one of the most ancient and diverse glyph panels in the West.

Photo advice: Some of the best pictures of El Morro can be taken as the trail passes close to the main spire at the end of the outcrop. A 28mm will do just fine there. The pool is also lovely and makes for a nice picture. Just past the inscriptions, you can elect to return to the Visitor Center or hike the Mesa Top Trail to the A'ts'ina Ruins.

Getting there: From I-40 at Grants take NM 53 south. It's a quick 41-mile drive. From I-40 at Gallup, drive south on NM 602 then east on NM 53 through Ramah. Both are lovely roads.

Nearby locations: Red Rock State Park is surrounded by red sandstone cliffs and an interestingly shaped pinnacle called Church Rock. Each year in early December, the park plays host to the second-largest balloon festival after Albuquerque.

Pasamos Por Aqui

Spectators watch from the top of a ridge as the balloons ascend toward them, coming very close on both sides. The park is also host to the yearly Gallup Intertribal Ceremonial. It is located 2 miles east of exit 26 on I-40, just outside of Gallup. It is within close proximity of the El Rancho Hotel, one of the most endearing icons of Route 66.

Driving westward on NM 53 after visiting El Morro, you may want to stop at the Pueblo of Zuni, the largest pueblo in New Mexico and the main center of the Zuni tribe. Of particular interest is the Mission of Our Lady of Guadalupe, built in 1629; it has a number of murals of Kachinas painted on its interior walls. The town has many shops offering exquisite Zuni jewelry and pottery and a chance to learn more about the tribe. None is better than the Museum, on the south side of Main Street, which has truly outstanding wares.

El Malpais

This vast but little-known National Monument preserves some remarkable geological features in a gorgeous setting. It is well worth a visit if you are willing to be a bit adventurous.

The monument sits right on top of the continental divide. As you cross the monument on NM 53, you'll see a sign indicating that you are crossing the divide at 7880 feet. A consequence of this high elevation is that you'll find clean air, beautiful skies, pleasant summer temperatures and nice stands of pine forest on the west side.

In a bizarre twist, there are two accesses into the park and they do not connect, at least not with a paved road, so most travelers see only one side of the monument.

The eastern section of El Malpais is administered by the BLM, which

The Sandstone Bluffs

maintains its own Visitor Center, 9 miles south of the Quemado exit on I-40. The view from the Sandstone Bluffs Overlook at mile 11 is spectacular; it's a must if you are in the area at sunset. At mile 18, you'll reach the La Ventana Arch. The shape of this large arch is unique and, although it can be easily observed from the road, it's best to take the short trail to photograph it from the large natural cave behind the arch. The arch is in the shade by mid-afternoon. A couple of miles further, you'll arrive at the Narrows. The Narrows are not a canyon, but simply a 2-mile long 500-foot high sandstone cliff. It is known as the Narrows because the road is squeezed tight between the cliff and the lava beds. The Narrows are an awesome view. The beige sandstone is particularly beautiful and photogenic at sunset, when it turns incredibly red. Extensive views of the lava beds can be seen along the Narrows Rim Trail, which starts at the south end of the Narrows.

The Narrows

In my opinion, the most formidable—though largely ignored—feature of the park is its extraordinary network of lava tubes, extending for miles underground in the west section. One tube is actually 17 miles long, although it is mostly collapsed. The lava tubes of El Malpais are on a par, if not better, than the tubes of Lava Beds Nat'l Monument in Northern California. Furthermore, they provide a sense of isolation and adventure that is now completely lacking in its California counterpart. The price to pay, of course, is that you must discover the tubes at your own risk and take the necessary precautions.

There are two easily accessible areas: the obvious one is El Calderon, a short detour from NM 53. Junction cave is a two-minute walk from your car and gives a quick but interesting glimpse into a lava tube. The 3-mile loop to the Bat Cave and the Cinder Cone is fun, but not particularly rewarding photographically.

The most spectacular spot to see lava beds is the Big Tubes area, located on the Chain of Craters Scenic Backway. The Big Tubes trailhead is located approximately 7 miles from the highway. The beginning of the road is a little rough, but passable by passenger car. This road is definitely impassable after a rain, so check its condition first by calling the El Malpais Ranger Station (see *Appendix*). Snow may also render the road impassable to passenger cars in winter. The entire Chain of the Craters Scenic Backway is 32 miles long. Most of it is maintained by the county and is in fairly good condition. It allows for a very pleasant 3-hour loop to or from the east side.

There is a very pleasant picnic area at the trailhead. The trail meanders up and down through a lava field but is well marked with cairns. You reach the first sign post at about 0.5 mile and from there you can make a 0.5-mile loop that will take you to noteworthy geological features. Big Skylight is the least impressive of the lot in my view. Seven Bridges is a must-see collapsed lava tube with seven bridges remaining in place over a length of half a mile. Four Windows is the most interesting cave to explore: It is also relatively easy to climb down into and explore on your own, even if you are not a caver. Inside, you'll find a superb lava tube.

The Bandera Volcano and Ice Cave are located a couple of miles down NM 53, on private land. An entrance fee is required. The hike to the top of the volcano yields a mildly interesting picture, but the adjoining ice cave shouldn't be missed. The ice cave remains at a steady 31° F (-1°C) year-round; the ice is 20 feet deep and that level hasn't changed for years.

Photo advice: For the western section of the park, limit the photographic equipment you're taking to a camera body with a wide-angle lens and a tripod. You'll find it difficult to convey a sense of depth, due to the stark color of the lava. There are several spots near the Seven Bridges signpost that allow you to get good shots of the bridges. To photograph the caves, you can shoot either into the cave from the outside or from inside the mouth of the cave looking out. In

both cases, you're faced with difficult shots because of the wide range of contrast. Avoid including very bright or very dark areas as much as possible. As you are walking in a circle, there will always be a cave entrance or a bridge that is well lit regardless of the time of the day. The cave interiors get a fair amount of light as the day progresses, so there are no standard exposure settings. You'll be working with exposures of a couple of seconds or more, so handheld photography is out of the question. Flash is also out of the question. Inside the lava tubes, you'll be in complete darkness; you'll need several camping lanterns to illuminate the tube. An 81B filter will help reduce the greenish cast of the long pause and including your partner(s) will provide a sense of depth to your images.

La Ventana Arch

Getting there: For the eastern section, from I-40 take Exit 89 to NM 117 and Quemado. For the western section, take NM 53 toward Zuni from Exit 81 on I-40, close to Grants. The Big Tubes area is located at the western edge of the monument on the Chain of Craters Scenic Backway, which starts 1.2 miles west of the sign for the Bandera Ice Cave.

Time required: 2 hours to visit the eastern section including a short walk to La Ventana Arch. 2½ to 3 hours to get a quick glimpse of the caves in the Big Tubes area. A full day to truly enjoy this wonderful area, including the Four Windows lava tube and a stop at the Bandera Ice Cave.

Special advisory: It is highly recommended that you do not venture into the caves on your

Bandera Ice Cave

own, especially off-season and during the week, when it might be days before someone else passes through. If you decide to explore a lava tube, each person should carry at least two flashlights with fresh batteries. The Park Service recommends wearing a hard hat for extra head protection. It is also essential that you have rugged footwear to walk on the hard lava.

Acoma Pueblo

Cleverly advertised under the catchy moniker of Acoma Sky City, Acoma Pueblo is an outstanding destination and a "must" for every visitor with an interest in Ancestral Puebloan culture.

Perched high on a flat mesa top, 430 feet above the valley floor, Acoma is a striking sight. You get your first glimpse of it after traveling on relatively monotonous ground and nothing prepares you for the incredible—albeit distant—vista of Acoma Mesa as you reach a high viewpoint on the road. The mesa rises up from the plain, surrounded by other interesting rock formations.

Like some of the Hopi villages in Arizona (*see chapter 11 in Volume 2*), Acoma claims to be the oldest continuously inhabited settlement in the United States. According to the tribe's literature, archeologists have recently "theorized" the occupation of Acoma to around 1150 AD.

The Pueblo is fraught with history and an uneasy relationship with the Spanish rulers, beginning with the terrible massacre of many of the inhabitants in 1598 at the hands of Oñate, first governor of the province of New Spain.

Nevertheless, one of the most spectacular sights in Acoma is the Mission of San Esteban del Rey, established in 1640 by a Franciscan friar. The sheer size of the mission is striking. It's all the more impressive when you consider that the massive beams forming the roof were carried all the way from Mt. Taylor, 30

Sky City (photo by Tom Till))

miles away, on the backs of Acoma's men.

The views from the mesa are spectacular, especially toward Mt. Taylor to the north and Enchanted Mesa to the east.

You can only visit the Pueblo in a group. A minibus takes you to the mesa and picks you up at the end of your guided walk. You may climb down on your own on a steep and rocky path, a 15 to 20-minute walk. Guided tours leave on the hour from 8 AM to 4 PM from November to March and to 5 PM from April to October. A morning tour is preferable as the front of the mission is in shade in the afternoon. In summer, you may find yourself in a group of 50 or more people, with your guide more preoccupied with crowd control than detailed explanations. Autumn is an excellent time to visit. Winters can be bitterly cold and spring often brings strong winds to the mesa.

Photo advice: The Acoma Tribe allows photography for personal use. There is an extra fee per camera on top of the visitor's fee. A commercial photography license is not available for purchase. Tripods are not allowed, so bring fast film or a digital camera. Video cameras, which are allowed at Taos Pueblo, are strictly forbidden at Acoma. The Acoma Pueblo houses and their traditional wooden ladders used to access rooftops are remarkably photogenic, but photography of the cemetery as well as inside the mission is prohibited.

Getting there: From I-40, take either exit 96, 15 miles west of Grants or exit 108, 52 miles east of Albuquerque. Another 15 miles on either road brings you to the Visitor Center at the base of the mesa.

Time required: 1 to 1½ hours for the guided walk, plus some time to linger. Count on at least 3 hours from I-40 and back.

Nearby location: The lovely little church of San Jose de Laguna, with its white facade, is located in Laguna Pueblo, close to Exit 114 on I-40. It's easy to photograph with a 24mm lens or wider angle. ✿

Egg Factory Dusk

Chapter 10

THE BISTI BADLANDS

Mineral World

THE BISTI BADLANDS

Introduction

I have to admit that I love the wonderful, whimsical Bisti Badlands. It's an extraordinary location that is very remote and not particularly well documented, so the place sees relatively few visitors. It conveys a great feeling of remoteness and solitude that I appreciate each time I return.

Bisti is a Navajo word signifying badlands. It is pronounced somewhere between Bis"tah" and Bis"tie". The Bisti Badlands moniker dates back from earlier times, when two separate wilderness areas were created: Bisti and De-Na-Zin. With the acquisition of additional land, both were merged in 1996, creating the huge 45,000-acre Bisti/De-Na-Zin Wilderness. For simplicity, I'll continue calling it Bisti Badlands or Bisti.

The Bisti area was once a coastal rainforest along the shore of an inland sea. Its latitude was probably close to Panama, before the continent drifted north. Starting somewhere around seventy million years ago, the sea dried up and the dinosaurs vanished. Through eons of geologic transformation, the forest/animal biomass became mixed up with sediments from the sea, deeply buried and subjected to unimaginable pressure. The Rocky Mountains emerged, lifting up the layers which eventually slowly eroded into what you see today. As in many other places in the Southwest, the decisive factor creating the amazing Bisti formations is the presence of harder sandstone caprocks protecting a much softer clay layer below. The clay erodes much faster from rains and wind action, creating these whimsical hoodoos. Petrified wood can be found in places, attesting to the ancient rainforest heritage of this place. Many fossils of ancient animal life can also be found.

You can explore the wilderness on foot in many different directions and you will come upon surprising sights at every corner. I have lost track of how many times I've been there, but with each visit I return with exciting new discoveries and photographs. I am always eager to go back, but there is one big caveat, time and distance.

Plates

Visiting the Bisti Badlands takes a bit of planning because of its remoteness, but if you like mineral landscapes and have time on your hands, you won't be disappointed. No permit is required and you are free to walk anywhere you want, as long as you don't climb on any of the delicate geological features.

While visiting the wilderness, be sure to have your ten essentials, plus extra water and a GPS, or at least a compass. Always take bearings on tall landmarks when exploring. Without paying close attention to where you're going, you could conceivably get lost in the Bisti Wilderness or you could waste a lot of precious time trying to find your way around. If you venture alone, be sure to let someone know what you're doing. Surprisingly, there is good cell phone reception from high points in the Bisti Badlands.

Photo advice: Spring or fall are the best times to photograph

Das Boot

Pedestal

the Bisti Badlands. Summers are too hot. I've been there several times in winter, but it can be risky. When it rains, the soft clay turns into a messy gumbo and you can forget about visiting the badlands. Regardless of the season, early morning or late afternoon to dusk is always the perfect time. Don't bother starting in the middle of the day, the light will be way too crude. The late afternoon light is better if you venture inside the wilderness area as most of the badlands taper down to the west. At the Bisti, you can use an entire panoply of lenses depending on what you see or want to convey in your photographs. You'll be using a wide angle most of the time, but a mild telephoto will also be very useful.

Getting there: Your best bet is to use Farmington as a base. It takes almost one hour to and from a motel in downtown Farmington, so you must plan on either rising very early or going to bed late. From Farmington, take NM 371 and reset your odometer at the San Juan River crossing. This road doesn't see much traffic, but there is an abundance of small wildlife before dawn, so be alert and don't drive too fast. You'll find County Road 7297 to the left at a bit over 36 miles. Coming from the south on NM 371, this turnoff is about 46 miles from Crownpoint. Follow the well-graded gravel road for 1.8 miles, then turn left at the T and continue 1.2 miles to the car park.

Marine Creature

There is good access from the east if you are coming from Chaco Canyon by way of CR 7500. This is also the fastest way to access the De-Na-Zin wilderness from Farmington. This dirt road is smooth, wide and mostly straight, but can be impassable after a rain. There is an easy-to-miss sign on the north side of the road and a small car park for the De-Na-Zin wilderness.

Time required: Two hours to a whole day just for scouting. Two days are better for photography, as it is materially impossible to hit all the good spots during the golden hour. I recommend spending two nights in Farmington. Check in at your motel in mid-afternoon and go directly to the Bisti to explore the northern section until dusk. If you are lucky enough to be there during full moon, a night walk is described as a fantastic experience by those who have done

The Seal

it. The next morning, you can photograph at dawn the section across the road from the entrance. You'll probably see some wildlife: mostly jackrabbits and rodents, but also foxes and coyotes. After this morning shoot, return to your hotel and relax or perhaps go visit Aztec Ruins. In the afternoon, you can return and explore the southern or eastern sections until dusk.

If the weather is not too hot, you may also choose to explore during the day and find spots to which you'll return to during the golden hour.

Bisti's Northern Section

I recommend that you begin your exploration with the northern section of the Bisti side (the west side of the Bisti/De-Na-Zin wilderness). It is relatively close to the previously mentioned car park, easy to find, and chock full of exceptional photographic opportunities.

After squeezing through the narrow barb-wired entrance, designed to prevent cattle from leaving, walk straight east from the parking area, following the obvious path on the flats. After about 0.3 mile, you'll be walking on the north side of the main Bisti wash, a dry, flat area about a quarter mile wide from north to south. Angle

Wings

Mask

a little bit northeast and follow the barbed-wired fence to your left for another 0.9 mile to where the fence makes a sharp angle to the north, skirting the water reservoir of the Gateway Mine (which may be empty during dry months).

Walk north, keeping the fence to your left. There are usually footsteps you can follow. If not, just pick a natural path between the large, soft badlands. To the west, you should be able to see an occasional post marking the boundary of the wilderness area. Continue north for about 10 minutes, noting a tall landmark to the east, with a bit of a sphinx profile. Climb out of the eroded clay hills onto the low plateau and within a few minutes, you'll come to a fantastic field of boulders, scattered about the landscape about 0.5 miles from where you skirted the Gateway Mine reservoir. This field looks positively moon-like in the late afternoon light (*see the double spread at the end of this book*). Immediately to the east of the boulder field, you see some tall, beautiful hoodoos with great caprocks, surrounded by all kinds of beautiful mushroom rocks. Continuing north past the boulder

Grand Canyon Mock-up?

field, aim just to the right of the "5836" mark on your USGS 7.5' map (36°16'45" 108°14'15"). You'll find an area containing some very photogenic hoodoos in the shape of wings. Returning the same way, walk southeast to reach a spot about 250 yards east of the previously visited boulder field. This is one of the very best spot in the whole Bisti wilderness for photography, with some of the weirdest clay sculptures. Be extremely careful with these fragile formations.

Overleaf: The Beasties go to Bed

Continue southeast to see many other spectacular formations in this area.

If you're running short of daylight (as you should be by now), just aim for the tall sphinx-like landmark to return to the Bisti wash. Don't try to take a shortcut to your car by walking directly west; chances are you'd bump into the fence on the north side of the reservoir and would have to backtrack to go around it. Instead, make sure you get to the wash first before turning west to the parking area.

Wall of Hoodoo

Bisti's Other Sections

Another good area to explore is due east in the Bisti wash and then south of it. Follow the same path as described in the previous section, but instead of turning north past the reservoir, continue east for less than a mile, then angle south toward the mesa and the obvious badlands that border it. Enter the broad canyon leading inside the badlands and walk for about 15 minutes until you find yourself completely surrounded by badlands. Everywhere you climb in this area, you'll reach great groups of hoodoos and mushroom rocks. Going up requires a bit of scrambling so be extra careful if you're by yourself.

Further east, but still on the south side of the wash, is a wonderful spot some call the Egg Factory, Egg Garden or Cracked Eggs (36°16'02" 108°13'26"). It's easy to miss if you don't stay close to the southern edge of the wash. It consists of a group of small eroded rocks (about 2 feet tall) with all kinds of fantastic shapes. Depending on the mood of the day, they could look like cracked eggs, giants shells, dinosaur bones, insects, etc... The rocks are at their best right before sunset, when they assume wonderful colors. From here, it is about 1.7 miles as the crow flies to the car park. It takes about 45 minutes to get back, so you might need your headlamp.

Clog

Of course, if you still have plenty of daylight after finishing the previously-described northern section of the Bisti, you can easily make a bigger loop by going just under the 5800 contour line of quadrant 33 on your USGS 7.5' map

Badlands Toffee

and dropping due south to the Egg Factory. This would make an action-packed 5-mile loop, but it's much preferable to do two outings on different days to benefit from the best light at each location.

Yet another good area can be explored easily by walking south/southeast into the badlands closest to the parking lot. It leads to beautiful formations in less than 20 minutes (for example 36°15'28" 108°14'43"). Follow any of the washes going south until you find something you like.

If you have little time, don't even bother walking into the wilderness area as you may come back empty-handed. Instead, concentrate on the western section's hoodoos that lay between the parking area and the highway. It's a very open area and it's well illuminated mornings and evenings. Just walk west/northwest in the direction of the paved road. In less than 10 minutes, you'll come to a remarkable area of hoodoos of all shapes and forms.

Besides these obvious walks, it's up to you to explore and find your own badlands and hoodoos, or it wouldn't be called a wilderness area. I'm not providing any additional waypoints, because I really don't think you need them to find plenty of great hoodoos and enjoy yourself. Walk in any direction and you're bound to find something that strikes your fancy within a mile or so.

De-Na-Zin Wilderness

About 20 miles further east from the Bisti side, the De-Na-Zin Wilderness offers almost guaranteed solitude. From the car park, follow the trail to the edge of the basin, then go down following an old jeep road. After 0.4 mile, turn left into a small wash and follow it west for about 0.8 mile until it meets with the larger De-Na-Zin Wash. There is a large amount of petrified wood in De-Na-Zin wash around 36°19'01" 108°01'08". The wash area is wide open for exploration. There are endless possibilities inside the De-Na-Zin wilderness, but I've yet to see scenery as attractive as on the Bisti side. ✿

Bandelier Ladder

Chapter 11

AROUND SANTA FE

Santuario de Chimayo

AROUND SANTA FE

This chapter and the next cover Spanish and Puebloan New Mexico, a land of soft light, high mountains and tremendous character, deeply rooted in history. I chose to split the descriptions across two separate chapters due to size constraints, but you can easily intermix them in the course of the same trip, based on schedule and areas of interest.

This chapter covers the northern section of Spanish and Puebloan New Mexico. Leaving Santa Fe, we'll visit outlying areas along the Rio Grande and the Sangre de Cristo Mountains, making a large clockwise tour. This land has plenty to offer to the photographer. Much of the attraction is in the feel and flavor of the towns: Fleeting moments having as much relevance in capturing the spirit of the land as do permanent icons of Spanish New Mexico such as plazas, missions, adobe houses with their blue doorways and colorful ristras.

Old Santa Fe

Santa Fe is your gateway to the exploration of this charming and history-laden part of Spanish New Mexico. It is the geographical, cultural and spiritual center of both Spanish New Mexico and the Pueblo civilization that formed along the Rio Grande. You cannot visit this part of the country without spending some time in Santa Fe.

Founded ca. 1610, it is the oldest capital city in the United States. It owes its origins to Governor-General Peralta, a name you're already familiar with from the Superstition Mountains chapter in *Photographing the Southwest-Volume 2*. Peralta chose the site to establish an administrative outpost for the northern part of New Mexico on behalf of the Spanish crown. He immediately set out to build the Palace of the Governors and the Plaza, at the convergence of the two commercial routes: The Old Santa Fe Trail coming from Missouri and El Camino Real coming from El Paso. The Plaza is near the oldest part of town and will serve as your beacon.

On the Plaza proper, you'll want to photograph the Palace of the Governors—the oldest U.S. public building still in continuous use. The one-story adobe building spans the entire north side of the Plaza and is very photogenic. The front portal is reserved for Native Americans artists and crafts people to sell their wares. They are there 360 days a year from 8 AM to dusk under a special program guaranteeing the authenticity of their products. Needless to say, there is a huge demand for photographs from visitors. If a scene strikes your fancy, ask for permission before taking photographs (never refused if you buy something).

The best way to discover and photograph the Old Santa Fe is on foot. It is not a large area and walking is easy. Parking in Santa Fe is never a problem, except during the annual Santa Fe Indian Market in July.

After the Plaza, walk up and down the Old Spanish Trail (aka Old Pecos Trail as it leaves town). In fact, if you are coming to Santa Fe by car from the south, I encourage you to get off I-25 at exit 284 and drive to the Old Town via the Old Pecos Trail Highway. There are many old houses along the trail and it sets the Santa Fe atmosphere right away.

On the south east corner of the Plaza is the famous La Fonda hotel: a grand old hotel with a superb interior. There is a great photo gallery in the basement that you shouldn't miss. And talking about galleries (including quite a few other photographic galleries),

Ristras & Blue Window

there are dozens of superlative art galleries in Santa Fe, all very inspirational. Just look at the local guides to locate them.

One remarkable building you'd have a hard time missing is the Inn at Loreto, close to the Chapel of the same name. It is a modern hotel, built entirely in the

Pueblo style of architecture. It's a great subject for photography, and not only from the front.

Cross the diminutive Santa Fe River and you'll find the Chapel of San Miguel at the corner with De Vargas Street. It was built in 1628, making it the oldest church in the U.S. This is also where you'll find the oldest house in the U.S. (at least the oldest house built by Caucasians). Both are highly photogenic. The entire neighborhood, called Bario de Analco, was built in the same era and is also presented as the oldest neighborhood in the U.S.

A little bit east of the Plaza on East Palace Avenue is the Sena Plaza complex, also one of the most photogenic areas of Old Town.

These are just a few obvious sights, to get you started in Santa Fe. There are many guidebooks that will help you with the details. One of them I recommend highly, having seen it grow and get better and better over the years: It's the remarkable *Journey to the High Southwest* by Robert Casey (see *Appendix*). This book has an excellent chapter on Santa Fe.

Bandelier National Monument

High in the beautiful Jemez Mountains (see *Around Albuquerque chapter*), Bandelier Nat'l Monument preserves outstanding Puebloan ruins occupied for nearly 500 years until the late 1500s.

Frijoles Canyon

This description focuses on Frijoles Canyon, where over 95% of the monument's visitation is concentrated. By way of introduction to this lovely canyon, there is a nice—albeit a bit distant—view from an overlook located just before the descent toward the Visitor Center.

There are essentially four groups of ruins preserved in this canyon. As you take the Frijoles Canyon Nature Trail from behind the Visitor Center, you'll first come upon the remains of the Tyuonyi Pueblo. This circular group of housings with only a foot or two of walls still standing gives a good idea of the overall architecture of the pueblo. The pueblo encircles a vast grassy area and a large kiva. It is best photographed from above, which brings us to the Talus House Loop Trail. The trail goes by a group of dwellings, consisting of a mix of man-made structures and cave dwellings carved or expanded in the soft pumice.

The trail goes right past Talus House and you are allowed to enter some of the cave dwellings, with their photogenic ladders. It also provides an outstanding view of Tyuonyi, with a nice foreground of cacti and cholla. The trail is very narrow in parts and requires careful foot placement, but it is never difficult.

A few minutes later, you'll be passing the Long House group of cliff dwellings, with its numerous windows carved into the cliff. This is a spectacular sight and a great place to photograph. After visiting Long House, you'll have to decide whether to return to the Visitor Center on the loop trail or extend your walk a half mile one-way on a shady trail, to the base of Ceremonial Cave. Before you make this decision, you should know that Ceremonial Cave is not visible from the canyon floor. Instead, it requires that you climb about 150 vertical feet on a series of four long wooden ladders. Although it is not too arduous if you pace yourself, keep in mind that you are above 7000 feet and that some exposed sections may not be suitable if you have fear of heights.

The climb is well worth it, however, and you'll be rewarded with the sight of a beautifully reconstructed kiva, tucked in under an alcove, that you can enter with a traditional wooden ladder.

In summer, particularly toward midday on weekends, the Visitor Center's relatively small parking lot can exceed its capacity and you may be forced to wait up to an hour to get a space. You may even be turned away by the Rangers if things get out of control.

Instead of waiting for the crowds to trickle out of the canyon, drive back to the Tsankawi detached section, which you passed earlier if you came from Santa Fe. Tsankawi is located 11 miles north of the main park entrance (right after the Truck Route for Los Alamos and 1 mile before the intersection with NM 502). A 1.5-mile primitive trail, including two short ladders, leads to a few yet to be excavated ruins and cliff dwellings, as well as views of Española Valley. Tsankawi remains undeveloped and little frequented. It is quite a spiritual expe-

rience to stroll on the ancient pathway, sometimes carved 10 inches deep into the soft rock by Puebloan footsteps of yore. After descending the second ladder, you'll explore cave dwellings carved into the cliffside before skirting a ledge decorated with faint petroglyphs.

Photo advice: Frijoles Canyon is an afternoon location. The ruins remain in shadow until late morning and are best photographed in late afternoon. You should

Ceremonial Cave

Troglodyte Dwellings

visit Ceremonial Cave early enough to catch great afternoon light, before the sun disappears above the canyon. Ceremonial Cave is best lit approximately 1 to 1½ hour before sunset. After photographing Ceremonial Cave, you can still get 20 minutes of good light if you hurry. Go back to Long House, where the cliffs above take on a wonderful golden hue.

At Tsankawi, the majority of the cave dwellings are lit by the sun in the morning.

Getting there: Coming from Santa Fe, drive north on US 285/84 to Pojoaque, then west on NM 502 and south on NM 4. The drive is 48 miles and will take about an hour. From Albuquerque, take I-25 to Bernalillo and US 550 northwest for almost 25 miles, then turn on NM 4 via the Jemez Mountains (see that section in the *Around Albuquerque chapter*).

Time required: A minimum of two hours at Frijoles Canyon, three if you include Ceremonial Cave, taking your time with photography. Add 1½ hour for Tsankawi.

Nearby location: The White Rock Overlook, located at the eastern edge of the town of White Rock, offers one of the most grandiose panoramas in northern New Mexico—although difficult to photograph. It is only a 4-mile round-trip detour from NM 4; simply follow the signs at the traffic light in town. From the Scenic Overlook, you can contemplate a 180° plus view, encompassing the Rio Grande—which winds its way through White Rock Canyon 900 feet below—and, beyond, the Sangre de Cristo Mountains, Black Mesa, as well as miles and miles of wilderness. It is a late afternoon location.

Abiquiu

Puebloans occupied the Abiquiu area for more than a thousand years; however, it was a more recent arrival who made this small town notorious. In the 1940s, Georgia O'Keeffe settled there and proceeded to paint some of her finest works, simply painting on canvas what she saw of her immediate surroundings. Today's photographers can be just as attracted by the landscape and the soft light.

One of her favorite subjects was the White Place—or Plaza Blanca—located just outside Abiquiu. On US 84 at the west end of town, take the first good dirt road to your right past the Rio Chama bridge and follow it for 2.3 miles. Turn left onto a bumpy road, then right at the fork to reach the car park. A short walk brings you to the base of white limestone cliffs and hoodoos, where you can photograph to your heart's content. To soften the bright white limestone and bring out definition, plan on being there early in the morning or late in the afternoon. If you'd gone left at the fork, you'd have reached Dar Al Islam, a beautiful adobe mosque built on the mesa top in the 1980s; the mosque harmoniously combines a Moorish look with the traditional Santa Fe style.

In the tiny heart of Abiquiu, on the other side of the O'Keefe house, don't miss the modern church built in classic adobe style. It photographs very well.

Almost 10 miles northwest on US 84 toward Chama, look to your right for one of the most colorful display of red rocks and badlands in New Mexico. These badlands are highly reminiscent of the Old Paria badlands in Southern Utah (See *Photographing the Southwest - Volume 1)*. About 2 miles further, between mileposts 224 and 225, make a right on the good dirt road leading to Ghost Ranch, a spiritual retreat center open to the public. Ghost Ranch sits on the grounds of a 20,000-acre property, which includes small museums, a retreat center, cabins, a campground and several hiking trails. From the top of the access road, you can get a good view of the yellow and red cliffs, with Chimney Rock at their west end. Behind the Ranch's museum, an easy 3-mile round-trip trail leads to the top of Chimney Rock's mesa. About 500 yards from the trailhead, you reach a small plateau where you can leave the trail on the left side and walk to the edge to photograph the Chimney Rock spires from a very nice angle, with the colorful badlands at their feet. At the end of the trail, you can enjoy a very nice panoramic view of the surrounding cliffs, the Chama River Valley and the Abiquiu Reservoir. Count about 1½ hour for this hike.

In the opposite direction, the 5-mile round-trip Kitchen Mesa Trail begins close to Long House, leading to the top of the impressive mesa above the Dining Hall. This is a more strenuous hike, requiring about 3 hours, with some steep portions and even a bit of scrambling at one point. However, as you reach the surprisingly white rock on the flat top, you'll be rewarded by a commanding view of Ghost Ranch, its side canyons,

Ghost Ranch's Chimney Rock (photo by Steve Larese)

colorful badlands, the Chama River Valley and the Jemez Mountains.

The sites on these two hikes are at their best in the early morning or from the middle of the afternoon on. This is also the best time to hike, as it can get very hot on these unshaded trails.

A few miles further on US 84, you'll come to a sign pointing to the Echo Amphitheater Recreation Area. The huge amphitheater with pastel colored sandstone walls has a large circular rocky bowl generating an interesting echo. It's a good morning location, but it's also a popular place and chances are you'll do your photography while some folks are shouting their lungs off.

Getting there: Take US 84/NM 285 north of Santa Fe, exit at Española and follow the signs to US 84 in the direction of Chama. Abiquiu is about 22 miles northwest of Española.

Time required: At least half a day to visit the Abiquiu area and do one of the Ghost Ranch hikes. Try scheduling an early morning visit, combining it with a mid-afternoon arrival at Bandelier Nat'l Monument, which is a great afternoon location.

Nearby location: At Santa Clara Pueblo, southwest of Española, you can visit the Puye Cliff Dwellings by permit. They have interesting ruins at the top and bottom of the Pajarito Plateau. Call beforehand to see if the area is open (see *Appendix*) or just drop by the Tribal office to obtain a permit.

The High Road to Taos

The so-called High Road to Taos is a very pleasant drive, making a good alternative to the crowded highway between Santa Fe and Taos. The High Road takes you through some spectacular high country, as well as several picturesque little towns. This area is rich in history, with many pueblos, missions and early Spanish settlements.

Although, the High Road officially starts in Española, following NM 76, I recommend that you leave Santa Fe by way of Washington Avenue, then Bishops Lodge Road, leaving the ski area road (NM 475) to your right.

Following Bishops Lodge Road (which becomes NM 590), you'll pass lovely Tesuque, which has good photography potential, before

Las Trampas

rejoining US 84. Leave US 84 at Pojoaque and turn east on NM 4. Soon, a short 1-mile spur leads to the old Nambe Pueblo, which has a small but nice plaza with a recently built adobe church. A few miles further on the spur road, you'll reach the Nambe Falls Recreation Area, which is popular for summer camping.

Follow NM 520 toward Chimayó, your next stop. Although, Chimayó's setting is not very attractive, a stop at the famous Santuario de Chimayó is a must. The church, built in 1816, has a simple but exquisite architecture and grounds that will delight photographers. The best light is in the morning.

Just outside Chimayó, follow NM 76 northeast toward Truchas, a picturesque village located at

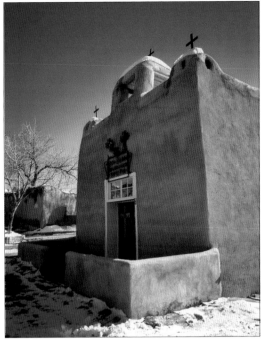

Talpa Church

8,600 feet on the edge of a canyon, with the Sangre de Cristo Mountains in the background. Here, the feeling of high elevation, the soft angle of the mountains and the beautiful light come together into classic Spanish New Mexico scenery. Truchas, started in 1754, probably hasn't changed very much since. On a side note, it has served as an outdoor location for Robert Redford's wonderful film: The Milagro Beanfield War.

Next is Las Trampas and the remarkable San José de Gracia church, a masterpiece of adobe architecture built in 1776—a must for photographers. The light is good at any time of the day. A wide angle is necessary to capture the church.

Turning left on NM 75 at Peñasco, take the short detour to Picuris Pueblo to photograph its lovely San Lorenzo church (after paying your fee, of course). Back on NM 76, continue on to NM 75 east and NM 518 north. Two more beautiful adobe churches await you before reaching Taos. First, the very small but lovely San Juan de Los Lagos is located on the left side of the road shortly after you enter Talpa. This small church is best photographed in late afternoon and its cramped location calls for a very wide angle lens. Next is the hugely famous San Francisco de Asis Mission, located on a lovely plaza in Ranchos de Taos just by NM 68, a few hundred yards to the left when coming from NM 518. The mission has been a source of inspiration for artists such as Georgia O'Keeffe, Ernest Blumenschein and Ansel Adams. The back of the church, with its massive adobe walls and buttresses, offers interesting angles and makes a great subject for photographers. Try using volume to shoot abstract compositions with a wide-angle. San Francisco de Asis is in good light throughout the day.

San Francisco de Asis (photo by Alan Plisskin)

Finally, you'll reach Taos. Despite its commercial trappings, Taos is still a wonderful little town full of great B&Bs, cafes, bookstores, galleries and museums. Its character and enchanting surroundings have made it a magnet for artists and visitors for decades. It is also renowned for its outdoor activities, which make it a popular year-round destination. In the historic district, photographers will be naturally drawn to shooting *ristras,* the colorful strings of red chili peppers hanging from beautiful adobe walls near colorful doors.

Time required: A whole day to fully appreciate the High Road from Santa Fe to Taos, coming back on NM 68 along the Rio Grande, a ±150-mile loop.

Taos Pueblo

Arguably the most spectacular pueblo from a visual standpoint is the illustrious Taos Pueblo—a model of multi-storied adobe architecture, with its beautiful dwellings fitting like building blocks in a 3D-model. Apply to this well-designed model the smooth angles and surfaces of richly colored adobe walls, a few wooden ladders, some beehive ovens to enliven the foreground and the magnificent backdrop of the Taos Mountains, you end-up with an eye-popping scene offering ideal perspective, warm tones and immense character. In short, the Taos Pueblo is a photographer's dream that no visitor to the Southwest should miss.

Photo advice: Strict rules govern picture taking at the Taos Pueblo. Whether you visit by yourself or on a guided tour, many parts of the pueblo are off-limits and you may not photograph inside the lovely San Geronimo church. The tribe has made a very good case of protecting their copyrights to their cultural heritage and offers a compromise to those who want to photograph their dwellings.

In addition to the entrance fee of $10, photographers pay a $5 fee per camera. This allows you to take pictures strictly for personal use. A $150 fee buys you one day of shooting and a license with limited reproduction rights. The personal use license prohibits usage of a tripod, greatly reducing the odds of taking home fine-art grade images.

Early to mid-morning and late afternoon are perfect for photographing the Pueblo. I tend to prefer early morning winter days when the light is low and soft and there are few visitors. In summer, the sun rises around 6 AM and the light is already a little crude, but you'll have no harsh shadows on the San Geronimo church. Except when tribal rituals require closure, the pueblo is open to the public from 8 AM to 4:30 PM.

Taos Pueblo (photo by Tom Till)

Getting there: Drive north through Taos' main thoroughfare and you'll see the sign for the Taos Pueblo just past the Kachina Lodge. The pueblo is located about 3 miles outside of town.

Time required: An hour or more; the commercial license is valid for one day.

Nearby locations: 12 miles northwest of Taos on US 64 to Tres Piedras and Chama, the impressive Rio Grande Gorge Bridge spans the deep gorge 650 feet above the river. The walls of the gorge are steep and dark and the river is in shadow most of the time. You can cross the bridge on foot; a number of observation points line up both sides along the way. The perspective is good from both sides. The best view of the bridge itself is from the picnic grounds located on the west side of the Rio Grande, just south of the ramadas.

Northeast of Taos, at the end of NM 150, the Taos Ski Valley is surrounded by New Mexico's tallest peaks, including its highest, the 13,161-foot Mt. Wheeler. This is a world-class location for alpine and cross-country skiing and a great location for fall colors.

Rio Grande (photo by Adam Schallau)

Pecos National Historical Park

It's a shame that the Pecos Pueblo was abandoned and left in ruins, because it would have been such a spectacular sight to see. In its heyday from 1450 to 1550 AD, Pecos was the largest Pueblo community in the present United States and was home to two thousand souls. The pueblo was an assemblage of large communal houses, four to five stories high and containing as many as 15 rooms each. The ground floor rooms were used for storage. Ladders gave access to the higher floors, which housed living quarters. According to an early Spanish visitor, you could actually walk from house to house on rooftops, completely encircling the plaza without setting foot outside.

Artists' renditions of the North and South Pueblos based on archaeological digs and analysis of the remaining structures reveal a majestic town of adobe walls similar to the Taos Pueblo further north, but many times larger. The pueblo's strategic location on a rise also gave it added majesty. Stonewalls encircled the town to protect it from intruders. Portions of these walls are still visible today.

Pecos was a major trading center that brought many Plains Indians from the east. There is also ample evidence that the town had regular contacts with Mesoamerican cultures. Later on, the Spaniards built a large mission just outside the town. Parts of the adobe church are still standing today.

Photo advice: A 1.25-mile loop trail leaving from the Visitor Center takes in the ruins of the pueblo and the mission. There are two rebuilt kivas, in which you can go down using a traditional ladder. The kiva located by the mission makes an excellent foreground to the church's massive walls for a late afternoon shot. If you don't have much time, park by the Park headquarters. They are only a quarter mile from the mission compound, which offers the most interesting shots.

Getting there: 20 miles east of Santa Fe on I-25, take exit 299 (Glorieta) to NM 50, and follow the signs for 8 miles.

Time required: About 1½ hour. ✿

Overleaf: Kiva & Church at Pecos Pueblo

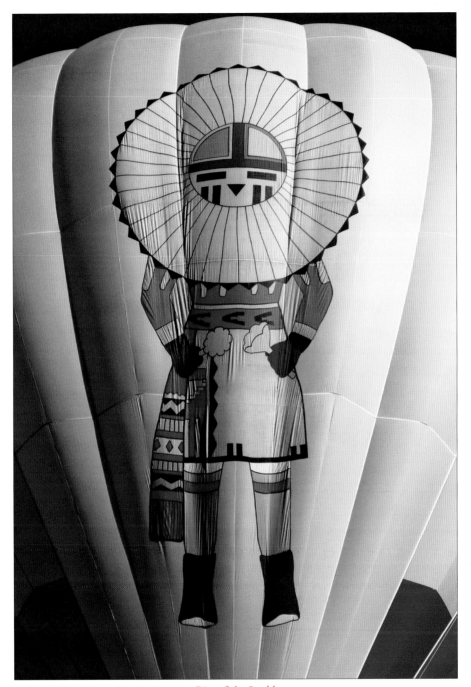

Rise of the Pueblo

Chapter 12

AROUND ALBUQUERQUE

Tent Rocks

AROUND ALBUQUERQUE

Old Town

Old Town is Albuquerque's historic center. The town was already a military outpost when the first Spanish colonists arrived in 1706 to farm the area along the Rio Grande. Old Town revolves around its lovely Central Plaza, surrounded by the church and many carefully restored traditional buildings. The one thing I appreciate in Old Town Albuquerque is that its restoration was understated. The Spanish Colonial character has a sense of authenticity but is never overwhelming to the senses. Granted, these are all tourist shops, but on the outside they all have character and are done in good taste. Wandering around the low adobe structures with protruding wooden beams, you discover hidden patios and shaded little gardens reached by narrow brick passageways. Flowers and ristras are everywhere. I have been there countless times and still always find it very refreshing.

The San Felipe de Neri Church, located on the north side of the plaza, is of major importance to us Southwest aficionados. Consider for a minute that it was the starting point for friars Dominguez and Escalante in their awesome and fascinating quest to find a northern passage to California. Yes, the same quest that led them to so many sites described in the Photographing the Southwest guidebooks—think of Canyon Pintado (*in Chapter 3*) and of the huge distance separating this church from that canyon near Dinosaur Nat'l Monument. It's in this church's quiet courtyard that Escalante planned his mission and this is where he returned after his incredible journey.

On the east side of the Plaza, under the original wooden beams of the Portico, there is always a group of Native American street vendors selling crafts, a tradition established since the early days of Old Town. Ask for permission before taking pictures.

A more modern aspect of Old Town is the popularity it gained when Route 66—the Mother Road—was built in the late 1920s. Some vestiges of the Route 66 heydays can make fascinating subjects for photographers. One great such structure, very close to Old Town, is the landmark El Vado Motel.

All in all, you'll find plenty of material for your photography in Old Town.

Time required: 1 to 3 hours

Nearby location: North of Old Town and I-40, the Indian Pueblo Cultural Center Museum is a good place to get to know the nineteen New Mexico Pueblo tribes that are represented.

The Balloon Fiesta

The Albuquerque International Balloon Fiesta is the largest gathering of balloons in the world. There are about seven hundred to a thousand balloons and well over a thousand pilots assembling over a period of ten days in early October, with sorties almost every morning, weather permitting. Enthusiasts come from all over the world to meet their peers, compete, learn and mostly have fun. The Fiesta also provides an opportunity for people to go beyond the "strictly balloon" activity and visit the great outdoors surrounding Albuquerque. For

photographers, this is one of the most famous, colorful and photogenic events in the Southwest, which is why I included it in this guidebook

Let's summarize what a normal day looks like at the Balloon Fiesta.

The day starts well before sunrise with the Dawn Patrol. About a dozen selected balloons leave the field approximately 45 minutes before sunrise, rising one by one in the cold morning air and dark sky. Once they've

Celestial Ascent

reached some elevation, the inside of the balloons are lit to make them look like nighttime glowworms. An additional purpose of the Dawn Patrol is to test wind currents and report on atmospheric conditions to balloonists. Meanwhile spectators converge in droves toward the launching field. On weekends, crowds top 100,000 people. I-25 looks like it's in grid-lock, but crowd processing is very efficient and soon every one finds a spot. One of the most remarkable aspects of the Balloon Fiesta is that you are free to wander around the field during the pre-launch and the mass ascension, mingling with the pilots and the chase crews, being at the center of the action. Mass ascension usually occurs on week-ends. During the week or in case of poor weather conditions, a few balloons just hover above the launch field. The go-ahead for the mass ascension is usually given to balloonists around 8 AM. A flurry of activity ensues as hundreds of balloons start inflating and heating up the air in a roar of propane burners, before lifting off. Depending on the direction of the wind, they will either take off toward the north or toward the south. The winds usually blow south at lower elevation and if that's the case, the entire city gets a fantastic free show for almost two hours, the time it takes for the mass ascension of over 700 balloons.

Bubbles

There are additional activities in the evening. Although static, they also offer great opportunities to photograph the balloons at close range, particularly during the night glow, when balloons are all lit up, while still on the field.

Photo advice: Let's face it, you're given the most extraordinary ingredients to start with: colorful balloons, wonderful shapes and the spectacular southwestern sky as a background. In most cases, this is sufficient to ensure that you'll come back with a bunch of excellent photos. But some additional tips may help you in fine-tuning your skills and getting even better results.

Digital is king at the Balloon Fiesta. First off, the subject matter lends itself remarkably well to digital photography, with its very high contrast and super-bright colors. Also, the average 1.5x crop factor of most dSLRs gives you an extra edge at the long end. You'll find the longer focal length given to your telephoto by the sensor's crop factor extremely useful.

On the ground, using a wide angle allows you to get closer to the balloons to avoid people in the picture. It allows shooting a huge balloon in the foreground, with smaller balloons already in the air. Once the balloons are high in the air, the telephoto zoom is invaluable to bring out details, getting rid of clutter by isolating your subject, tightening your compositions or compressing the perspective. Next, you can quickly check your results on your LCD and compensate if necessary. Finally, you can shoot to your heart's content, without worrying about the cost of film. Tripods are too cumbersome and too slow here. You will need to move about the field quickly, pointing your lens to capture a certain combination in the sky, turn around, and shoot in the other direction. The tripod is too stationary for that, except during the Night Glow. However, you also need a fast shutter speed to ensure crispness of the moving balloons and the sky is still dark at the beginning of the balloon release. This is why a gyro-stabilized lens or camera will work wonders, easily giving you 2 to 3 stops, enough to make the difference between a blurred shot at 1/60th and a very crisp one at 1/250th. If you don't have one, you'll need to push the ISO sensitivity, running the risk of introducing noise in the sky. This depends on your camera, of course, and modern dSLRs have a huge advantage over consumer digicams in that department.

Now, let's talk about specific aspects, starting with the sky. The good news is that you don't have much to worry about the sky. The balloons are only ascending in the early morning, so the sky is always well saturated. The sun rises from behind the Sandia Mountains (see *Turquoise Trail* section below) so it's best to shoot north or south for great side lighting with a muted velvet sky. This imparts incredible depth and texture to your images. If you want more saturated color against a deep blue sky, shoot more toward the west. Even shooting against the light works, if you have to do so to photograph a particular balloon or group of balloons rising to the east of you. If you fill your frame with one or more balloons while shooting against the light, adding 1/3 or 1/2 f/stop is enough to prevent your meter from being fooled. If you leave a substantial amount of sky in your composition, compensate by 1.5 to 2 f/stops more. A quick glance at your LCD will reassure you that what you're doing is right.

As far as your main subject (the balloon) is concerned, be sure to have a balanced composition if you're shooting a cluster. If you're shooting only one balloon, off-center placement creates a more dynamic balance. Above all, my main advice is: avoid clutter. You don't want distracting details. In the midst of action, it's hard to balance shooting fast and leaving out unwanted balloons. Fortunately, thanks to the even skies, a bit of post-processing can take care of those gremlins.

For best results, review your work, see what works and what doesn't, and come back the next day if you can.

Getting there: Exit I-25 at Alameda on week-ends and Tramway on week-days and follow the traffic. If you would rather not drive,

Buzzing Around

there are convenient Park-N-Ride locations throughout Albuquerque.

Time required: It's best to arrive by 5:30 AM to enjoy the Dawn Patrol and avoid being caught in traffic. You'll be out by about 10 AM.

Petroglyph National Monument

Petroglyph Nat'l Monument is a small park located just northwest of the city of Albuquerque, consisting of two separate sections: Boca Negra Canyon and Rinconada Canyon. It preserves thousands of petroglyphs carved over centuries by the Rio Grande's Pueblo people and their hunter-gatherer descendants and later by Spanish shepherds and travelers. If you don't have much time, Boca Negra Canyon is your best choice. It has three short trails, with the Mesa Trail offering the most interesting petroglyphs.

With a bit more time, you can also hike the Rinconada Canyon Trail, an easy 2.5-mile round-trip loop. There are many petroglyphs carved on boulders toward the end of canyon, but they are not always obvious to spot.

Photo advice: From a photographic standpoint, the fact that the petroglyphs are carved mostly on lava boulders strewn about the land makes for original pictures under the right light. You will mostly be using a wide-angle lens. A polarizing filter will help bring out the relief of the glyphs when they are in bright sunshine.

Getting there: Coming west from I-40, exit at Unser (Exit #154) and drive 2.7 miles north until you see the sign for the Visitor Center. Coming from Santa Fe, it's easier and probably just as fast to take I-25 south all the way to I-40 west and follow the previous instructions. Boca Negra Canyon is located about 2 miles North of the Visitor Center on Unser Boulevard, while Rinconada Canyon is located about a mile south. There is no fee to visit Rinconada.

Time required: About 1 hour for the three Boca Negra Canyon trails. 1½ hour to get a good glimpse of the petroglyphs in Rinconada Canyon.

Nearby location: The western section of Petroglyph Nat'l Monument provides protection for several beautiful little volcanoes. Three of them, Vulcan, Black and JA, are easily accessible by car and a short walk. These volcanoes are the source of the lava flows where the rock art is located down below. Time permitting, consider paying a visit to these volcanoes, which offer pleas-

Rinconada Petroglyphs

ant walking and a great view of Albuquerque and the Sandia Mountains. To do so, take I-40 west from Albuquerque and exit at Paseo del Volcan (Exit #149). Drive 4.8 miles north on Paseo del Volcan and turn right at the unmarked gate leading to the ramadas visible from the road. From there follow the 0.5-mile trail to the base of the volcanoes. A couple of footpaths continue up to the crater of each volcano. Vulcan is the most easily accessible. Count on 45 minutes to an hour from your car.

Coronado State Monument

Coronado Painting

This New Mexico State Monument, on the right bank of the Rio Grande, warrants a visit for one good reason: it harbors some very rare 14th to 17th century paintings found on the walls of a kiva. The murals have been removed from their original location and are now displayed behind protective glass in their own museum. Although the colors are very faded, the designs are very original and kiva murals are a rare occurrence in the Southwest. The original Kuaua settlement was abandoned in 1680 and its Great House, the third largest in the Southwest, was entirely wiped out. The ruins you see outside the Visitor Center have been artificially constructed to provide some sense of what the compound may have looked like. One bright point is that the kiva harboring the murals has been reconstructed and that you can descend in it using a classic pueblo ladder to admire replicas of the paintings on its walls.

Getting there: 16 miles north of Albuquerque on I-25, take exit 242 in Bernalillo to US 550 and follow the signs to the monument for another 3 miles.

Time required: 1 hour.

The Jemez Mountain Trail

The Jemez Mountain Trail (NM 4), a National Scenic Byway, crosses the Jemez Mountains then skirts the southern tip of the Valles Caldera, leading to Bandelier National Monument (see the *Around Santa Fe chapter*) and Los Alamos. It's an exceptionally pleasant road, which you'll certainly enjoy driving if you can spare the time. What makes the Jemez Mountain Trail so interesting is a combination of rugged, scenic beauty and several noteworthy stops right alongside the road.

In San Ysidro, the southern gateway to the Jemez Mountain Trail, the nicely-restored Spanish adobe church is worth a photograph for its lovely facade.

About 5 miles north of San Ysidro, you'll find Jemez Pueblo. The fairly spread-out village has a pleasant, casual atmosphere; it's a good place to stop for a rest before tackling the mountainous part of the road. The heart of Jemez Pueblo is the Ancestral Puebloan village of Walatowa. Don't expect any photogenic old structures, but the modern Walatowa Visitor Center—set in front of the scenic Jemez Red Rocks—is attractive and informative.

About 12 miles after leaving Jemez Pueblo you'll come to Jemez Springs, at the heart of the Cañon de San Diego. The whole area is dotted with several mineral hot springs, due to past volcanic activity. Jemez Springs is a relaxed little art community; it has galleries, inns, various retreat houses and a historic bathhouse. Just above the village is the Jemez State Monument which protects some Puebloan ruins. Almost next door is the 17th century Spanish Mission of San José de los Jemez. Less than a mile past the monument is Soda Dam, a natural dam formed by mineral deposits blocking the Jemez River. A path leads to a natural cave next to the dam, from which you can take an interesting shot of the river, framed by the travertine. About 3.8 miles past the Soda Dam, the road delivers a surprise: Battleship Rock, a startling cliff rising abruptly above the Jemez River like the prow of the ship. It is particularly striking in mid-afternoon, coming from the south.

About 3 miles past Battleship Rock, the Jemez Mountain Trail winds its way out of the canyon after passing NM 126 on the left and the landscape changes radically. The road now follows the edge of the vast Jemez Caldera, the Valle Grande, part of the Valles Caldera National Preserve. The preserve protects a 14-mile wide caldera, one of the largest volcanic calderas in the world, the result of a gigantic eruption 1.2 million years ago. Also inside the preserve is Redondo Peak, one of New Mexico's tallest mountains at 11,254 feet. There are excellent photo opportunities during the golden hour.

Getting there: Continuing west on US 550 past Coronado, you'll pick up the Jemez Mountain Trail at San Ysidro, at the junction of US 550 and NM 4, a 24-mile drive northwest from Bernalillo and I-25.

Time required: At least half a day from Albuquerque to Los Alamos.

Nearby location: Cuba, a picturesque little town further to the northwest on US 550, is the gateway to the northern section of Santa Fe National Forest, which has several Puebloan ruins from the Gallina culture, including the photogenic Nogales Cliff House. CO 96 links Cuba with US 84, allowing a loop with Ghost Ranch and Abiquiu (see *Around Santa Fe chapter*).

Tent Rocks

The official name of this recently designated National Monument is Kasha-Katuwe Tent Rocks, but most people refer to it as Tent Rocks, and in this particular case, I have decided to go with the flow.

The Tent Rocks are white hoodoos made of a particularly brittle ash tuff. In many instances, their hard layer cap rocks have vanished and they have been strangely eroded into perfectly conical shapes, similar to teepees. These unique formations are actually very reminiscent of the

Teepees

Capadocce area in central Turkey. Unlike the latter, however, the Tent Rocks are relatively small.

The Tents Rocks are very easily accessible and should be visited by every photographer passing through on I-25, between Albuquerque and Santa Fe.

The most interesting group of Tent Rocks is found on the Canyon Trail. After following a sandy wash and passing through a nice little slot canyon with a beautifully striated rock surface, you reach a small group of less than a dozen eroded "tents" right at the end of the canyon. The trail continues up, allowing you

to view and photograph the cluster of tents from above. At some point, you need to negotiate three easy moki steps and the trail forks to the left. This is probably the best spot to photograph the Tents Rocks with a moderate wide-angle lens. Continue up to the plateau to reach Lookout Point. On the way, you will pass a point where you gain a 360° view of the area, with the Cochiti Valley in front of you, the Sandia Mountains in the distance and the Jemez Mountains behind you. This

Coneheads

Son of Cocky Hoodoo

is truly spectacular. From Lookout Point, there is also an interesting view of different Tent Rocks if you look back. On your way back, shortly after passing the main tents, look up to the left for a small but spectacular hoodoo. It makes for a very nice photo with a 200mm lens when the sun sets on it. Past the canyon, take the Cave Trail Loop to the right. The cave itself is mildly interesting, but as you get closer to the trailhead, you'll pass a very nice group of small Tents Rocks and you'll have an open view of the cliff, which has a large concentration of interesting hoodoos.

Photo advice: A cloudy day would work best to photograph the very white rock. You won't get any sense of depth when it's flooded with too much light. Late afternoon is best to photograph the main concentration of Tent Rocks on the Canyon Trail; Early morning will work fine elsewhere.

Getting there: Coming from Albuquerque, drive north on I-25 about 35 miles from downtown, get off at Exit 259 (Cochiti Reservoir) and follow NM 22 for 12 miles to Cochiti Pueblo. At the foot of the dam, turn left and follow the signs to the monument. The 5-mile graded dirt road at the end is suitable to all vehicles, but drive slowly.

Time required: 2 to 3 hours to walk the loop. The monument closes at 6 PM but there is an always-open exit route.

The Turquoise Trail

The high desert road (NM 14) between Albuquerque and Santa Fe, known as the Turquoise Trail, is a very pleasant alternative to the I-25 freeway. It gets its name from turquoise deposits found in abundance in the Cerrillos area. Turquoise was a major source of trade between Ancestral Puebloans and Plains Indians and also had a major impact on the settling of the area by the Spaniards. Later on, the discovery of gold brought thousands of newcomers to the area near the little community of Golden, in what was to be the first gold rush west of the Mississippi, almost twenty years before the California gold rush. At the turn of the 19th century, coal mining provided yet another boom for the area near Madrid and Cerrillos.

Six miles north of Tijeras on I-40, the Turquoise Trail provides access to the Sandia Mountains on the 12-mile long Sandia Crest Scenic Byway (NM 536). There are spectacular views along the road, which passes through four different life zones, including high alpine scenery. The view of Albuquerque from Sandia Crest at 10,678 feet is truly more spectacular than photogenic.

It's the northern section of the Turquoise Trail, however, that provides the most interesting sights. In Golden, don't miss the charming white Church of San Francisco, up on the east side of the road. Next, the little community of Madrid, formerly a bustling mining town turned ghost town, has been taken over by artists and craftspeople who have made the place charming and unique.

Just 3 miles north of Madrid and 0.5-mile west of NM 14 is Cerrillos, an interesting little village with picturesque houses lining unpaved streets. There are still many relics of the past, such as old hotels, saloons and general stores, but the Old West atmosphere has been left unspoiled. This is an excellent place for photography.

Just north of Cerrillos lies a small but spectacular area of badlands, faults and hogbacks called the Garden of the Gods (no relation with its more famous namesake outside of Colorado Springs). You can just park on the side of the road to take a picture of the formations as the land is private property.

Getting there: From Albuquerque, drive 15 miles east on I-40, take Exit 175 (Tijeras) and follow NM 14 north for about 45 miles until it reaches I-25.

Time required: At least half a day to truly enjoy the trail, including the side trip to Sandia Crest.

The Salinas Missions

Salinas Pueblo Missions National Monument protects three separate sets of Puebloan ruins and Spanish missions to the southeast of Albuquerque. Spanish Franciscans built these missions in the early 17th-century in the heart of what were then thriving communities. However, by the late 1670s, both the Spaniards and the Ancestral Puebloans had left. What remains today are rather austere but quite photogenic ruins of the mission churches and few of the kivas and structures of the Puebloans.

The three missions, Abó, Quarai, and Gran Quivira are quite distant from each other and each has its own Visitor Center. They are little

Abó Mission

Quarai

known to the general public and see very little traffic, but those who come can't fail to be impressed by the clean, geometric lines of their architecture.

Gran Quivira, which is the most distant and hardest to get to, seems to receive the most traffic. Formerly known as Las Humanas, it was a major trade center, with many buildings and kivas. It is still the largest of the three today, but it has none of the striking red walls of Abó and Quarai.

The Quarai unit receives very few visitors, which contributes to its enjoyment, I must say. I find the Quarai unit very impressive and interesting to photograph.

The Abó unit is the closest to Albuquerque. The mission's ruins stand tall and impressive, with the Manzano Mountains in the distance. They are photographically very appealing.

Photo advice: At Abó, a telephoto works extremely well to isolate the tall walls against the mountains, but a wide-angle works as well. The grounds at Quarai are smaller than at Abó, so it's more wide angle and normal lens territory. Likewise at Gran Quivira where the structures are shorter than at the others.

Getting there: From Belen on I-25, south of Albuquerque, take NM 47 for about 22 miles to US 60, then drive 12 miles east and 0.5 mile north on NM 513 to reach Abó. Back on US 60, continue east for almost 10 miles to the town of Mountainair, then drive 8 miles northwest on NM 55 and 1 mile west at the sign to reach Quarai. The Gran Quivira ruins are 26 miles southeast of Mountainair on NM 55.

Time required: For just a quick visit with little photography involved, the bare minimum would be 30 minutes at Abó and Quarai and 45 minutes at Grand Quivira which requires a short walk. Add to this the transit time between the three units. At a more comfortable pace, consider spending almost 4 hours to see the three missions. ✿

Yucca Solitaire

Chapter 13

SOUTHERN NEW MEXICO

Nuclear Blast

SOUTHERN NEW MEXICO

Valley of Fires

The Valley of Fires Recreation Area is a nice and easy stop when driving around south-central New Mexico. The park preserves over 125 square miles of lava beds, part of a much vaster flow extending 10 miles northwest of Carrizozo and 35 miles south into the Tularosa Basin, at the latitude of Three Rivers. The flow is between 4 and 6 miles wide and the lava is 160 feet deep at its thickest. One striking aspect of this lava flow is its remarkable "youth" in terms of geologic time. It is estimated that the main flow occurred about 5,000 years ago, following repeated eruptions of Little Black Peak, a volcanic vent located a mere 5 miles north of US 380. This makes it the youngest lava field in the continental United States. The developed area is located on a "kipuka", a small ridge of older rock that was too high for the molten lave to submerge. It provides a commanding view of the lava flow below.

I highly recommend Valley of Fires to folks who want to hike lava beds but are not in shape to hike a long time. Unlike El Malpais—the Southwest's king of lava beds—which we discovered in the Northwest New Mexico chapter, it is very approachable: It's a short 0.7-mile hike on a paved trail and you're always in view of the observation deck on the ridge. Also, it is highly vegetated, in contrast to the much starker El Malpais. I find the flowers, grasses, tall yuccas and small cacti very attractive compared to other lava flows. Wildlife is present, although only in the early evening and at dawn, due to the intense daytime heat. You can observe a great diversity of birds especially during winter and spring.

My only regret is that this nice little park doesn't have at least one lava tube that you can enter, for those who have never experienced the joy of exploring such.

Valley of Fires

Finally, Valley of Fires has the best public campground around, including a large, immaculately clean shower area, a boon for those used to sleeping in their vehicles. All of this for a very small fee, which is moreover halved for Golden Eagle Pass holders. Hats off to the BLM on this one.

Photo advice: The nature trail is located on the west side of the ridge and is best photographed in late afternoon to avoid harsh contrast and dark shadows.

Getting there: Drive 4 miles west of Carrizozo on US 380.

Time required: 30 minutes for a quick hike. 2 hours for extensive photography.

Three Rivers Petroglyph site

With an estimated 20,000+ glyphs, the Three Rivers Petroglyph Site preserves one of the largest number of petroglyphs in the Southwest. But sheer quantity is only part of the story. The site is more remarkable for its remote location, tight concentration and, above all, for the diversity and interest of the glyphs. The glyphs were pecked between approximately 900 and 1400 AD by people from the Jornada Mogollon group.

Bighorn Petroglyph

Stella

Most of the art can be seen along a short and easy 1-mile round-trip trail straddling a narrow basalt ridge. There is an incredible variety of figures: humans, plants, and animals such as birds, insects and fish, as well as numerous geometric and abstract designs. The trail has numbered markers identifying the main petroglyphs and you can read about them in a very detailed trail guide available at the trailhead.

All of the descriptions I could give you of the Petroglyph Site can be found in this excellent booklet, so there is not much use repeating it here. Instead, I'll concentrate on what the booklet does not tell you. It is possible to see even more petroglyphs by hiking to the very end of the ridge. There is a shortcut to do that. Leave the main trail right past the bridge and take the footpath to the right. Follow it for 0.9 mile, keeping to the right side of the fence enclosing the Petroglyph site, until you reach a perpendicular fence marking the beginning of State land. Go under the fence and continue for less than 0.2 mile until you reach a small wash with badly eroded banks. Look for a large rock on the left side of the path with some petroglyphs on it. This is your cue. Leave the wash here and climb toward the end of the ridge. You'll find the area between the wash and

Mask

the ridge top full of very nice petroglyphs. One interesting specimen you may stumble upon is an uncommon goggle-eyed creature pecked on a low-lying rock. It has been beautifully shot at twilight by the master David Muench. Return the way you came.

Across the road from the picnic area is a small, partially excavated site called the "Village", consisting of a couple of small structures and a pit house.

Speaking of the picnic

area, it's nice to know that you are allowed to camp here if you're self-contained. It's highly convenient to be on the trail at dawn. It costs a meager $2 and it's even free to Golden Eagle pass holders. If you're coming in at night and somehow miss the sign, do not make the mistake of driving to the Three Rivers Campground, which is 8 miles farther east inside Lincoln Nat'l Forest.

Photo advice: The ridge is oriented north/south. Serious photography at Three Rivers can only be done successfully at sunset or sunrise. I suggest starting about 30 minutes before sunrise. This will provide a nice alpenglow in the background and give you even lighting, plus you'll have the place to yourself. If you're there later in the day, you might want to use a small reflector to minimize harsh contrast areas. Sierra Blanca—the tallest peak in southern New Mexico—provides a nice backdrop to the east during sunset.

Getting there: Drive 17 miles north of Tularosa or 28 miles south of Carrizozo on US 54. Turn east at Three Rivers on CR B30, cross the railroad tracks and continue for about 5 miles until you see the sign on the left.

Time required: 1½ to 2 hours including driving time for the main ridge. Add another 1½ hours to see the area on State land at the end of the ridge.

Bosque del Apache

From early November to mid-February, tens of thousands of birds—including sandhill cranes, snow geese, and many kinds of ducks—gather at the Bosque del Apache National Wildlife Refuge to spend the winter. In short, it goes like this: At dawn, thousands of snow geese fly-out at the same time in an explosion of sound to feed in the adjoining fields. They are followed later by sandhill cranes taking off in much smaller groups. Both return in late afternoon to roost in the Refuge's marshes.

So why should a landscape photographer or Southwest fan be interested in this? The short answer is that it is a unique, exhilarating, visual and sensorial experience, even if you are not a birder or wildlife photographer. I'll try to give you a description of how things happen, but words are not enough to describe the deep connection to nature you're bound to experience at Bosque del Apache.

It all begins at the first glimmer of dawn on a cold

Pre-dawn Fly-out

winter morning with a few calls from various parts of the pond. Soon, this turns into a loud cacophony, as the entire Arctic geese colony erupts into a

high-decibel wall of sound in preparation for their fly-out. The calls settle down a bit before building up to an even louder racket, leading you to believe that the birds are going to take off. Wrong, these false alarms may occur two or three times. Suddenly, with no warning, thousands of birds take to the air in a thunderous explosion of wings and honks. In a matter of seconds, the marsh is totally empty of geese and the colorful dawn sky is full of them. Wave upon wave of geese from other ponds fly

Sandhill Cranes on Frozen Lake

over your head in formations, flying at different altitudes and honking like mad. A computer animator's dream, except it's real. Soon the roar subsides and the geese fade out in the distance. You're left a bit shell-shocked at the suddenness of it all, puzzled by the now eerie quietness. Soon, you are ecstatic at having witnessed this incredible scene. Someone was not impressed, however: As the marsh becomes immersed in warm light, the reluctant sandhill cranes slowly, very slowly, wake up, sending sleepy calls at each other. Finally, groups of them will get in line, like jets waiting for their turn on the runway, before taking off one by one to the air. No curtain falls, but you know the play is over.

Photo advice: Being essentially a landscape photographer, I have only limited expertise with wildlife photography. To me, shooting at Bosque is no different from shooting any other scene of the natural world. The birds are simply part of it. The only difference is that I shoot with a longer lens. I've just related my experience so you can get an idea of what to expect. If you are a serious birder or wildlife photographer you probably know more than me and won't need this advice. If you've never done bird photography before, the following tips should be enough to give you a good basis.

You may have heard the saying that "most photographers are late for work", meaning they arrive on location after the best morning light has come and gone. Well, this saying proved accurate in my case.

On my very first morning at Bosque, I watched in disbelief as I saw wave after wave of snow geese flying out over my car in almost complete darkness, a full half hour before sunrise. Don't let this happen to you. You must be on location a full 45 minutes before sunrise at the very least. In most years, the fly-out occurs closer to sunrise but you can't take any chances. This is something you'll find out while you are in the field.

The Flight Deck, located less than a mile north of the pay station, is generally the best location to observe the morning fly-out. It is a long wooden platform built onto the largest marsh in the Refuge, usually harboring over ten thousand birds. You are unlikely to be disappointed by the Flight Deck. Things change from year to year, however; and it doesn't hurt to call the rangers and verify that this information is still accurate at the time of your visit. One thing I really like about the Flight Deck is that you are shooting against the light, with a wonderful gradient of orange, to dark red to blue velvet in the pre-dawn sky.

If you are at the Refuge late in the day and plan to shoot the next morning, one good way to track where the birds will be at the time of your morning shoot is to find out where they are roosting. Once they have settled for the night, they won't fly out until morning.

Although 90% of the action takes place at dawn and dusk, there are always birds to be observed during the day. Along the water channels, there are two self-drive roads. They are the 7-mile Marsh Loop to the south and the 7.5-mile Farm Loop to the north. Both can be driven separately or as one big loop. The Farm Deck, at the north end of the Refuge, is usually a very good spot during the day. The Wildlife Refuge has agreements with local farmers to grow crops around the refuge's perimeter for wintering birds. It's a good arrangement. The farmer gets the alfalfa or whatever he chooses to grow and the birds get the worms. There

is usually an abundance of birds in that field. The main drawback of the Farm Deck is that the scene can be quite distant.

For the evening fly-in, I like to take position along one of the permanent ponds located along the west side of NM 1, north of the Visitor Center. This location offers outstanding flexibility to photograph the birds coming in for a landing. Unlike the morning fly-out, which occurs so suddenly, you can spot the birds coming in

The Cranes' Fly-in

from afar and prepare accordingly. Furthermore, you are in close proximity of the ponds so the geese and cranes pass just a few feet above your head on their final approach. There are ponds on each side of the road, but those to the west are closest, allowing you to shoot against the evening light, which produces beautiful photographs with warm hues.

As you can imagine, serious bird photography is the domain of powerful telephotos. A 300mm is the bare minimum to photograph flocks in the ponds or in flight, and that's if they are close by. A 400mm is a more reasonable entry-level focal length, while 600mm offers much more flexibility to isolate birds in the ponds. There are always many pros and well-heeled amateurs at Bosque del

At Roost

Apache and you'll see some astounding long lenses around you. You'll also see folks shooting from their cars with special devices to hold their long lenses. Digital SLRs, especially those with a 1.5 or 1.6x crop factor now reign supreme, and they are indeed a formidable tool. With such a high crop factor, a "standard" (and much more affordable) 400mm telephoto turns into a 600mm power-house, while remaining much easier to wield and focus. Also, it maintains its constant aperture, allowing you to get more light in. With a gyro-stabilizer and a high ISO, you are pretty much guaranteed to bring back many excellent shots.

If you don't have a dSLR or a long lens, you can also achieve very good results with a small long-zoom gyro-stabilized digicam. Some have 400mm+ at the long end and can even accept telephoto extensions. The plus side is that they generally cost under $500 with a good, versatile lens. The downside is that they don't operate as fast and produce considerably more noise than a dSLR at high ISO. Still, if you're not planning on doing much wildlife photography, this could be an economical alternative.

Getting there: From Socorro, take I-25 south to San Antonio Exit 139, then US 380 east for 0.5 mile and turn right on NM 1 going south for 8 miles to the refuge. From downtown Socorro motels, it takes roughly 15 minutes to reach the north ponds on NM 1 and 20 minutes for the main entrance and the Flight Deck. From the south on I-25, take the San Marcial Exit 124 and go north on NM 1 for about 9 miles.

Time required: You can get away with one evening and one morning shoot, but to really enjoy Bosque del Apache, I suggest you spend at least a couple of mornings and evenings. Even if you are not a birder, Bosque will grow on you and you may well find it hard to leave. The Refuge is open daily from one hour before sunrise until one hour after sunset.

White Sands National Monument

White Sands Nat'l Monument is a place of exceptional beauty. The fantastic white gypsum, exotic-looking yuccas and beautiful ripple patterns in the sand all contribute to a truly unique experience, unlike any other dune system.

The 8-mile long Dunes Drive cuts deep into the heart of the dunes, providing a great initial contact with this strange environment. However, to truly enjoy the experience and immerse yourself into this otherworldly ecosystem, you'll need to walk the marked trails that lead into the dunes, or better yet, make your own solo adventure by hiking away from the crowds wherever your fancy takes you.

Two of the four trails stand out: the Big Dune Nature Trail (aka Dune Life Nature Trail) located about 2.75 miles from the Visitor Center and the longer Alkali Flat Trail located at the end of the park road.

The vegetation on the 1-mile Big Dune Nature Trail is spectacular. There is an abundance of soaptree yuccas, rising tall over the surface of the sand, saltbrush and rabbitbrush fill interdunal areas. The contrast of the vegetation over the stark white gypsum makes for spectacular photographs. Yet, you should save enough time for the next trail.

Closer to a wilderness-type experience, the 4.6-mile round-trip Alkali Flat Trail is considerably longer but takes you deep into the heart of the sands and onto the "playa" environment, ending at the dry lake bed of Lake Otero. There is no veg-etation in this area, just stark naked dunes that seem to go on forever. It's fun to follow the orange mileposts that are sometimes quite distant from each other. You don't have to hike the entire trail to enjoy the spectacular scenery.

You are allowed to walk anywhere you want in the monument, as long as you park your car in one of the numerous pullouts. This is essentially how you'll do most of your photography. As you walk on the dunes, your vehicle will quickly be out of sight, so be sure to carry and

Spanish Bayonets at Dusk

use a GPS or a compass or, at least, carefully orient yourself to natural landmarks such as different mountain ranges. If a strong wind is coming, turn back immedi-ately as blowing sand can reduce visibility to a few feet, making it easy to get lost. Needless to say, a hat, sunscreen, a pair of dark sunglasses and plenty of water are

Overleaf: Zen Yucca

essential, even under cloudy skies. Although the sand may feel wonderfully soft and cool in the early morning, you should wear shoes on all hikes or you'll burn your feet as soon as the sun rises.

Ranger-led full moon programs are very popular, but you'll probably want to do your own moonwalk at your own pace, even if it is not a complete full moon. Just remember the closing time of the Dunes Drive, officially 9 PM during summer. The White Sands rangers show quite a bit of flexibility in letting people stay past that, especially those picnicking at the end of the Dunes Drive, as long as everybody is out by 10 PM. Do not abuse this tolerance; use it responsibly to squeeze a little bit more evening photography into your schedule, while keeping an eye on your watch. Allow plenty of time to exit the park before it closes. During the rest of the year, the official closing time is sunset and you have to be outside of the park half an hour after dusk.

If you are lucky enough to join a ranger-led car caravan to Lake Lucero, which is the "birthplace" of the White Sands, by all means do it. These trips are usually organized once a month on Saturday (sometimes also Sunday) and must be reserved in advance. You can usually reserve the day before but it is better to do it sooner if you can. You'll cross the White Sands Missile Range in your own vehicle under a special group permit. The trip takes 3 to 4 hours round-trip depending on how long the group lingers at the lake. Lake Lucero is a beautiful playa, which occasionally fills with water. When the water evaporates, the gypsum turns into selenite crystals.

Photo advice: First and foremost, be very aware of potential underexposure pitfalls when photographing the white sand. If you let your camera meter automatically, it will be fooled and you'll end up with gray sand. The stronger the luminosity, the more you'll need to overexpose. Your exposure compensation should be at least 1/2 stop under covered skies and up to 2 stops under intense light; you'll have to be your own judge. To avoid being disappointed with your results, simply bracket your exposure. Twilight photography on the dunes creates fantastic shadows and colors and should not be missed. Late afternoon thunderstorms create huge contrast between dark gray skies and the intense white sand, but be wary of lightning if you carry a tripod on the dunes. The dunes are absolutely stunning in a rain. A hard rain will erase the ripples and pelt the sand with a multitude of tiny holes, making the surface look like it's been raked like a Zen garden. Avoid the period from February through May, when very strong winds create dust clouds that make good photography almost impossible, not to mention damaging your equipment. Winters are mild to very cold, but uninspiring for photography. I prefer summer and autumn, when there are more clouds and stormy skies.

Getting there: Your base is Alamogordo only 15 miles away on US 70 and two hours north of El Paso. Las Cruces is only an hour away to the southwest. Although a primitive backcountry campsite is available in the park to backpackers with a permit, it will be impractical with your photographic equipment.

Time required: Devote at least one evening and one morning to the monument, so you can walk both trails and photograph under different lighting conditions.

Try to time your arrival in mid-afternoon, leaving in mid-morning the next day. Otherwise you'll be stuck a large part of the day when the high sun and high temperatures make photographing miserable. If that is the case, consider visiting the following nearby locations.

Nearby locations: Cloudcroft is a small resort town, located in an old-growth forest, high (9,200 feet) in the Sacramento Mountains, 18 miles east of Alamogordo. Shady trails abound, providing welcome relief from Alamogordo's oppressive heat. Right before entering town on US 82, you'll see a high wooden trestle across the canyon; this is the only remaining trace of the Sacramento Railway Line. You can walk to this trestle from the Trestle Recreation Area (0.5 mile further) where you can also catch a distant vista of the valley, including White Sands.

The Organ Mountains

The Organ Mountains, a beautiful range of rugged granite spires, lies 30 miles southwest of White Sands. On the east side, Aguirre Springs National Recreation Area is a great base to explore the lusher side of the mountains. The park offers a nice campground and two main trails: The Pine Tree Loop is a pleasant 4-mile loop, ascending to the base of the spires and a sparse ponderosa pine forest. The 12-mile round-trip Baylor Pass Trail traverses the range to the west side. The Pine Tree Loop is arguably more photogenic, although the Baylor Pass Trail does pass close to the Rabbit Ears, a distinct landmark resembling their namesake, and offers distant views of Las Cruces, White Sands and Sierra Blanca.

The western side houses Dripping Springs Natural Area, a day-use park that provides excellent trails and views of the photogenic western side. Additionally, the area preserves an old sanatorium from the early 20th century.

Photo advice: The Organ Mountains are best photographed at sunrise or sunset on their respective east and west sides. Since the gates to both parks open and close during daylight hours, taking pictures from the parks is difficult. Luckily, a vast majority of the land skirting both parks is BLM-owned. On the access road to Aguirre Springs, it's easy to park at a safe pull-off and shoot sunrise. Respect all private property signs and be sure not venture onto White Sands Missile Range!

The Organ Mountains (photo by Benjamin Parker)

Getting there: For Aguirre Springs, make a south turn off of US-70 about 1 mile after crossing the San Augustine Pass coming from Las Cruces), and drive about 5 miles to the fee area. To reach Dripping Springs, exit US-70 at Baylor Canyon road and travel south on the well-maintained Baylor Canyon dirt road. After 6.5 miles, make a left on University/Drippings Springs road and head east less than 2 miles towards the park.

City of Rocks

The City of Rocks is a striking concentration of large boulders rising incongruously in the middle of a grassy high plateau in southern New Mexico. The "city" is not very large and can be easily circumnavigated on foot in less than an hour. This can also be done by car if you are in a hurry and want to do some quick scouting of locations. More interesting than circumnavigating, however, is wandering through the heart of the city. It is sheer fun to walk around and make your way through this maze of ancient volcanic rock. There is ample space to walk between the boulders—some squat little trolls, some towering fifty feet high—changing directions on a whim and feeling like a child. The City of Rocks is an extraordinary natural playground. Don't worry if you have young children with you, the city is too small to get lost. All they have to do is walk uphill to catch a bird's eye view of the city and get their bearings. There are small groups of rocks off to the side of the main city. These little clusters of suburbia make great campsites as well as great pictures.

Photo advice: The outskirts of the city are actually used as remote campsites. On a busy spring or autumn week-end this could interfere with your photography, but when I was there shortly after Labor Day, the place was practically empty. There is plenty to photograph in the city proper. The boulders provide very good traction and are easy to scale. Thirty three million years of erosion have removed most of the rough edges and you won't scratch your hands; so just climb up and take pictures. The rocks are well lit in early morning and late afternoon, but expect a lot of contrast. A slight haze will soften the shadows, but it's a rare occurrence in this pristine high plateau environment. If photographic conditions are not good, just enjoy the place. Be sure to drive to the lookout point outside the city, which provides a great panoramic view.

City of Rocks

Getting there: From Deming on I-10, drive 24 miles northwest on US 180. Turn right on NM 61 and drive 5 miles to the park. It's all very well marked.

Time required: 1 hour for just a quick walk through. 3 hours for an in-depth visit with enough time for photography.

Gila Cliff Dwellings

You will have to drive a long time to get to the Gila Cliff Dwellings National Monument, but what a drive it is. From the Mimbres Valley, the constantly winding road climbs high on the Continental Divide, affording spectacular vistas of the vast and remote Gila Wilderness—the first federally-designated wilderness area in the country.

Gila Cliff Dwellings

The setting of these Mogollon dwellings is beautiful, a lovely canyon, with plenty of shade and the wonderful west fork of the Gila River. It is arguably the most hospitable environment of all cliff dwellings in the Southwest—except for the fact that winters must have been bitterly cold.

An easy 1-mile loop takes you across the river to a couple of natural caves on the cliff face where the dwellings are located. The main cave is quite deep and the trail lets you wander through the ruins it shelters. The most remarkable feature of the main cave is a square structure located under a natural arch in the cave. It is easily photographed from various spots on the trail, so act responsibly and don't wander around.

Photo advice: Sunshine begins to hit the Gila Cliff Dwellings about an hour after sunrise. This is the best time for photography. By late morning the shadows will be too intense. By mid-afternoon the dwellings will be in the shade. You'll need a wide angle to photograph the dwellings, a 24mm will work best.

Getting there: From Deming on I-10, follow the route to the City of Rocks and continue 23 miles to San Lorenzo. Take NM 35 northwest for 27 miles to Lake Roberts, turn north on NM 15 and follow it 19 miles to the Gila Cliff Dwellings. Coming from Silver City, it is 44 miles to the dwellings, and you'll travel via the longest and windiest section of NM 15. From either San Lorenzo or Silver City, you'll need about 1½ hour to Gila Cliff Dwellings.

Time required: Approximately 1½ hours to see and photograph the cliff dwellings at a slow pace; however, factoring the driving time and remoteness of the area, it takes a whole day round-trip to come from the largest city—Las Cruces—which puts you at the dwellings at the worst time of the day. There are some motels and lodges on the way and very nice campgrounds inside the monument as well as in the surrounding National Forest. To avoid a hectic pace and maximize your enjoyment, consider spending a couple of days in the area.

Carlsbad Caverns National Park

I can't think of any cave system as big, spectacular and easy to visit as Carlsbad Caverns. In addition, Carlsbad Caverns National Park offers a unique attraction: Half a million bats spend the summer inside one of the caves and, at sunset, they fly out of the natural entrance in search of insects, in one seemingly unending black cloud. As flash photography disturbs the bats, cameras (including video cameras) are not allowed at the Bat Flight without a special permit.

The Chandelier

The best way to visit the caves on your own is to take the two self-guided routes, starting with the Natural Entrance route and finishing with the Big Room route. Both routes end up at the underground rest area, where you can catch the elevator back to the Visitor Center. The Big Room route can be visited from 8:30 to 5 PM (entrance time) from Memorial Day to Labor Day and 3:30 PM the rest of the year. The Natural Entrance route closes 1½ hour sooner. Visitors with little time should do only the Big Room route.

The Natural Entrance route is steep in places, but paved and well graded. There are many spectacular formations along the 1-mile trail. Soon after entering, you'll pass the warm and smelly Bat Cave, descending into Devil's Spring, before reaching the Green Lake overlook. Green Lake is located in a room that can only be visited on the Kings Palace ranger led-tour.

The Big Room is the main attraction of the park and many visitors are content to limit their visit to the 1-mile walk around the perimeter of this huge chamber.

Opposite page: Hall of Giants

Blue Grotto

It can be directly accessed via elevator if you don't take the Natural Entrance route. While many of the sights in the Big Room are phenomenal, it is also crowded. The most spectacular sights along the easy trail are the huge Twin Domes in the Hall of Giants, Crystal Spring Dome—the largest active stalagmite in the caverns—and the colorful Painted Grotto.

To see the so-called Scenic Rooms, you'll need a reservation on the Kings Palace ranger-led tour. During this 1½-hour tour, you'll visit the fabulous Green Lake Room, which is the home of one of the most awesome sights in the park: the Veiled Statue—a spectacular column resulting from the fusion of a stalagmite and stalactite. The Kings Palace and Queens Chamber are both exceptionally ornate, with very delicate formations. The Papoose Room is remarkable, with its army of soda-straw stalactites.

Photo advice: Although flash photography is allowed, you'll get better results using the caves' artificial lighting. Flash tends to put way too much light on the closest formations and wash out contrast and relief on those that are at the correct distance. If you shoot digital and handheld, I recommend using ISO 400, which yields crisp shots as long as you have a gyro-stabilizer. Without stabilization, ISO 800 would be safer. The artificial light tends to play havoc with the digital cameras' automatic white balance. Overall, I tend to get more pleasant results shooting transparency film, but in that case a tripod is mandatory. Daylight film works just fine; there is no need for tungsten film. An 81a or 81b filter can also produce excellent results.

Getting there: 20 miles southwest of Carlsbad or about 140 miles east of El Paso on US 62/NM 180 to NM 7, then 7 miles to the Visitor Center.

Time required: 3 hours for both self-guided tours; 1½ hour, plus wait, for the Kings Palace tour. Longer if you stay and watch the bats fly out at sunset.

Nearby location: The Living Desert State Park, on the outskirts of Carlsbad, is a great place to observe the fauna and flora of the Chihuahuan Desert. One of the highlights of this small park is its outstanding wolf exhibit. ❧

Balanced Rock in Big Bend NP

Chapter 14

A FORAY INTO TEXAS

El Capitan Sunrise (photo by Mike Norton)

A FORAY INTO TEXAS

Hueco Tanks

Hueco Tanks, a Texas Historic State Park, has beautiful Mogollon rock art, in particular, finely drawn pictographs of Tlaloc, the Rain God and other masks and anthropomorphs. It is becoming increasingly popular with El Paso residents, as well as with rock art aficionados and rock climbers. Despite its small size, the park is a microcosm of the Chihuahuan desert, harboring many birds, some wildlife and very nice flora specimen if you take the time to explore the higher ground. The park gets its name from large natural potholes that retain water after rain storms, called *huecos* in Spanish. The presence of water in such a harsh desert environment acted as a magnet over centuries, attracting early Native Americans, followed by Mexican and Anglo ranchers, Apache and even Kiowas from the distant plains of Oklahoma.

Despite constant struggle with vandalism, many of the pictographs have survived or have been restored, offering an interesting display to the modern-day hiker and photographer.

To protect the rock art and fragile terrain, there is a quota of 70 visitors a day without a guide in the North Mountain section—the only section in which you are allowed to wander freely. It has some very nice *huecos* and surprising plateaus with rich vegetation in its upper reaches. Except for the Blue Trail around the northern border, there are no trails; the terrain is moderately difficult and requires occasional scrambling. After your compulsory orientation, ask the ranger to point out the general location of rock art, then set out on your own discovery.

A guided tour is a better alternative to photograph pictographs as well as the only way to see other sections of the park. There are also guided bouldering and hiking tours, as well as birding tours. Tours are given several days a week by volunteers. Call the park to find out times and to reserve.

Photo advice: Some of the rock art is hidden in cracks, with little available light, so a tripod is a must. Hueco Tanks is a wonderfully lush little oasis so there is much more than just photographing rock art. Among other subjects, there is great sunset photography of North Mountain.

Getting there: The turnoff is located 24 miles east of El Paso on US 62 and is well marked. The park is located at the end of a good 8-mile access road.

Time required: 2 hours just to walk on the Blue Trail, which doesn't have much rock art; a full day to enjoy a guided tour, then wander on your own.

Nearby locations: I have been to a great number of border crossings in the Southwest, from Tijuana on the West Coast to Matamoros on the Gulf, but none are as interesting and exotic as Ciudad Juarez. In fact, you don't even have to cross over to the Mexican side. The area around the U.S. side of Downtown El Paso's border crossing is remarkably full of life and offers interesting opportunities for street photography.

Hueco Tanks Masks

Guadalupe Mountains National Park

Guadalupe Mountains National Park offers plenty of good photography, even on a tight schedule, as far away from the crowds as any National Park in the Continental United States. The park's highest point is Guadalupe Peak, also the highest peak in Texas at 8,749 feet. However, it is eclipsed by the lower, more visible and impressive El Capitan: a huge limestone formation rising majestically from the desert floor and contrasting with the stark desert surroundings. The park literature does a great job of explaining the amazing geology of El Capitan—an ancient reef covered by the sea during the Permian era, petrified under sediment

when the waters receded, and later eroded into its present form by the elements.

From the Pine Springs Visitor Center, separate trails leave for the top of Guadalupe Peak and the base of El Capitan, but the trails from the Frijole Ranch Trailhead are more rewarding for the photographer. The strenuous 9.1-mile loop climb to the Bowl offers classic alpine scenery of Ponderosa Pine and Douglas Fir. The very relaxing 2.3-mile Smith Spring loop hike offers a remarkable sampling of the rich high-

Snow on El Capitan

Chihuahuan ecosystem after so many harsh desert miles.

In the northeast corner of the park, McKittrick Canyon offers an easy 6.8-mile round-trip walk to the Grotto picnic area, alongside a perennial stream. Be sure to pick up a trail guide at the Contact Station. This hike is interesting in all seasons, due to the remarkable diversity of vegetation you encounter over such a short distance. You go from typical Chihuahuan spiky cacti, through a transition zone of grassland and finally thick woodlands. The last mile to the small Grotto has a surprising number of trees usually found in more temperate ecosystems. However, McKittrick Canyon shines in the fall when the trees explode with rich color. McKittrick Canyon is the only trail that sees any real

crowds during the off-season. While sparse during the rest of the year, they can be fierce during fall colors. The Grotto is a white limestone cave with weird formations. It is in direct sun relatively early in the morning and the contrast with the darker parts of the cave becomes a real challenge. Along the way, the Pratt Cabin makes a good stop although there isn't much left to photograph. All

McKittrick Fall Colors (photo by QT Luong)

of the Guadalupe trails offer good opportunities for bird watching.

If your time is limited, you can take the short nature trail to the Pinery—a former site of the Butterfield Stage line, used by the Pony Express riders to carry mail from coast to coast. This trail is very nice in the early morning sun.

Guadalupe has an excellent campground.

Photo advice: The best place to photograph El Capitan is from one of the two picnic areas along US 62 a little bit over 4 miles south of the Pine Springs Visitor Center road. The view is best at sunrise, but can also be photographed successfully in late afternoon when the entire west side of the Guadalupe Mountains is lit sideways. A moderate wide-angle to normal lens works well to capture the length of the forbidding El Capitan promontory.

Salt Basin Dunes (photo by QT Luong)

All the above-mentioned hikes offer good opportunities and are never crowded, except during late-October and early-November which sees an influx of visitors for the outstanding fall colors along McKittrick Canyon. Winters are usually mild, but storms can dump quite a bit of snow on the mountains. Summers are hot, as can be expected, but wildflowers are out in force after the monsoon storms.

Getting there: The Visitor Center road is off US 62, about 110 miles east of El Paso. To reach the McKittrick Canyon area, turn off 7.5 miles northeast of the Visitor Center road and continue 4 miles to the parking area. Coming from the south, note that TX 54 between Guadalupe and Van Horn on I-10 isn't a good road to take in case of thunderstorms. There are numerous dips that can become flooded, potentially delaying your progress by several hours.

Time required: 3 hours to cross the park and hike the Smith Spring loop; add another 3 to 4 hours to hike McKittrick Canyon. The gate to McKittrick Canyon closes at 6 PM in summer and 4:30 PM the rest of the year, so it's better to do a morning hike. The full loop to the Bowl takes a good 6 hours.

Nearby location: The grey/white gypsum dunes of the Salt Basin, near the small community of Salt Flat, 24 miles west of the Visitor Center road, provide an interesting foreground to the west side of the Guadalupe Mountains in late afternoon. There is talk of integrating the Salt Basin into Guadalupe Nat'l Park. Wind storms can be fierce in the area, blowing sand all over the road and sometimes obscuring it entirely.

BIG BEND NATIONAL PARK

Big Bend is one of the least visited national parks. This is due partly to its remoteness and partly to the fact that it has few grandiose landmarks or universally recognized vistas like so many parks of the southwest. Big Bend is a park that slowly grows on you, however, to the point where you find it hard to leave it when the time comes. Perhaps, it has to do with the warm wind whispering in your ear, the absence of crowds, the cheekiness of the ubiquitous *paisanos* (roadrunners), the presence of another world just a few feet across the Rio Grande, or perhaps I've watched Lone Star too many times.

Big Bend is also one of the largest national parks in the U.S., at over 1,250 square miles. When you combine this with its remoteness, it becomes obvious that you just don't pass through it casually, it has to be a deliberate decision. Given the time, effort and cost involved, I suggest that you spend a minimum of two days in the park. However three or four days would be a lot better to do it justice. If you go through the pain of driving about 325 miles one-way from El Paso, better maximize your time inside the park.

There are two main entrances to the park: from the west and from the north. I have arbitrarily decided on the western one. We'll enter Big Bend from Study Butte (aka Terlingua) on TX 118 and follow what I refer to as the main park road, traversing the park from west to east. Along the way, we'll take side-trips along the

Camino del Rio

Ross Maxwell Scenic Drive to Castolon and Santa Elena Canyon, the Grapevine Hills, and the Chisos Basin, ending up at Rio Grande Village. We'll exit the park to the north via US 385. I believe this approach gives the best first impression of the park and allows one to concentrate quickly on its best features.

Coming to Big Bend from Alpine on TX 118, you'll get really spectacular views of the Chisos Mountains starting about 20 miles north of Study Butte. Study Butte itself is tiny, but it has a couple of motels. The two border crossings of Santa Elena and Boquillas del Carmen were closed as of this writing.

Before we enter Big Bend National Park, we'll visit a relatively seldom seen location just outside the National Park: Big Bend Ranch State Park.

Big Bend Ranch State Park

Covering over 450 sq. miles, this State Park is the largest in Texas, but it likely is the least well-known and least visited. Many visitors who have already covered huge distances to come to Big Bend National Park are not particularly eager to do more miles outside the park. The other reason is that many people are not aware of its existence, despite the fact that it is an international biosphere reserve.

From a visitor's standpoint, there are two parts to the park: The one most people see is the scenic Camino del Rio, which more or less follows the Rio Grande. The second, the Solitario, is a vast wilderness said to be the least populated area in the Continental United States.

The Ubiquitous Paisano

The Camino del Rio is a 50-mile drive along RR 17 through the border section of Big Bend Ranch, between Presidio to the west and Lajitas to the east. It is a very scenic and pleasant drive. Chances are you won't stray far from the road, which is the main attraction of the park and has good views of the Rio Grande in its eastern part. On the west side, you'll pass above Colorado Canyon, where Study Butte outfitters run 1 or 2-day canoe and raft trips.

The most popular short trail along the road is the Closed Canyon Trail, just off RR 170 near the East Rancherias trailhead, about 30 miles from Presidio. The 1.4-mile round-trip hike takes you from the mouth of Closed Canyon to some interesting narrows. While its shape is reminiscent of some Southern Utah narrows, the canyon feels distinctly different with its barren walls of porous volcanic material and its ground that feels dry as a bone. It is not as photogenic as sandstone narrows, but just as enjoyable to hike. Retrace your steps when you reach the *tinajas* and drop-off.

On the east side of the park, the road follows the Rio Grande more closely. Mexico is just a stone's throw away on the other side of the surprisingly narrow river. It's a bit eerie to see a border with no fence whatsoever.

Just outside the east entrance to the State Park on RR 170 is the tiny village of Lajitas. Lajitas has caught the eye of developers and has an old town movie set, a resort and the closest golf course to a border anywhere. There is even an "International Airport". Just east of Lajitas is the Barton Warnock Visitor Center, which is a good stop for interpretation of the Big Bend landscape.

Going from Lajitas toward Study Butte, the Old Terlingua Ghost Town (not to be mixed up with Terlingua Abajo, which we'll see later on) is worth the 12-mile round-trip detour. Terlingua sees a huge influx of visitors every year in November during its famous chili cook-off.

Getting there: There are two ways to come to Big Bend Ranch SP. If you're coming from El Paso or Guadalupe Nat'l Park on US 90, turn right in Marfa and drive south about 60 miles on US 67 to Presidio, then follow RR 170 along the Rio Grande and through Big Bend Ranch State Park to Lajitas. You can also come from Alpine on TX 118 to Study Butte, continuing on RR 170 to Lajitas and exiting through Presidio or simply do a shorter trip inside the park between Lajitas and Closed Canyon.

Time required: Up to 4 hours from Presidio to Lajitas, with plenty of time for stops and photography. A couple of hours are enough for a short trip to the east side from Lajitas.

Nearby location: US 90 is dotted with picnic areas at regular intervals. One of these picnic areas, 9 miles east of Marfa on the way to Alpine, was specially built so motorists could observe the "Marfa lights", which have become a major tourist attraction.

The Ross Maxwell Scenic Drive

At the Maverick Junction, almost 4 miles southeast of Study Butte, you are faced with a couple of choices. You can either continue east on TX 118 toward most of the sites in the park, or you can take the Old Maverick Road directly to Santa Elena Canyon. I recommend the first alternative for several reasons. Continuing on the main park road through the more richly vegetated plain to

Mule Ears Dusk

Santa Elena Junction to catch the Ross Maxwell Scenic Drive is a much better introduction to the park. There is a great concentration of ocotillos near the Maverick entrance station and the road is lined with the ubiquitous purple-tinged Prickly Pear cacti, sotols, and lechuguilla that are the trademarks of the Chihuahuan desert. Another reason is that you'll be so pleased with the Ross Maxwell Scenic Drive that you may decide to drive it in both directions and pass on the Old Maverick Road (described in a later section).

From Santa Elena Junction, the excellent Scenic Drive road leads south to the Castolon area and Santa Elena Canyon. After about 2 miles, look to your left toward the Chisos Mountains and you'll notice a V-shaped notch. This is the famous Window, which I'll describe later in the Chisos Basin section.

After about 3.8 miles from the junction, you'll find a road heading east toward the Chisos, about 0.1 mile past

Cerro Castellan (photo by Mike Norton)

the Sam Nail Ranch pullout. This rough road ends at a locked gate. A high-clearance vehicle is a must. Walk past the gate toward Oak Springs and look for the small sign pointing to the Cattail Falls. The falls are a perennial waterfall, but only come into their own after a rain. In dry weather, they could be little more than a trickle. Seen within the context of the park's Chihuahuan environment, the falls are a pristine little vortex of lush vegetation and cool, clear water and the Park Service prefers to keep it that way. The water is the source of a unique and fragile ecosystem that exists in the drainage below, a world away from the desert floor. Just tread lightly and do not play in the stream and the pool below the falls. The stream's water is apparently also being used as a source of drinking water for the park. The visible section of the falls is about 40 feet tall, but there are other segments higher up. There is a small pamphlet available at the Panther and Chisos Visitor Centers. Park Rangers will provide it only if you ask specifically about the falls by name. Finding the falls is easy, however, as they are referenced on the 7.5' USGS map, including the path leading to them.

Resuming your drive, the road climbs steadily through the base of the Chisos Mountains' west side. Stop at the Homer Wilson Ranch pullout for a view of the homestead at the bottom of Blue Creek Canyon. There is a trail following an old jeep road, going down to the nearby ranch.

Soon after that, take the spur road to the Sotol Vista Overlook for a spectacular, though distant, panoramic view of the plains. Back on the main road, you begin dropping fast on the other side. Take the marked side road leading in 1.5 miles to the Burro Mesa Pouroff Overlook. Although you can see the pouroff from here, it's only a short 1-mile round-trip hike to the base of the photogenic 40-foot pouroff, rendered slick by eons of floods.

About 1.2 miles south of the Burro Wash junction, stop at the Chimneys trailhead pullout. It's an easy 4.8-mile round-trip to the weird outcroppings—part of an old volcanic dike. The formations can be seen from the trailhead in the distance. This hike should be done during the golden hour.

Santa Elena Canyon Sunrise (photo by Mike Norton)

Your next stop is at the Mule Ears Viewpoint, 2.7 miles further. A short spur road leads to the viewpoint, providing a distant view of the Mule Ears, which are best seen in late afternoon. The Mule Ears Trail is 3.8 miles round-trip to the spring of the same name. It's a very easy, well-constructed trail through classic Chihuahan desert scenery. After about 1.3 mile, a very good view of the dark twin peaks opens up, with some good desert vegetation mix in the foreground. As you continue on the trail toward the spring, the view becomes progressively worse as the northern peak masks the other one. Even if you don't feel like walking the whole trail, walk just 500 feet from the car park and follow the faint footpath to the right to a little promontory with a more open view of the Mule Ears than from the car park. You'll need a long telephoto, something in the order of 200mm, to photograph the Mule Ears. In late afternoon, there is also an excellent view of the Mule Ears from about 2 miles south on the road, looking back at the twin peaks.

About 1 mile before Castolon, stop along the road to admire Cerro Castellan, a tall volcanic peak rising 1,000 feet above the plain below. Cerro Castellan appears as a butte from Castolon.

Castolon has a small Visitor Center and a great old store. The Visitor Center has an interesting collection of old photographs of the Texas Rangers and U.S. Army presence at the time of the Mexican Revolution. The Castolon store was established in a former army barrack after the Mexican Revolution ended. It looks right out of the 1920s inside and out, with a nice antique gas pump in front. It's a fun place to stop for a drink or to get some food if you're camping at the lovely Cottonwood campground.

Time required: Count on spending a full day on the Ross Maxwell Scenic Road, but two days are necessary if you want to do all the hikes including Santa Elena Canyon, as described next.

The Old Maverick Road

After entering Big Bend from Study Butte and reaching Maverick Junction, you can choose to drive directly to Santa Elena Canyon using the Old Maverick Road heading southwest for 13 miles. However, for reasons explained above and because this road isn't particularly spectacular, I don't really recommend it. Nevertheless, It is doable as a major shortcut between the Santa Elena Canyon/ Castolon area and Study Butte, allowing you to make a clockwise loop without retracing your steps.

Old Maverick Road is a fairly good gravel road, suitable for passenger cars in good weather, but it is rather washboardy. A spur road takes you to the ghost town of Terlingua Abajo, along Terlingua Creek. The Sierra Ponce Mountains inside Mexico look great from the ruins, cut deeply by Santa Elena Canyon. Further north, you'll pass Luna's Jacal, the almost collapsed house of one of Big Bend's early settlers.

Time required: About 1 hour.

Santa Elena Canyon

The paved road coming from Santa Elena Junction, or the Old Maverick road, bring you to the Santa Elena Canyon Overlook.

The trailhead for Santa Elena Canyon is located at river level near Terlingua Creek. At the parking area, note the marker located 7 feet above the ground on one of the restrooms. It shows the high water mark reached by the Rio Grande and Terlingua Creek in October 1990.

The easy Santa Elena Canyon Trail is only about a 1.5 miles round-trip. A couple of minutes into the walk, you actually cross Terlingua Creek. Fortunately, it is only a trickle most of the time and chances are you'll barely get your soles wet. Past Terlingua Creek, the trail ascends a few concrete steps to reach a platform at the mouth of the canyon. From here a level path continues inside the canyon, about 40 feet above the Rio Grande. It's surprising how slow-moving and quiet the river is. The opposite wall, inside

Inside Santa Elena Canyon

Mexico, feels very close. In a few minutes, you reach a pleasant point at river level. There are some rocks providing a good foreground to photograph the narrow limestone canyon. You can continue for a couple of minutes to a second river level point at the end of the trail but it is less photogenic than the first one.

You may be in luck and see some boaters or kayakers coming out, after their run through the canyon from Lajitas. Come to think of it, you may yourself want to canoe Santa Elena Canyon with an outfitter. I haven't done this trip, but it is obviously an excellent way to see much more of the 8-mile long canyon. Several outfitters in Study Butte offer 1-day trips.

Photo advice: There is a great shot of Sierra Ponce with the mouth of Santa Elena Canyon at sunrise from the Santa Elena Canyon Overlook. The best time to photograph the inner canyon is late afternoon.

Time required: About 1 hour.

Balanced Rock

From the Grapevine Hills trailhead, it's an easy 2.2-mile round-trip hike on a sandy path, except for the last 0.25 mile which requires some moderate scrambling to reach the big rocks of the Grapevine Hills. As you gain elevation, you find yourself in the midst of a vast jumble of granite boulders. None of them are as strange and spectacular as the trademark Balanced Rock, a huge oblong stone stuck precariously on two vertical boulders, much like a Celtic *dolmen.* There are distant views of the barren Rosillos Mountains to the north.

Balanced Rock

Photo advice: The Balanced Rock is best photographed in the morning from the back side, which is more photogenic. It can also make a worthy photograph in the afternoon from the front side, especially if you photograph it against the sun to reveal only its interesting outline.

Getting there: From Santa Elena Junction, drive east for about 9 miles on the main park road toward Basin Junction. Turn northeast on improved Grapevine Hills Road for about 7 miles until you reach the trailhead to your right.

Time required: About 1 hour from the trailhead.

The Chisos Basin

How about a radical change of scenery, going from the hot Chihuahuan desert to the wonderful sub-alpine environment of the Chisos Mountains. This incredible contrast is, to me, the most striking feature of Big Bend.

Along the Chisos Road

The 6-mile road leading from TX 118 to the Chisos Basin is remarkable, not only for its scenic beauty during the golden hour, but also for the abrupt transition between ecosystems. There are great views of Pulliam Peak on the west side of the road along Green Gulch in the early morning. As you near Panther Pass in the shadow of Casa Grande Peak, the landscape changes in front of your eyes in a matter of minutes.

Once you emerge on the other side and lay your eyes for the first time on the Chisos Basin, you can't help being astonished at how green it is. The Basin has many great hikes and views and it's worth spending at least one night here, if only for the change of scenery. There is a good campground, a great lodge and a nice store, so it's easy to extend your stay and relax here in the cool air.

From the Window View Overlook behind the store, there is a great view of the so-called Window. The Window is a V-shaped opening revealing the vast Sotol Valley far below. It can be photographed in the early morning, before sunrise, when the valley is already irradiated by sun rays. The view is equally interesting, albeit harder to photograph, in the evening when you can see the sunset through the Window.

If you only have a little time to hike in the Basin, take the Basin Loop, an easy 1.6-mile round-trip trail offering nice views, but nothing better than the Window View. For a different and more rewarding perspective of the Basin, take the 4-mile round-trip Window Trail from the Basin Campground. It brings you right to the notch you see from above. It is the pour-off of Oak Creek, which drains the entire Chisos Basin. From the pour-off, the view of the desert side is somewhat limited and marred by the presence of the giant water tank near Oak Springs. The Window Trail connects with the primitive Oak Spring Trail, which starts off the Ross Maxwell Scenic Drive. A short hike up the Oak Creek Trail provides a better view of the Window from above.

There is a high probability of seeing wildlife on the Window Trail, particularly javelinas. I have encountered javelinas on this trail and along the road

Window Sunrise

near Park Headquarters and have found them eager to get out of sight. Less frequent, but far from uncommon, are black bear and mountain lion encounters. As of this writing, reported mountain lion sightings had increased dramatically throughout the entire park, averaging about 15 per month. However, due to an abundance of prey, instances of attacks on humans are almost non existent (an average of 1.5 per decade).

Getting there: The Chisos Basin road heads south from Basin Junction, about 10 miles east of Santa Elena Junction.

Time required: About 3 hours in late afternoon, plus 2 hours the next morning.

Rio Grande Village & Boquillas Canyon

Coming back down from the Chisos Basin, we continue our exploration along the main park road toward the east side. This road is characterized by the flatness of the landscape, compared to the west side. Still, it's a very pleasant drive through rich Chihuahuan Desert. There are great views of the Chisos Mountains lit by the sun in the morning.

Hot Springs (photo by QT Luong)

About 6 miles past Panther Junction, on the north side of the road, the Dugout Wells are worth the short detour to see the surprisingly verdant oasis in the middle of the desert.

A couple of miles past the Dugout Wells turnoff, there is a remarkable Ocotillo forest. This is one of the best concentration of ocotillos I've ever seen in the Southwest. It is worth stopping here just to wander around the dense cacti. Late March and April are usually best to observe them in bloom, but they can often spring to life after a good rain.

As you approach the Rio Grande Village area, turn right at the sign for the Hot Springs and follow the gravel road for a little over 1 mile to the springs, located right alongside the Rio Grande. The springs used to be part of the private and long-gone Hot Springs Village, but are still accessible and functional and you're free to use the remaining shallow pool. It's fun to soak in the 105°F mineral water, while looking at the Rio Grande just a few feet below.

Boquillas Canyon

About 2 miles past the Hot Springs turnoff is the Rio Grande Overlook. It has a fair view of the jagged Sierra del Carmen. It's too bad the Sierra is so distant because its jagged profile is quite striking. You can try a long telephoto shot but the sky is often hazy over the Rio Grande.

The Rio Grande Village area is by far the most developed in the park. It has a well-stocked modern store and you can buy gas. There is a large, well developed campground. It's a major motorhome haven and a bit crowded for my taste, but it's a very convenient place to spend the night. Behind campground site #18, you'll find the trailhead for the Rio Grande Village Nature Trail. Don't miss this short nature trail, which packs a lot of photographic potential in only 0.7-mile round-trip: riparian wetlands crossed on a boardwalk and a great view of the Sierra del Carmen and the Rio Grande at the end. It's a very popular gathering spot for sunset. You won't be alone, but it's well deserved.

Close to the end of the road, the Boquillas Canyon Overlook has an expansive view of the Rio Grande and border area, but not of the canyon proper.

Lastly, at the end of the road, is the Boquillas Canyon trailhead. The trail is a short and easy 1.4-mile round-trip entering the mouth of Boquillas Canyon. It ends up on sandy bluffs a bit above the river. With the border crossing now closed, Mexican nationals routinely wade across the Rio Grande to sell trinkets at the foot of the small hill located at the beginning of the hike.

Photo advice: It is difficult to photograph Boquillas Canyon during the day due to the harsh shadows contrasting with brightly lit areas. It is best to go early in the morning or in late afternoon to get an even light.

Time required: About 2 hours for the drive one-way from the Chisos Mountains Basin junction, including stops. 1 hour for Boquillas Canyon.

Panther Junction to Persimmon Gap

Inside the park, there aren't too many photo opportunities along the 26 miles between Panther Junction and the north entrance of the park at

Persimmon Gap; the views of the distant Chisos Mountains aren't that great. Persimmon Gap, however, is the preferred gateway if you want to go directly from Marathon to the Chisos Basin or Rio Grande Village. The Persimmon Gap is a narrow opening in a series of mountain ranges that semi-encircle the northern section of the park. There is a small Visitor Center next to the entrance station.

Almost 13 miles north of Panther Junction, the Dagger Flat Auto Trail is a well-maintained 14-mile round-trip gravel road, suitable for passenger cars in dry weather. The pleasant drive on the narrow, winding road is essentially a nature trail for non-hikers, with some good photographic opportunities during the golden hour. The best feature along, and especially at the end of the road,

Yucca in Bloom

are the various yuccas, and in particular the giant Dagger Yuccas, which are truly spectacular when they are in bloom and best photographed in late afternoon. This happens normally in late March and April, regardless of how much it rained.

Getting there: From Marathon on US 90, take US 385 south, driving 39 miles to the park entrance at Persimmon Gap. This approach is just as long and deserty as from Alpine.

Time required: Less than 1 hour one-way from Panther Junction to Persimmon Gap. Up to 1½ hour for the Dagger Flat Auto Trail.

Nearby location: Marathon is a very tiny town compared to Alpine, and there isn't much to photograph, with the exception of the old Gage Hotel. It has a long, shady courtyard that is very photogenic. ❀

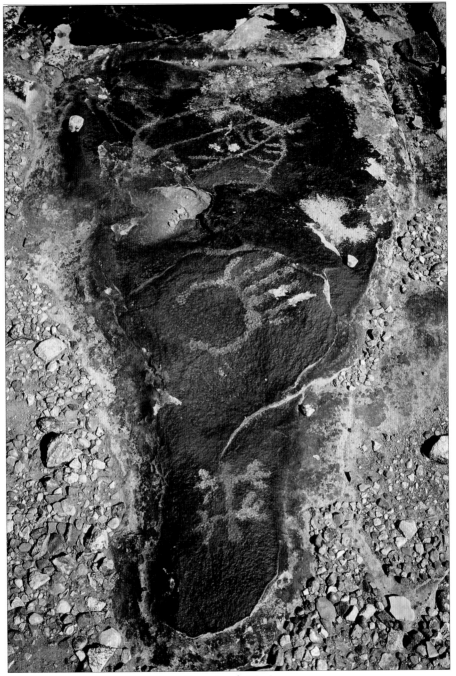

Footprint & Glyphs

APPENDIX

APPENDIX

Maps

Large scale road maps: The best general road map to visit the Southwest is without doubt the Indian Country Guide published by the American Automobile Association (AAA). This remarkable guide/map is a sheer pleasure to read and use. It contains a surprising amount of dirt and gravel roads, with very accurate mileage and it does an excellent job of referencing little-known locations. Unless you intend to do some heavy-duty hiking or four-wheeling, this map is quite sufficient for an ordinary car-based tour of the "Four Corners" area. Unfortunately, coverage doesn't extend to northern Colorado, the Rockies, and southern New Mexico. Sites located in these areas are adequately covered by the AAA Colorado and New Mexico maps. You can obtain these maps from any AAA office and many of the bookstores in the National Parks and Monuments.

National Park and Monument miniguides: These wonderfully concise miniguides are packed with all the essential information about the parks, their history, geology and fauna. You can get them at the park entrances or at Visitor Centers. They will help you find your way around on roads and trails.

National Park topographic maps: If you plan on adventuring along the trails and roads in distant parts of the national parks, the topographic maps of the Illustrated Trails series, printed on waterproof paper, are extremely well made and highly recommended. I always use them for hiking in the parks.

National Forest maps: The Pawnee National Grassland map can be ordered from the Forest Service web site at http://www.fs.fed.us/r2/maps/maporderform.pdf

Topographic maps on CD-ROM: These digital maps are a fantastic resource to plan your trip beforehand. The maps print spectacularly well and you can mark your intended route. Great to enter way points in your GPS. Delorme, Maptech and National Geographic make topographic mapping software on CD-ROM or DVD using Digital Rasterized Graphics. National Geographic's Topo! State Series is particularly good; I have them permanently loaded on my laptop. Mapsource City Navigator and Topo 24K work great with Garmin GPS units and so does MapSend on Magellan units. On the web, topozone.com allows you to display at no charge small portions of topographic maps using GPS coordinates and to print them on your own equipment. This site and others, such as backpacker.com, offer a paying service allowing you to download and print personalized maps.

Other road maps: Rand McNally Road Explorer software allows you to print express maps of Colorado and New Mexico and generate detailed roadbooks for your own use or for the benefit of friends or groups.

Selected Bibliography - Guidebooks

National Geographic Guide to the National Parks: Southwest, published by the National Geographic Society, ISBN: 0-792295-39-0

Journey to the High Southwest by Robert Casey, published by Globe Pequot Press, ISBN 0-762740-64-7

A Guide to Colorado's Best Photography Locations by Andy Cook, ISBN 0-976089-30-0

Rocky Mountain National Park: The Complete Hiking Guide by Lisa Foster, published by Westcliffe Publishers, ISBN 1-565795-50-4

Rocky Mountain National Park Dayhiker's Guide, published by Johnson Books, ISBN 1-555661-10-6

Hiking Colorado's Weminuche Wilderness by Donna Ikenberry, published by Falcon Press, ISBN 1-560447-16-8

The Essential Guide to Great Sand Dunes National Park by Charlie & Diane Winger, published by Colorado Mountain Club Press, ISBN 0-972441-31-x

The Essential Guide to Black Canyon of the Gunnison National Park by J. Jenkins, published by Colorado Mountain Club Press, ISBN 0-972441-34-4

Scenic Driving New Mexico by Laurence Parent, publisheed by Falcon Press, ISBN 0-762730-31-5

Hiking New Mexico by Laurence Parent, published by Falcon Press, ISBN 1-560446-76-5

New Mexico's Wilderness Areas: The Complete Guide, by Bob Julyan, published by Westcliffe Publishers, ISBN 1-565792-91-2

100 Hikes in New Mexico by Craig Martin, published by Mountaineers Books, ISBN 0-898867-90-8

Route 66 Traveler's Guide and Roadside Companion by Tom Snyder: a fun and informative guide for driving Route 66

Santa Fe in a Week: More or Less by Joel B. Stein, published by Clear Light Books, ISBN 1-574160-72-9

Hiking Carlsbad Caverns & Guadalupe Mountains National Parks by Bill Schneider, published by Falcon Press, ISBN 1-560444-01-0

Hiking Big Bend National Park by Laurence Parent, published by Falcon Press, ISBN 1-560442-86-7

Selected Bibliography - Other Recommended Reading

Centennial by James Michener, published by Fawcett Books, ISBN 0-449214-19-2

The Milagro Beanfield War by John Nichols, published by Owl Books, ISBN 0-805063-74-9

The Southwest Inside Out by Thomas Wiewandt and Maureen Wilks, published by Wild Horizons Publishing, ISBN 1-879728-03-6

New Mexico: An Interpretive History by Marc Simmons, published by University of New Mexico Press, ISBN 0-826311-10-5

Ghost Ranch by Lesley Poling-Kempes, published by University of Arizona Press, ISBN 0-816523-47-9.

Valley of the Shining Stone: The Story of Abiquiu, by Lesley Poling-Kempes, published by University of Arizona Press, ISBN 0-816514-46-1.

Albuquerque: A City at the End of the World by V.B. Price, University of New Mexico Press, ISBN 0-826330-97-5

Architecture of the Ancient Ones by A. Dudley Gardner and Val Brinkerhoff, published by Gibbs Smith, ISBN 0-87905-955-9

Mysterious Chimney Rock - The Land, The Sky, The People, published by Chimney Rock Interpretive Association, ISBN 1-4276-0159-3

On the Go Resources

These resources are intended as a quick way of finding further information about the sites described in this guidebook while you're on the road, by calling the appropriate agency. The phone numbers have been verified shortly before we went to press; however, phone numbers can change and this information may be obsolete by the time you read it. I hope you find this list useful in your travels. It is just a convenient way to call from the road and I have purposely avoided presenting a formal list of web sites.

National Parks & Monuments in Colorado
   Black Canyon of the Gunnison NP (970) 641-2337
   Colorado NM (970) 858-3617
   Curecanti NRA (970) 641-2337
   Dinosaur NM (970) 374-3000
   Florissant Fossil Beds NM (719)748-3253
   Great Sand Dunes NP (719) 378-6399
   Mesa Verde NP (970) 529-4465
   Rocky Mountain NP (970) 586-1206 (main)
   Rocky Mountain NP (970) 586-1242 (backcountry)

National Parks & Monuments in New Mexico
   Aztec Ruins NM (505) 334-6174
   Bandelier NM (505) 672-3861
   Capulin Volcano NM (505) 278-2201
   Carlsbad Caverns NP (505) 785-2232
   Chaco Culture NHP (505) 786-7014
   El Malpais NM (505) 783-4774 or (505) 876-2783
   El Morro NM (505) 783-4226

Gila Cliff Dwellings NM (505) 536-9461
Pecos NHP (505) 757-6414
Petroglyph NM (505) 899-0205
Salinas Pueblo Missions NM (505) 847-2585
White Sands NM (505) 679-2599 or (505) 479-6124

National Parks & Monuments in Texas (partial list)
Big Bend NP (915) 477-2251
Guadalupe Mountains NP (915) 828-3251
Rio Grande WSR (432) 477-2251

State Parks in Colorado (partial list)
Golden Gate Canyon SP (303) 582-3707
Ridgway SP (970) 626-5822
Rifle Falls SP (970) 625-1607
Roxborough SP (303) 973-3959
San Luis Lakes SP & Wildlife Area (719) 378-2020

State Parks & Monuments in New Mexico (partial list)
City of Rocks SP (505) 536-2800
Coronado SM (505) 867-5351
Elephant Butte Lake SP (505) 744-5923
Jémez SM (505) 829-3530
Living Desert Zoo & Gardens SP (505) 887-5516

National Forests in Colorado

Arapaho & Roosevelt National Forests
Boulder Ranger District (303) 541-2500
Canyon Lakes Ranger District (970) 295-6700
Clear Creek Ranger District (303) 567-3000
Sulphur Ranger District (970) 887-4100

Grand Mesa, Uncompahgre and Gunnison National Forests
Grand Valley Ranger District at Grand Junction (970) 242-8211
Grand Mesa Visitor Center (970) 856-4153
Gunnison Ranger District at Gunnison (970) 641-0471
Gunnison Ranger District at Lake City (970) 641-0471 or (970) 944-2500
Ouray Ranger District (970) 240-5300
Norwood Ranger District (970) 327-4261
Paonia Ranger District (970) 527-4131

Medicine Bow & Routt National Forests
Hahns Peak/Bears Ears Ranger District (970) 879-1870
Parks Ranger District at Walden (970) 723-8204

Parks Ranger District at Kremmling (970) 724-3068
Yampa Ranger District (970) 638-4516

Pawnee National Grassland (970) 346-5000

Pike & San Isabel National Forests
Leadville Ranger District (719) 486-0749
Pikes Peak Ranger District (719) 636-1602
Salida Ranger District (719) 539-3591
San Carlos Ranger District
South Park Ranger District (719) 836-2031
South Platte Ranger District (303) 275-5610

Rio Grande National Forest
Conejos Peak Ranger District (719) 274-8971
Divide Ranger District at Del Norte (719) 657-3321
Divide Ranger District at Creede (719) 658-2556
Saguache Ranger District (719) 655-2547

San Juan National Forest
San Juan Public Lands Center (970) 247-4874
Columbine East Ranger District (970) 884-2512
Columbine West Ranger District (970) 884-2512
Dolores Ranger District (970) 882-7296
Pagosa Ranger District (970) 264-2268
San Juan Mountains Center at Silverton (970) 387-5530

White River National Forest
Aspen Ranger District (970) 925-3445
Blanco Ranger District (Meeker area) (970) 878-4039
Sopris Ranger District (Carbondale area) (970) 963-2266
Rifle Ranger District (970) 625-2371

National Forests in New Mexico

Carson National Forest
Camino Real Ranger District (505) 587-2255
Jicarilla Ranger District (505) 632-2956
Questa Ranger District (505) 586-0520
Tres Piedras Ranger District (505) 758-8678

Gila National Forest
Black Range Ranger District (505) 894-6677
Glenwood Ranger District (505) 539-2481
Quemado Ranger District (505) 773-4678
Gila Wilderness Ranger District (505) 536-2250

Cibola National Forest
Magdalena Ranger District (505) 854-2281
Mountainair Ranger District (505) 847-2990

Mt. Taylor Ranger District (505) 287-8833
Northwest New Mexico Visitor Center (505) 876-2783
Sandia Crest Visitor Center (505) 248-0190

Lincoln National Forest
Smokey Bear Ranger District (505) 257-4095
Guadalupe Ranger District (505) 885-4181
Sacramento Ranger District (505) 682-2551

Santa Fe National Forest
Coyote Ranger District (505) 638-5526
Cuba Ranger District (505) 289-3264
Española Ranger District (505) 753-7331
Jemez Ranger District (505) 829-3535
Pecos/Las Vegas Ranger District (505) 425-3534

BLM Offices in Colorado
Anasazi Heritage Center, Dolores (970) 882-5600
Arkansas Headwaters Recreation Area, Salida (719) 539-7289
Colorado State Office, Lakewood (303) 239-3600
Columbine Field Office BLM/USFS, Durango (970) 385-1368
Glenwood Springs Field Office, Glenwwod Springs (970) 947-2800
Grand Junction Field Office, Grand Junction (970) 244-3000
Gunnison Field Office, Gunnison (970) 641-0471
Gunnison Gorge NCA, Montrose (970) 240-5300
McInnis Canyons NCA, Grand Junction (970) 244-3000
Mancos/Dolores Field Office BLM/USFS, Dolores (970) 882-7296
Pagosa Field Office BLM/USFS, Pagosa Springs (970) 264-2268
Royal Gorge Field Office, Canyon City (719) 269-8500
San Juan Public Lands Center, Durango (970) 247-4874
Uncompahgre Field Office, Montrose (970) 240-5300
White River Field Office, Meeker (970) 878-3800

BLM Offices in New Mexico
Albuquerque District Office, Albuquerque (505) 761-8700
Carlsbad Field Office, Carlsbad (505) 887-6544
Cuba Field Station, Cuba (505) 289-3748
Farmington Field Office, Farmington (505) 599-8900
Grants Field Station, Grants (505) 287-7911
Las Cruces District Office, Las Cruces (505) 525-4300
New Mexico State Office, Santa Fe (505) 438-7400
Rio Puerco Field Office, Albuquerque (505) 761-8700
Roswell Field Office, Roswell (505) 627-0272
Socorro Field Office, Socorro (505) 835-0412
Taos Field Office, Taos (505) 758-8851

Indian Pueblos (partial list)

Acoma Pueblo (505) 552-6604
Indian Pueblo Cultural Center in Albuquerque (505) 843-7270
Jemez Pueblo (505) 834-7235
Laguna Pueblo (505) 552-6654
Nambe Pueblo (505) 455-2278
Picuris Pueblo (505) 587-2519
Santa Clara Pueblo (505) 753-7326
Taos Pueblo (505) 758-1028
Zuni Pueblo (505) 782-4481

State Visitor Centers

Colorado Welcome Center at Cortez (970) 565-4048
Colorado Welcome Center at Dinosaur (970) 374-2205
Colorado Welcome Center at Fort Collins (970) 491-3583
Colorado Welcome Center at Fruita (970) 858-9335
New Mexico Anthony Welcome Center (505) 882-2419
New Mexico Chama Welcome Center (505) 756-2235
New Mexico Gallup Welcome Center (505) 870-0249
New Mexico Lordsburg Welcome Center (505) 542-8149
New Mexico Raton Welcome Center (505) 445-2761
New Mexico Santa Fe Welcome Center (505) 827-7336

Others

American Rock Art Research Association (888) 668-0052
Chimney Rock Interpretive Program (970)264-2287
Colorado Road & Weather Information (877) 315-7623 or (303) 639-1111
Crystal Mill Tours (970) 963-1991
Cumbres & Toltec Scenic Railroad (888) 286-2737
Durango & Silverton Narrow Gauge RR (877) 872-4607 or (970) 247-2733
Georgetown Loop Railroad (303) 569-1000
Surface Creek Valley Historical Society (970) 856-7554

Note: Most National Parks and Monuments and most travelers' bureaus will send you free documentation anywhere in the world to prepare your trip.

RATINGS

Using a scale of 1 to 5, the following ratings attempt to provide the reader with an overall vision of each location, in order to facilitate comparisons and choices. Obviously, the ratings alone don't tell the whole story about a location and should be used only in conjunction with the explanations of each section.

The ratings are assigned on the basis of four different criteria: overall interest of a location, based mostly on its scenic value (or its beauty and interest in the case of rock art and ancestral dwellings), photographic potential for those of you who happen to carry a camera :-) and level of difficulty to access each location with your vehicle and/or on foot.

The objectivity of ratings done by an author tend to be somewhat tainted by the individual's personal preferences. To minimize personal bias, I arrived at the ratings through a concensual process with a team of knowledgable friends and photographers. We based our assessments on the criteria below and I think we achieved even-handed results. I hope you'll find the ratings helpful in preparing your trip(s) to the Southwest.

Rating	Scenic Value
–	Of no particular interest
♥	Mildly interesting, visit if nearby and/or time permitting
♥♥	Scenic location, worthy of a visit
♥♥♥	Very interesting, scenic or original location
♥♥♥♥	Remarkably scenic or rewarding location, a highlight
♥♥♥♥♥	World-class location, absolutely tops

Rating	Photographic Interest
–	Of no particular photographic interest
♦	Worthy of a quick photo
♦♦	Good photo opportunity
♦♦♦	Good photographic potential and scenic subjects
♦♦♦♦	Outstanding photographic potential, highly original or scenic subjects
♦♦♦♦♦	World-class photographic location, "photographer's dream"

Rating	Road Difficulty
–	Paved road, accessible to all normal-size vehicles
♦	Dirt road accessible without difficulty by passenger car (under normal conditions)
♦♦	Minor obstacles, accessible by passenger car with caution (under good conditions)
♦♦♦	High-clearance required, but no major difficulty
♦♦♦♦	High-clearance 4WD required, some obstacles, no real danger
♦♦♦♦♦	High-clearance 4WD required, some risk to vehicle & passagers, experienced drivers only

Rating	Trail Difficulty
–	No or very little walking (close to parking area)
♠	Easy short walk (<= 1h r/t), for everybody
♠♠	Moderate hike (1 to 3h r/t) with no major difficulty or short hike with some minor difficulties
♠♠♠	Moderate to strenuous (3 to 6h r/t) and/or difficulties (elevation gain, difficult terrain, some risks)
♠♠♠♠	Strenuous (> 6h r/t) and/or globally difficult (elevation gain, difficult off-trail terrain, obstacles, risks)
♠♠♠♠♠	Backpacking required or for extremely fit dayhikers

Location	Page	Scenic Value	Photogr. Interest	Road Difficulty	Trail Difficulty
Moraine Park	97	♥♥♥	♦♦♦	–	♣
Moraine Park - Cub Lake Trail	97	♥♥	♦♦	–	♣♣
Moraine Park - Fern Lake Trail	97	♥♥	♦♦	–	♣♣♣
Sprague Lake	98	♥♥♥	♦♦♦	–	♣
Bear Lake	98	♥♥	♦	–	–
Bear Lake to Fern Lake Trailhead thru-hike	99	♥♥♥♥	♦♦♦	–	♣♣♣♣
Dream Lake	100	♥♥♥♥	♦♦♦♦♦	–	♣
Emerald Lake	100	♥♥♥	♦♦♦	–	♣♣
Lake Haiyaha (entire loop)	100	♥♥♥	♦♦♦	–	♣♣♣
Alberta Falls	101	♥♥	♦♦	–	♣
Mills Lake	102	♥♥♥	♦♦	–	♣♣
Black Lake	102	♥♥♥	♦♦	–	♣♣♣
The Loch	102	♥♥♥	♦♦♦	–	♣♣
Glass Lake	102	♥♥♥	♦♦♦	–	♣♣♣
Sky Pond	103	♥♥♥	♦♦	–	♣♣♣♣
Chasm Lake	103	♥♥♥♥	♦♦♦♦	–	♣♣♣♣
Copeland Falls	104	♥♥	♦♦	♠	♣
Calypso Cascades	104	♥♥	♦♦	♠	♣
Ouzel Falls	104	♥♥♥	♦	♠	♣♣
Kawuneeche Valley - Road & viewpoints	105	♥♥♥	♦♦♦	–	–
Kawuneeche Valley - Timber Lake	106	♥♥	♦	–	♣♣♣♣
Kawuneeche Valley - Big Meadows	106	♥♥	♦♦	–	♣♣
Kawuneeche Valley - Granite Falls	106	♥♥	♦♦	–	♣♣♣♣
Kawuneeche Valley - East Inlet Trail	106	♥♥	♦♦	–	♣♣♣♣
Mt. Goliath Nature Area	107	♥	♦♦	–	♣
Mt. Evans to summit	107	♥♥♥	♦♦♦	–	–
Georgetown	108	♥♥	♦♦	–	–
Guanella Pass	108	♥♥	♦♦	–	–
Peak-to-Peak Byway	108	♥♥♥	♦♦	–	–
Brainard Lake	108	♥♥♥	♦♦♦	–	–
Golden Gate Canyon SP - Gap road	109	♥	♦	–	–
Cache La Poudre Scenic Byway	109	♥♥♥	♦♦	–	–
Roxborough SP	110	♥♥♥♥	♦♦♦	–	♣♣
Red Rocks Park	111	♥♥♥	♦	–	♣
Devil's Backbone - Wild Loop	111	♥♥♥	♦	–	♣♣
Pawnee National Grassland	112	♥♥	♦	♠	♣

6 Southern Colorado

Location	Page	Scenic Value	Photogr. Interest	Road Difficulty	Trail Difficulty
Garden of the Gods	114	♥♥♥♥♥	♦♦♦♦♦	–	♣
Pikes Peak	118	♥♥	♦♦	♠	–
Manitou Cliff Dwellings	118	♥	♦♦	–	–
Florissant Fossil Beds	118	♥♥	♦	–	♣
Gold Belt Scenic Bwy - Phantom Canyon	119	♥	♦	♠♠	–
Gold Belt Scenic Bwy - Shelf Road	120	♥♥	♦	♠♠♠	–
Victor	120	♥♥♥	♦♦	–	–
Royal Gorge Bridge	120	♥	♦	–	–
Highway of Legends - Cuchara Pass	120	♥♥♥	♦	–	–
Capulin Volcano	121	♥♥	♦♦	–	♣
Great Sand Dunes NP - Top of dunes	123	♥♥♥♥	♦♦♦	–	♣♣♣
Great Sand Dunes NP - Medano Creek	123	♥♥♥♥	♦♦♦	–	♣
Great Sand Dunes NP - Medano Pass	123	♥♥♥	♦♦	♠♠♠♠	–
Zapata Falls	125	♥♥	♦♦	♠	♣
Cumbres & Toltec RR (train or road)	125	♥♥	♦♦	–	–
Wheeler Geologic Area - via trail	126	♥♥♥	♦♦♦	♠	♣♣♣♣
Wheeler Geologic Area - via 4WD road	126	♥♥♥	♦♦♦	♠♠♠♠	♣♣
Silver Thread Scenic Byway	128	♥♥	♦♦	–	–
Chimney Rock	129	♥♥♥	♦	–	♣

Location	Page	Scenic Value	Photogr. Interest	Road Difficulty	Trail Difficulty
7 San Juan Mountains					
Dallas Divide - Main Road (CO 62)	133	♥♥♥	♦♦	—	—
Dallas Divide - County Roads 5, 7 & 9	133	♥♥♥♥	♦♦♦♦	♠♠	—
Last Dollar Road	135	♥♥♥	♦♦♦	♠♠♠	—
Telluride - Town	136	♥♥♥	♦♦	—	—
Telluride - Alpine Village & gondolas	136	♥♥♥	♦	—	—
Telluride - Jud Wiebe Trail	137	♥♥	♦♦	—	♣♣
Telluride - Wilson Mesa	137	♥♥	♦	♠	—
Alta Lakes & ghost town	137	♥♥♥	♦♦♦	♠♠♠	♣
Gold King Basin	137	♥♥♥	♦♦♦	♠♠♠	♣
Ophir Pass	138	♥♥♥♥	♦♦♦	♠♠♠♠	—
Lizard Head Pass	138	♥♥♥	♦♦♦	—	—
Western Skyway - Rico to Cortez	138	♥♥	♦♦	—	—
Southern Skyway - Cortez to Durango	139	♥♥	♦	—	—
Durango & Silverton RR	139	♥♥♥♥	♦♦	—	—
Animas Overlook Trail	140	♥♥	♦	—	♣
Old Lime Creek Road	141	♥♥	♦♦	♠	—
Molas Pass & lakes	141	♥♥	♦♦	—	—
Silverton	141	♥♥	♦♦	—	—
Silverton to Animas Fork - along Animas River	142	♥♥	♦♦	♠♠	—
Silverton to Animas Fork - via California Pass	142	♥♥♥	♦♦	♠♠♠♠	—
Ice Lake Basin (wildflower season)	143	♥♥♥♥	♦♦♦♦	♠	♣♣♣♣
Red Mountain Pass	143	♥♥♥♥	♦♦♦	—	—
Guston & Yankee Girl Mine	143	♥♥♥	♦♦♦	♠♠	—
Ironton	144	♥	♦	♠	—
Crystal Lake	144	♥	♦♦	—	—
Ouray	144	♥♥	♦	—	—
Bear Creek Trail to Grizzly Mine	145	♥♥	♦	—	♣♣♣
Yankee Boy Basin (wildflower season)	146	♥♥♥♥	♦♦♦♦	♠♠♠♠	♣
Blue Lakes Pass	147	♥♥♥	♦♦	♠♠♠♠	♣♣♣
Governor Basin	147	♥♥♥♥	♦♦♦	♠♠♠♠	—
Imogene Pass	147	♥♥♥♥	♦♦	♠♠♠♠♠	—
Alpine Loop - North (via Engineer Pass)	148	♥♥♥♥	♦♦♦	♠♠♠♠	—
Alpine Loop - South (via Cinammon Pass)	149	♥♥♥	♦♦♦	♠♠♠♠	—
Lake City	149	♥♥♥	♦	—	—
American Basin	150	♥♥♥♥	♦♦♦♦	♠♠♠♠	♣♣
Handies Peak (to the summit)	150	♥♥♥♥	♦♦♦	♠♠♠♠	♣♣♣
8 Mesa Verde NP					
Mesa Verde Rim overlooks	153	♥♥♥	♦	—	—
Far View ruins	154	♥♥	♦♦	—	—
Chapin Mesa - Cliff Palace	156	♥♥♥♥	♦♦♦♦	—	♣
Chapin Mesa - Spruce Tree House	157	♥♥♥♥	♦♦♦♦	—	♣
Chapin Mesa - Balcony House	158	♥♥♥♥	♦♦♦	—	♣♣
Chapin Mesa - Square Tower House	159	♥♥♥	♦♦♦	—	—
Wetherhill Mesa - Long House	159	♥♥♥♥	♦♦♦	—	♣
Wetherhill Mesa - Other ruins	160	♥♥	♦♦	—	♣
Ute Tribal Park (full day)	160	♥♥	♦♦	♠	♣♣
Canyon of the Ancients - Sand Canyon Trail	161	♥♥♥	♦♦	—	♣♣♣
Canyon of the Ancients - Lowry Pueblo	161	♥♥	♦	♠	—
Hovenweep NM - Main group	163	♥♥♥	♦♦♦♦	—	♣♣
Hovenweep NM - Holly group	163	♥♥	♦♦	♠	♣♣

Location	Page	Scenic Value	Photogr. Interest	Road Difficulty	Trail Difficulty
9 Northwest New Mexico					
Aztec Ruins	166	♥ ♥ ♥	♦ ♦	–	♣
Shiprock	167	♥ ♥ ♥ ♥	♦ ♦ ♦ ♦	♠ ♠	♣
Chaco Canyon - Pueblo Bonito & Overlook	169	♥ ♥ ♥ ♥	♦ ♦ ♦	♠	♣ ♣
Chaco Canyon - full Pueblo Alto loop	171	♥ ♥	♦ ♦	♠	♣ ♣
Angel Peak	172	♥ ♥	♦ ♦	♠	–
Zuni Pueblo	172	♥ ♥	♦ ♦	♠	–
El Morro - Inscription Rock loop	173	♥ ♥ ♥	♦ ♦ ♦	–	♣
El Morro - Mesa Top loop	173	♥ ♥	♦ ♦	–	♣ ♣
Red Rock SP	173	♥ ♥	♦ ♦	♠	♣ ♣
El Malpais - Eastern section	174	♥ ♥ ♥	♦ ♦ ♦	–	♣
El Malpais - Big Tubes area	175	♥ ♥ ♥	♦ ♦	♠ ♠ ♠	♣ ♣ ♣
El Malpais - Bandera cave & volcano	176	♥ ♥ ♥	♦ ♦	–	♣
Acoma Pueblo	177	♥ ♥ ♥ ♥	♦ ♦ ♦ ♦	–	♣
Laguna Pueblo	178	♥	♦ ♦	–	–
10 Bisti Badlands					
Bisti Badlands - Northern section	182	♥ ♥ ♥ ♥	♦ ♦ ♦ ♦ ♦	♠ ♠	♣ ♣ ♣
Bisti Badlands - Other sections	187	♥ ♥ ♥ ♥	♦ ♦ ♦ ♦ ♦	♠ ♠	♣ ♣ ♣
Bisti Badlands - De-Na-Zin Wilderness	188	♥ ♥ ♥	♦ ♦ ♦	♠ ♠	♣ ♣ ♣
11 Around Santa Fe					
Old Santa Fe	190	♥ ♥ ♥	♦ ♦ ♦	–	♣
Bandelier NM - Frijoles Canyon	192	♥ ♥ ♥ ♥	♦ ♦ ♦	–	♣ ♣
Bandelier NM - Tsankawi section	193	♥ ♥	♦ ♦	–	♣ ♣
White Rock Overlook	194	♥ ♥	♦	–	–
White Place	195	♥ ♥ ♥	♦ ♦	♠	♣
Abiquiu Church	195	♥ ♥	♦ ♦	–	–
Ghost Ranch	195	♥ ♥ ♥	♦ ♦	–	♣ ♣
Echo Amphitheater	196	♥	♦	–	–
High Road to Taos (as a whole & churches)	196	♥ ♥ ♥ ♥	♦ ♦ ♦	–	–
Taos Pueblo	198	♥ ♥ ♥ ♥	♦ ♦ ♦ ♦	–	–
Rio Grande Gorge Bridge	199	♥ ♥	♦	–	–
Pecos Nat'l Historical Park	202	♥ ♥	♦ ♦ ♦	–	♣
12 Around Albuquerque					
Old Town Albuquerque	204	♥ ♥ ♥	♦ ♦	–	♣
Balloon Fiesta	205	♥ ♥ ♥ ♥ ♥	♦ ♦ ♦ ♦	–	♣
Petroglyph NM - Boca Negra	208	♥ ♥	♦ ♦	–	♣
Petroglyph NM - Rinconada	208	♥ ♥	♦ ♦	–	♣ ♣
Petroglyph NM - Volcanoes	208	♥	♦	–	♣
Coronado SM	209	♥ ♥	♦ ♦	–	–
Jemez Mountain Trail	209	♥ ♥	♦	–	–
Tent Rocks	211	♥ ♥ ♥ ♥	♦ ♦ ♦ ♦	♠	♣ ♣
Turquoise Trail	212	♥ ♥	♦	–	–
Salinas Missions - Gran Quivira	214	♥ ♥	♦	–	♣
Salinas Missions - Abo	214	♥ ♥	♦ ♦	–	♣
Salinas Missions - Quarai	214	♥ ♥	♦ ♦	–	♣
13 Southern New Mexico					
Valley of Fires	216	♥ ♥	♦ ♦	–	♣
Three Rivers Petroglyph Site	217	♥ ♥	♦ ♦ ♦	–	♣ ♣
Bosque del Apache (November to February)	219	♥ ♥ ♥ ♥	♦ ♦ ♦ ♦	–	–
White Sands NM - Big Dune Nature Trail	223	♥ ♥ ♥ ♥	♦ ♦ ♦ ♦	♠	♣
White Sands NM - Alkali Flat Trail	223	♥ ♥ ♥	♦ ♦ ♦	–	♣ ♣ ♣
White Sands NM - Lake Lucero	226	♥ ♥ ♥	♦ ♦	♠ ♠	♣
Cloudcroft	227	♥ ♥	♦	–	♣
Organ Mountains - Aguirre Springs NRA	227	♥ ♥ ♥	♦	–	♣ ♣
Organ Mountains - Dripping Springs NRA	227	♥ ♥ ♥	♦	♠	♣ ♣
City of Rocks	228	♥ ♥ ♥	♦ ♦	–	♣
Gila Cliff Dwellings	229	♥ ♥ ♥	♦ ♦ ♦	–	♣
Carlsbad Caverns NP	230	♥ ♥ ♥ ♥ ♥	♦ ♦ ♦ ♦	–	♣ ♣

Location	Page	Scenic Value	Photogr. Interest	Road Difficulty	Trail Difficulty
14 A foray into Texas					
Hueco Tanks	234	♥♥♥	♦♦	—	♣♣
Guadalupe Mtns NP - Roadside	235	♥♥	♦♦♦	—	—
Guadalupe Mtns NP - Pine Springs trails	236	♥♥	♦♦	—	♣♣♣
Guadalupe Mtns NP - Smith Spring loop	236	♥♥	♦♦	—	♣♣
Guadalupe Mtns NP - McKittrick Canyon (Fall colors)	236	♥♥	♦♦♦	—	♣♣♣
Guadalupe Mtns NP - Salt Basin	237	♥	♦	—	—
Big Bend Ranch SP - Camino del Rio Drive	239	♥♥	♦♦	—	—
Big Bend Ranch SP - Closed Canyon Trail	239	♥♥♥	♦♦	—	♣
Ross Maxwell SD - Drive only	240	♥♥♥	♦	—	—
Ross Maxwell SD - Cattail Falls	241	♥♥	♦	♠♠♠	♣♣
Ross Maxwell SD - Chimneys	242	♥♥	♦♦	—	♣♣
Ross Maxwell SD - Mule Ears Trail	242	♥♥	♦♦	—	♣♣
Old Maverick Road	243	♥	♦	♠♠	—
Santa Elena Canyon	243	♥♥♥	♦♦	—	♣
Balanced Rock	244	♥♥♥	♦♦♦	♠♠	♣♣
Chisos Basin - Drive only	245	♥♥♥	♦	—	—
Chisos Basin - Windows View Overlook	245	♥♥	♦♦♦	—	—
Chisos Basin - Windows Trail	245	♥♥♥	♦♦♦	—	♣♣♣
Panther Junction to Rio Grande Village	246	♥♥	♦	—	—
Boquillas Canyon	247	♥♥	♦♦	—	♣
Panther Junction to Persimmon Gap	248	♥	♦	—	—
Dagger Flat Road	248	♥♥	♦♦	♠♠	—

Warning: Road Difficulty ratings are for normal, dry conditions. Driving conditions can change dramatically during or after a rain or a snowstorm, even more so on clay roads or roads that follow the course of a wash. As an example, the popular and well-used Last Dollar Road—rated 3 in difficulty—can become impassable after rain or snow, even with 4WD. Severe weather can dramatically alter conditions for extended periods of time. When the road was last maintained also has a huge impact on its condition and can alter the rating by 1 level in either direction. Always check current road conditions with local authorities before you leave.

INDEX

A not so brief blip about the Author

I was born in Paris, France. Thanks to an open-minded family, I attended school in Paris, London, Barcelona and several cities in Germany. I hold degrees in modern languages and international business.

A couple of years after college, I did the best thing a young person can do to widen his/her horizons and gain an understanding of our world and its wonderful diversity: I set out on a 20-month trip around the world, photographing extensively.

From 1976-1981, I lived in Tokyo, becoming a permanent resident of Japan and teaching at Sophia University. During that time, I also worked as a freelance photographer and pursued my research on the origins of Sumo and its ties with the Shinto religion, resulting in my book *Sumo – Le Sport & le Sacré*

Laurent & his wife Patricia

published in 1984. My years in Japan have had a profound influence on my life, my philosophy, and my photography.

I immigrated to the United States in 1982, settling in Southern California and creating Graphie Int'l, Inc, specializing in software, multimedia and, later on, internet technologies. Constant exploration and photography of the Southwest resulted in the publication of *Land of the Canyons* in 1998. In 1999, I permanently switched my focus from the software industry to a full-time career as a fine-art photographer, author and publisher, spending a good deal of my time in the Southwest.

I have been photographing since the age of eleven, paying my dues to the B&W chemical lab for many years. While in Japan, I became an early adopter of Cibachrome, enlarging and processing my own prints.

I prefer shooting 2¼" medium format. Although I have shot Hasselblad and Mamiya in the past, I now do the majority of my photography with two Fuji 645 rangefinder cameras, which I find well-suited to my style. In the past, I have also used a 35mm Olympus OM-4 system extensively, especially for extreme wide-angle and long-telephoto shots. More recently, I have used Canon and Olympus dSLR cameras. When shooting film, I use Fujichrome Velvia and Astia exclusively. In my work, I seek to challenge the imagination with images characterized by bold colors, unique textures and a striking sense of depth, ranging from starkly minimalist compositions to complex abstracts. ✿

Intentionally left blank for notes